# Shrine Of The Black Madonna Celebrates 50th Anniversary

A'Lelia P. Bundles, great-great granddaughter of Madam C.J. Walker, hair care pioneer, will be the guest author Saturday, July 20, 2-4 p.m. at the Shrine of the Black Madonna Bookstore, 946 Abernathy Blvd., S.W. Ms. Bundles, a producer with ABC's World News Tonight, will sign copies of her book "Madam C.J. Walker, Entrepreneur," the first book length biography ever written about Madam Walker.

## Double Column Editors To Autograph Book

## Happy Birthday Garvey!

Because most of you who read this column already know much about Marcus Garvey, and because you know what he stood for and what he did, this is not a history lesson. For those of you who are not as familiar with Brother Garvey as you would like to be, please go to a Black bookstore and get a few of the many books written about this giant.

hood Arts Center. Later, the same building housed the Timbuktu Book Store, the first all African bookstore in Atlanta.

**PLAN TO CIRCULATE NEGRO BOOKS**

---

# Dick Gregory Speaks On Obama, Health, Gas Prices

## Seale To Speak At Shrine

Bobby Seale, co-founder and past National Chairman and chief spokesman of the Black Panther Party for Self-Defense (Bpp), will be the guest speaker at the Shrine of the Black Madonna Bookstore, 960 Gordon St., SW, on Sunday, October 13, 6:00 p.m.

Seale's visit comes on the eve of the 25th anniversary of the founding of the Black Panther Party and coincides with the recent reprinting of his book." SEIZE THE TIME: THE STORY OF THE BLACK PANTHER PARTY AND HUEY P. NEWTON."

## Author Connie Porter To Sign "Addy" Series

She will sign her three new books "Addy Saves the Day," "Happy Birthday, Addy," and "Changes for Addy" on Sunday at Medu Bookstore at Greenbriar Mall from 3 p.m. to 5:30 p.m. Also, she will have a booksigning at Oxford Book-Store, 360 Pharr Road in Atlanta, from 10 a.m. to 1 pm.

# NEGRO BOOKS

## Author At Local Bookstore

# BOOK NOOK

### Shrine Of Black Madonna Begins Search For Descendants Of Slaves From Ga.

The Shrine of the Black Madonna Bookstore is searching for descendants of slaves from Georgia listed on documents in the Shrine of the Black Madonna's Black Holocaust Exhibit.

HUNDREDS NEEDED to sell Negro Books. Excellent market. High Salary. No experience necessary. Write Robinson. Box 1880 GPO, NY 1, NY.

---

# Books More Popular Since Arrest Of Jamil Al-Amin

Many publishers are fearful that Negro books will not sell. Many readers have become accustomed to th stereotype picture of the Negro are difficult to win over to books which tell more the truth.

Marita Golden, author "of Migrations of the Heart and Long Distance Life," will be the guest author Wednesday, July 24, 7:30 p.m. at the Shrine of the Black Madonna Bookstore, 946 Abernathy Blvd., SW. Ms. Golden will read from her soon-to-be released book Do Remember Me and will authograph copies of her present works.

## Spelman Alumna Has Book Signing

# The World Is At Your Fingertips

*First World Bookstore at Underground Atlanta 50 Alabama Street*

# The World Of Books

Walter Mosley stands outside of Black Books Plus.
Courtesy of Benjamin Cotten/Algodon Photographics.

KATIE MITCHELL

presents

# PROSE TO THE PEOPLE

## A CELEBRATION OF BLACK BOOKSTORES

Principal photography by Julien James
Foreword by Nikki Giovanni

Clarkson Potter/Publishers
New York

Published in the United States by Clarkson Potter/
Publishers, an imprint of Random House, a division
of Penguin Random House LLC, New York.
clarksonpotter.com

CLARKSON POTTER is a trademark and POTTER with
colophon is a registered trademark of Penguin
Random House LLC.

Library of Congress Cataloging-in-Publication Data
is available upon request.

ISBN 978-0-593-58134-6
Ebook ISBN 978-0-593-58135-3

Printed in China

Editors: Sahara Clement and Emma Brodie
Designer: Mia Johnson
Production editor: Liana Faughnan
Production manager: Phil Leung
Compositors: Merri Ann Morrell
and Hannah Hunt
Copy editor: Andrea Peabbles
Proofreaders: Rachel Markowitz, Eldes Tran,
Hope Clarke, Sigi Nacson, and Tess Rossi
Publicist: Felix Cruz
Marketer: Monica Stanton

10 9 8 7 6 5 4 3 2 1

First Edition

Cover design by Mia Johnson

Cover photographs by Julien James and courtesy
of Garbo and Auna Hearne, Los Angeles Times
Photographic Archive, UCLA Library Special
Collections, Vera Warren-Williams, Paul Coates,
The Daphne Muse Collection, Benjamin Cotten/
Algodon Photographics, Yvonne Blake, Glenderlyn
Johnson, Christina Gandolfo, Alta Journal,
Desiree Sanders, and Jennifer Lawson

For LC, Annie Lee, Katie Mae, and 'nem
For Black bookstores past, present, and future

# CONTENTS

## CHAPTER 1

## THE NORTHEAST

## CHAPTER 2

## THE DMV

# FOREWORD

## BY NIKKI GIOVANNI

We hear stories before we are born. Our mothers and our grandmothers sing to us; sometimes spirituals, sometimes jazz to keep our coming in rhythm with our ancestors. We are born and everyone who loves our family comes around to drink and eat and sing. We are happy.

By the time we begin our own dreams, we are given illustrated books that stoke our imaginations. Whether people give us books, money to buy books, or paper to draw on, we find ways to make up our own stories. Some of these stories are still with us. Others have been lost or destroyed by time or close-mindedness. But their essence lives on in memory, history, libraries, and bookstores.

Libraries are the university of the people. I loved going into the wood-floored, green-lighted rooms where index cards awaited. There were so many worlds in those cards, and I could pick any one of them to venture into.

When I learned how to drive, I could go to the bookstore. I'd drive downtown, park, and go in looking grown-up. I was always neat, and I always spoke to the owners. I got to know bookstore owners across America the same way I got to know my librarians.

I had an old clunker, but gas was less than a dollar a gallon, so I could drive from New York City to Detroit to Chicago to Denver to Portland and down the California coast, meeting bookstore owners along the way. Coming back home, I took the southern route: Houston, Dallas, St. Louis, New Orleans, Mississippi, Cincinnati, Pittsburgh.

There were Black bookstores on almost every corner, from Una Mulzac's Liberation Books and Lewis Michaux's famous and necessary National Memorial African Bookstore in Harlem, to Vaughn's Bookstore in Detroit. My goodness, did I leave out Washington, D.C.? Every Black community had a Black bookstore. And we had pride. We had poetry. We had song. We had readings. Nothing was more important than the bookstores, except perhaps the churches.

Most of the buildings have been taken but not forgotten. Marcus in Oakland still stands, as does Medu and the Shrine of the Black Madonna in Atlanta, and there are new bookstores opening across the country. The songs are still being sung.

*Prose to the People* reminds us that "Black is Beautiful," as Mr. Michaux liked to say, "but knowledge is power."

OPPOSITE: Nikki Giovanni shows off her "Thug Life" tattoo at Afrocentric Bookstore. Courtesy of Desiree Sanders.

LEFT: Nikki Giovanni poses at Black Books Plus. Courtesy of Glenderlyn Johnson.

# INTRODUCTION

**BLACK PROTESTS FEED BLACK BOOKSHOPS LIKE RIVERS DO THEIR BANKS,** like volcanoes do their valleys—through floods and fires, through eruptions and deluge, through burnings and drownings powerful enough to turn the barren and bleached, fertile and Black. For when our movements surge, when Black folks' gurgling pain swells into the streets, that same pain flows through our pens. It turns our subjugation into our subjects, our pain into our prose. It turns life sentences into lyrical sentences. It turns everyday speech into extraordinary speeches. This creative cycle began churning sixty years ago—the Civil Rights Movement gave way to the Black Arts Movement, the flood of marches nourished the poets, the fire of rioters fertilized the novels, and our resistance fueled our renaissance.

In the late 1960s, Black bookstores emerged as cultural hubs of Black art and thought, as the incubators for Black aesthetics and Black Power, as the physical spaces where the modern artistic movements of slam poetry, spoken word, and hip-hop were first seeded. And today, just as the Black Art's bookshops bloomed from the tumult of the Civil Rights era, a new generation of Black bookstores is blossoming amid the upheaval of the Movement for Black Lives.

For the past two years, I have traveled to Black bookstores across the United States gathering the accounts of shops old and new, talking with elders and upstarts, and collecting love letters, poems, histories, pictures, essays, and art from those whose stories unfold in these stores. What follows is a quilting of those narratives, interviews, and discussions revealing Black bookstores as a mosaic as diverse as the

Tina McElroy Ansa signing a book at Pyramid Art, Books & Custom Framing. Courtesy of Garbo and Auna Hearne.

Courtesy of Jennifer Lawson.

Black community, as institutions reflecting all of our character, joy, humor, tears, scars, and ideas in motion. All at once, Black bookstores are resilient and radical. They're motley yet mingled. They're all of our identities, refracted innumerable times, across millions of pages all across this nation.

Their history runs deep. Along with Black colleges and Black churches, Black bookstores have sustained us through unspeakable oppression. When libraries banned us, they were our catalogs; when museums barred us, they were our exhibitions; when archives forbade us, they cradled our histories. Black bookshops—crafted in the shadows of slavery and segregation—created cathedrals for Black art, ideas, and resistance. They were our counter-publics. They were our brain trusts. They held our intellectual pasts, presents, and futures in a country denying our intellects, pasts, presence, and futures. And today, in America—where teaching Black people to read was once illegal and where teaching many Black books still is—Black bookstores remain as vital as ever.

This book presents a wide sampling and a survey of this remarkable institution. However, the stories featured herein are more exemplary than exhaustive. A full accounting of all the nation's Black bookstores is a project beyond this book's scope. The profiles adhere to Rosemary M. Stevenson's definition of a Black bookstore in *Black Bookstores: A Cultural History*, as one that "specializes in Black publications as opposed to [being] merely Black-owned." This work stands on the shoulders of many scholars, scribes, and community historians, and would have been impossible without the aid of many friends, old and new. To all those who made this book possible, I'm eternally grateful, and to all those who are about to discover the extraordinary story of the Black bookstore, I am proud to present *Prose to the People*.

# THE FIRE
What I Say to My Friends About Racism
## DON LEMON

## BLACK LIKE ME

# THE NEW NEGRO

## DEATH of INNOCENCE

# Uncle Tom's Cabin

## To be a SLAVE

# THEAST

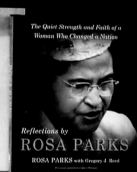
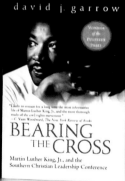
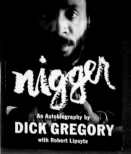

The Quiet Strength and Faith of a
Woman Who Changed a Nation

Reflections by
## ROSA PARKS
ROSA PARKS with Gregory J. Reed

david j. garrow
## BEARING THE CROSS
Martin Luther King, Jr., and the
Southern Christian Leadership Conference

## nigger
An Autobiography by
### DICK GREGORY
with Robert Lipsyte

NATIONAL BESTSELLER
# DEFINING MOMENTS IN BLACK HISTORY
## READING BETWEEN THE LIES
### DICK GREGORY

Dick Gregory's Political Primer
Edited by
James R. McGraw

# THE WISHING POOL
...her Stories

# THE KEVIN POWELL READER
Essential Writings
and Conversations

## STANDING AT THE SCRATCH LINE

WHEN NOTHING ELSE

THE EVERYTHING

# D. RUGGLES BOOKS

In the burgeoning metropolis of 1830s New York, Southern slave catchers prowled the streets, scouring for Black bodies. Whether a freeman or a runaway, Black New Yorkers feared being kidnapped and sold into eternal servitude.

Yet while those who beat slaves stalked the streets, those who wanted to beat slavery congregated in reading rooms and literary societies, working tirelessly to promote reading among the Black population and disseminate knowledge about the abolitionist movement.

David Ruggles, the first known Black bookstore owner in the United States, emerged as one of the most influential abolitionists in New York due to his brazen and courageous anti-slavery tactics, and his shop, D. Ruggles Books, inaugurated Black book vendors as epicenters of Black freedom. Unsurprisingly, Ruggles's store at 67 Lispenard Street bustled with the sale of anti-slavery publications, some of which he penned and printed in his own print shop.

In 1835, merely a year after the opening of D. Ruggles Books, this sanctuary of abolitionist literature burned to ashes in a suspected act of arson. Although no one claimed responsibility for the fire, Ruggles's relentless efforts in the fight against slavery drew countless enemies, particularly those exposed within his *New York Slaveholder Directory*—a publication that unmasked esteemed white citizens whose "servants" were, in truth, kidnapped Black people.

White New Yorkers threatened, harassed, and assaulted Ruggles, yet his commitment to freedom endured. In a November 24, 1835, advertisement in the *New York Emancipator*, Ruggles stated the following:

Agency Office, 67 Lispenard Street, New York—the friends of human rights are respectfully informed that in consequence of the destruction of my books, pamphlets, and stationery by fire, I am compelled for the present to discontinue the sale of books and the circulating library, but will abide in the same place and continue my agency for all Anti-Slavery Publications.

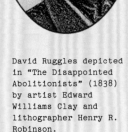

David Ruggles depicted in "The Disappointed Abolitionists" (1838) by artist Edward Williams Clay and lithographer Henry R. Robinson.

Ruggles continued his abolitionist work as the secretary of the New York Committee of Vigilance, an integrated group that monitored the Underground Railroad in the city. Ruggles's home was one of the main stations. Ruggles assisted hundreds of runaways, including Frederick Douglass.

In his Pulitzer Prize–winning biography of Douglass, Yale historian David W. Blight recounts how as a runaway in New York City Douglass felt "numbed by loneliness" and "trusted no one" before he met David Ruggles.

Douglass had been hiding from slave catchers. He was unhoused ("for at least one and possibly two nights, Frederick slept among the barrels at the wharf") until a Black sailor directed Douglass to Ruggles's house on Lispenard Street. There, Ruggles sheltered Douglass, helped him change his slave name (then Bailey), sent for Douglass's wife, Anna, in Baltimore, hosted their wedding, gave the couple some cash, exposed them to the life of abolitionism, and, "sensing that Frederick had no plan other than some vague idea of going to Canada, firmly urged the newlyweds to move up the New England coast, to New Bedford, Massachusetts, a whaling port, where Frederick could find work as a caulker, and the couple would find a welcoming fugitive-slave and free-black community."

As Douglass himself wrote, "I speak of David Ruggles as my old friend. [He] assisted me as well as many other fugitive slaves, on the way from slavery to freedom." Douglass described Ruggles as a "whole-souled man, fully imbued with a love of his afflicted and hunted people."

By 1837, Ruggles had spent seventeen months in jail, awaiting trial for sheltering a runaway. With failing health and deteriorating eyesight, he resigned from the New York Committee of Vigilance and went on to treat his progressive blindness with hydropathy, erecting the first building in the nation dedicated exclusively to the technique. Advertisements for Ruggles's water cure establishment ran in his former "cargo's" newspaper, *The North Star*.

Ruggles envisioned a free society and believed books could break slavery's chains. As the father of stateside Black bookstores, Ruggles served as a lighthouse for later booksellers seeking freedom through literacy. David Ruggles and D. Ruggles Books mark the genesis of the storied history of Black bookstores in the United States and their key role as sites for Black liberation.

An ad for Ruggles's bookstore.

# YOUNG'S BOOK EXCHANGE

Young's Book Exchange advertisement, index to the Schomburg clipping file, Schomburg Center for Research in Black Culture, Jean Blackwell Hutson General Research and Reference Division.

Before Malcolm X lindy-hopped at the Savoy Ballroom, before Mahalia Jackson testified at the Apollo Theater, before Harlem earned the nickname "Black Mecca," George Young opened Harlem's first Black bookstore, Young's Book Exchange—also called Young's Book Emporium—in 1915.

The former Pullman porter crammed upward of 10,000 volumes into the "dingy and drab . . . enterprising little shop" at 135 West 135th Street (and later in his home at 255 West 144th Street) by visiting bookstores in every city his work took him. Riding the rails, Young built a national supply chain that would catalyze the Black bookstore into a global business model.

In a 1921 *New York Evening Post* article, he detailed his procurement process: "I believe I've been in the bookstores of every major city in the U.S. I was a porter with the Pullman Company, and I used to go out on private [train] cars all over the country. Sometimes I'd have a week waiting in a place, and then I'd go out and scout around and pick up books and bring them home with me."

Young sourced Black books to "instill into the race a devotion to the literature." He advertised his "Mecca of Negro history and literature" in local and regional newspapers, attracting scholars and laymen alike. Even President Hoover read from Young's Book Exchange's shelves. In 1930, Hoover expressed his thanks to Young for sending him of copy of *The Life and Times of Frederick Douglass* and described George Young as "perhaps the foremost collector and dealer in old and rare books and objects concerning Negroes."

According to Richard B. Moore, a fellow Harlem-based collector and the Frederick Douglass Book Center's owner, these books included *The History of the Yorubas* by Rev. Samuel Johnson, *The Lone Star of Liberia* by F.A. Durham, and *Christianity, Islam and the Negro Race* by Edward Wilmot Blyden.

Like Indian spices or South African diamonds, the vast, rare collection at Young's Book Exchange soon generated international demand. The *New York Times* noted in his obituary that Young "was known to thousands in all parts of the world as one of America's foremost exponents on education for Negroes. . . . He had customers in almost every country in the world."

As the first Black bookstore in Harlem, Young's Book Exchange modeled the possibility for the domestic and international sale of Black books and helped transform New York into the Black literary capital of the world.

# THE SCHOMBURG SHOP AT THE SCHOMBURG CENTER FOR RESEARCH IN BLACK CULTURE

In Arturo Schomburg's 1925 essay, "The Negro Digs Up His Past," he writes, "The American Negro must remake his past in order to make his future. History must restore what slavery took away."

After Schomburg's fifth-grade teacher solemnly remarked, "The Negro has no history," Schomburg started collecting all the evidence he could find that proved that Black people had a long and honorable past. He found this evidence in books and established himself as Harlem's preeminent Black books collector.

Much like the hordes of exuberant Garveyites parading through Harlem's streets, Arturo Schomburg's collection of nearly 3,000 volumes and more than 1,100 pamphlets inspired the neighborhood's awe.

The New York Public Library (NYPL) cataloged Schomburg's collection in the Division of Negro Literature, History and Prints of the 135th Street Branch in 1926. By 1932, Schomburg served as the collection's curator, a position he held until his death in 1938.

Two years after Schomburg's death, NYPL renamed the division the Schomburg Collection of Negro Literature, History and Prints. And in 1972, the Schomburg Collection was designated as one of the Research Libraries of the New York Public Library and became the Schomburg Center for Research in Black Culture.

A gleaming indie bookstore beckoning pedestrians from Malcolm X Boulevard, the Schomburg Shop was once a mere closet, as current manager Virginia Mixon remembers: "I was a volunteer in the nineties when the shop was virtually a closet in the lobby. The books were on a shelf in the closet and there was a little table in front and people would come and buy books like *The Autobiography of Malcolm X* and books by James Baldwin—the classics."

Since the mid-aughts, the Schomburg Shop operates the independent bookstore arm of the research center. "The vision for the shop is to stock any books by Black or Caribbean authors or books that are on the subject of the global Black experience," former Schomburg Shop manager Rio Cortez told the American Bookseller Association in 2017.

Now, the Schomburg Center for Research in Black Culture helps usher in such books—including this one—through its extensive archives, proving not only that Black people have a history but that we are the future. Like the Apollo Theater, Abyssinian Baptist Church, and Sylvia's Restaurant, the Schomburg radiates as a cultural gem of Harlem, the Black Mecca.

Where every month is Black History Month.

Schomburg Center for Research in Black Culture's K. C. Matthews.

Schomburg Shop manager
Virginia Mixon.

Customers browse
books on Black
history and culture.

# HEAVEN, TO LEAVE WITH A BOOK

## BY RIO CORTEZ

I prefer waking up to sunlight
than to curtains drawn.
I prefer to let my body decide
and if it says so to lay in bed
for a very long time in stillness
and total quiet, I listen. If my body says
to Play Héctor Lavoe, I listen then too.
I prefer cool linens and satin pillowcases
and for someone I love to say
*good morning*, and to light a stick
of copal next to an open window.
I prefer to do nothing for a long time
and then, finally, to go for a walk
in the neighborhood. The walk
would end up, preferably,
at a bookstore. And wouldn't it
be so lovely to belong, to see
familiar brown faces, on and off
the shelves. To receive the perfect
recommendation, after staring
a weirdly long time at the poetry
section. And then to find
a little spot in the corner, where I'd
prefer to stay until sunset. And then,
Heaven, to leave with a book.
And walk home, without remark.
I prefer that someone else
has cleaned the house already. And
that dinner was delicious and
there's nothing left to do but pour
a glass of Vinho Verde
and open up the book where I left off.

# "Black is beautiful, but knowledge is power."

# NATIONAL MEMORIAL AFRICAN BOOKSTORE

It's rare to refer to a singular person as an institution, but Lewis Michaux fits the bill. Michaux's focus on Black liberation educated generations of readers in Harlem, the United States, and the world.

The self-taught Harlem historian and bookstore owner's personality befitted that of an eccentric bibliophile—always ready for a debate, speech, or protest. He was a self-proclaimed Black nationalist who spoke in rhymes and aphorisms (sometimes rhyming aphorisms) that seared into Harlem's collective memory. The *Amsterdam News* eulogized him as "the little, sharp-tongued philosopher."

Long before he earned his moniker "The Professor," uttered a pithy saying, or gained his one-man-institution status, Michaux worked as a deacon at the Church of God, which was founded by his evangelical brother, Lightfoot Solomon Michaux. Lewis Michaux eventually left the church and gave up religion (*"The only lord I know is the landlord."*) and set out to make a life in the book business.

Legend holds that Michaux decided to sell books after seeing some through a window display during his time as a window washer. He started small, with only a handful and a wagon to drag his inventory up and down Harlem's streets during the beginning of the Great Depression. Despite poor profits (only a dollar or two each day), Michaux's brother allowed him to use an old Church of God office storefront on Seventh Avenue to sell books. As an homage to his brother, Michaux named the bookstore after Lightfoot Solomon's failed farm co-op, the National Memorial to the Progress of the Colored Race in America. Thus, the National Memorial African Bookstore—called "the House of Common Sense and the Home of Proper Propaganda" by Lewis, and simply "Michaux's" by the neighborhood—was born. And it made Harlem its home for around forty years.

The way to hide something from the Black man
is to put it in a book.

**—LEWIS MICHAUX**

Despite the store's longevity, most didn't believe a store with books by and about Black people could succeed. Even Michaux thought Black folks didn't prioritize reading, but he strived to get Black people to read, think, and develop more self-confidence. "The average reader has not been taught to read and appreciate good books. You've got to go out and tell him the inspiration he can get from good literature about his people," Michaux told the *Afro-American* in 1945.

And inspire he did. The National Memorial African Bookstore housed the Afro-American Hall of Fame, large posters with the likenesses of famous Black people such as George Washington Carver, Paul Robeson, and, curiously, President

Eisenhower, who Michaux claimed was part Black. The store featured Black Santa and Black Jesus' portraits with a sign that read: "Christ is Black." Newly formed African nations' flags crowded shelves bursting with titles like W.E.B. Du Bois's *The Souls of Black Folks*, James Weldon Johnson's *Black Manhattan*, and William Melvin Kelley's satirical *Dem*, and copies of *Jet*, *Ebony*, the *Liberator*, and *Challenge*. The narrow and deep storefront held more than 200,000 texts, the largest Black literature collection in the world, complete with rare and out-of-print texts Michaux acquired during the Harlem Renaissance. In a 1953 *Chicago Defender* review of Harlem bookstores, Langston Hughes noted of Michaux's, "the very sight of so large a display of literature by or about Negroes is almost breathtaking" and "I find the National Memorial Book Store one of the most fascinating book shops I have ever seen."

WORLD'S HISTORY BOOK OUTLET ON 600 MILLION COLORED PEOPLE

NATIONAL MEMORIAL BOOK STORE
2107 Seventh Ave
New York, N. Y.

THE NEGRO AND HIS MANY DISADVANTAGES AND BURDENS.

BE PATRIOTIC

Buy books by and about Negroes; build a library in your home; help us display pictures and busts of noted Negro leaders before the public; also in the home and business of every patriotic Negro in America, for a memorial and inspiration to youth.

Visit us and know the Negro from his landing to his present standing and progress.

We specialize in Negro History and Music by noted writers and composers.

Free Admission Daily to the World's Only Negro Hall of Fame

National Memorial African Bookstore brochure, Black Print collection, Stuart A. Rose Manuscripts, Archives, and Rare Books Library, Emory University.

> The white man's dream of being supreme
> has turned to sour cream.
>
> —LEWIS MICHAUX

Though National Memorial received recognition from scholars and book lovers the world over, Michaux's militancy threatened those who expected Black people to be meek and subservient. An August 9, 1966, article in the *Daily Home News* about Michaux's featured the headline "Black Power Bookstore Is Headquarters for Harlem Bitterness." In it, the journalist reported that Lewis Michaux represented "militant extremists . . . with an almost neurotic contempt for 'Whitey'" and bemoaned a sign in the shop's window: "Move on over, white man, or we'll move on over you!" The bookstore served as the self-proclaimed Repatriation Headquarters for Marcus Garvey's Back to Africa Movement and an important meeting place for Black activists to learn and strategize. By the 1950s, the FBI took notice of Lewis Michaux, claiming he was "responsible for about 75 percent of the anti-white material which is distributed in Harlem." Oftentimes, activists and other community members spouted pro-Black ideas on soapboxes outside the store, an area Lewis Michaux named Harlem Square.

> Black is beautiful, but knowledge is power.
>
> —LEWIS MICHAUX

Michaux's goal of encouraging Harlem to read unfolded at National Memorial and spilled out into the streets. Malcolm X frequented the store and held rallies at Harlem Square.

Michaux hosted autograph parties for the likes of Eartha Kitt, Joe Louis, and Louis Armstrong. He encouraged all his customers to start home libraries, and if someone didn't have money to pay, he'd let them read books in their entirety in the store or give them away for free. In the 1940s, Michaux had a trailer he'd take out every Saturday to sell books on the street. "I feel that this is a good opportunity to meet the people and talk to them," he told the *Afro-American*.

But it wasn't just home libraries Michaux supplied books for. Black bookstore owners trekked to Michaux's to stock up on inventory and wisdom from the seasoned bookseller. In a Facebook post, Paul Coates described meeting with Michaux during his time owning Baltimore's The Black Book: "He drove hard bargains, but would most often let me win, taking pity on this young bookseller breaking into the trade that he

pioneered." Coates went on to assert, "Michaux remains our greatest bookseller."

While National Memorial African Bookstore and Lewis Michaux were synonymous, Michaux did have assistance from employees and family members. His wife, Bettie, whom he met at the store, and his son Lewis Michaux Jr. chipped in around the shop along with two of Michaux's sisters, Margaret and Ruth. Michaux described Helen Brown, the store's secretary, as "a help to all who passed through the shop's doors." Olive Batch, Michaux's future niece by marriage, also worked at the House of Common Sense and the Home of Proper Propaganda.

```
        Only a tree will stand still
       while it's being chopped down.
```

**—LEWIS MICHAUX**

In 1974, the legendary bookstore closed after getting evicted by the state of New York to expand the State Office Building. Harlem protested the forced removal, with community groups

fundraising and gathering ideas on how to save the store. Despite their efforts, Michaux was getting older and made the difficult decision to let go of National Memorial.

```
    It's my baby, but it's got too heavy for me.
```

**—LEWIS MICHAUX**

After Malcolm X's 1965 assassination, Michaux hung a sign outside National Memorial African Bookstore that read:

```
Man, if you think Bro. Malcolm is dead,
you are out of your cotton picking
   head.
Just get up off your slumbering bed,
and just watch his fighting spirit
   spread.
Every shut eye ain't sleep, Every
   good-bye
ain't gone.
```

The same could be said for Lewis Michaux and his bookstore. Like Malcolm X, Lewis Michaux burned as a lodestar for liberation and literacy. National Memorial African Bookstore continues to inspire new generations of booksellers and readers. Michaux lived long enough to see Black writers honored for their literary contributions at the first annual Lewis H. Michaux Book Fair in 1976.

To this day, National Memorial African Bookstore remains the standard-bearer for what a Black bookstore can be.

B.S.S. #526-M

November 28, 1962

From:      Detective William K. De Fossett, #631, B.S.S.

To:        Commanding Officer, Bureau of Special Services

Subject:                                            THE NATIONAL
                                                    , N.Y.C.

    1. From                                    r 27, 1962,
the unders                                area with the
following

    2.  T                                    ed at 3:50
P.M. and a                                  ck Nationalists
were found                                  eetings of any
significan                                  eet meetings,
outside hi                                  uitable.

ABOVE: James E. Hinton. "Stokely Carmichael and H. Rap Brown in
Michaux's Bookstore in Harlem, 1967." Courtesy of Emory University
Rose Library.

BACKGROUND: New York Police Department surveillance report on Lewis
Michaux, owner of the National Memorial African Bookstore in Harlem.
Courtesy of the New York City Municipal Archives.

    2.  The National Memorial Bood Store was visited at 3:50
P.M. and again at 6:10 P.M.  The usual group of Black Nationalists
were found in and around the store.  There are no meetings of any
significance planned by Mr. Michaux.  The usual street meetings,
outside his store are held whenever the weather is suitable.

                                    William  K.  De Fossett
                                    Det. #631,  B.S.S.

# MY GREAT-UNCLE LEWIS MICHAUX AND HARLEM'S GREATEST BOOKSTORE

## BY VAUNDA MICHEAUX NELSON

"Knowledge is power! You need it every hour! Read a book!"

"If you don't know and you ain't got no dough, then you can't go and that's fo' sho'!"

With words like these, how could I have resisted falling under Lewis Michaux's spell?

I believe books saved my great-uncle Lewis. As a reader, librarian, and writer, I was drawn into his story.

Lewis was independent-minded, some might say stubborn, from the time he was a child. As a boy, he refused to work in the fields for twenty-five cents a day. Instead, he found more profitable, sometimes illegal, ways to make money. Lewis's self-directed nature may have led to dangerous risk-taking in his youth, but it served him well when he found his calling in books.

I did not experience the kind of troubles Lewis had growing up, but, like him, books were crucial in the making of me.

My early inspiration to read and write came from my parents. They read to me and my four siblings every night. Most times my mother read the next chapter of our current book, but sometimes Dad would recite poetry from memory, some his own. My parents gave me their love of stories. And they taught me the power of words—how they can lift up and tear down—"so be careful with them," they said.

Thanks to my older sister, Regina, when I started school at the age of five, I could read. The ability to read gave me more access to the stories my parents had inspired me to love. Reading led to writing; the rest is my life.

Knowing what I know now, I have no doubt that my father's love of literature, particularly poetry, was encouraged by his uncle Lewis. My mother, who worked in the bookstore before marrying my dad, most certainly caught the fever as well. I may owe Lewis more than I know. It's possible that I am a writer today because of his distant influence.

Lewis once said, "Where did I get that literary idea? I could have been an iceman." How providential that he was not.

The National Memorial African Bookstore was successful because Lewis knew and loved his stock, but more so because he loved his community and made it his business to connect with people. He gave as much time to those who came to look or talk as to those who bought. Lewis fostered a space where customers came to connect with other regulars. His bookstore became a gathering place, and closing time wasn't dictated by the clock.

I didn't know my great-uncle well, but in the summer, my family would pile into our Chevy station wagon and drive from Pittsburgh to New York for a weeklong visit. We spent most of our time at my grandparents' home in Port Chester or playing in the sand at Rye Beach. I may have been at the bookstore more than I recall, but I have only one clear memory.

Lewis Michaux with (*from left to right*) Margaret Banks (Lewis's sister), Olive M. Batch (Vaunda's mother), and Miss Duffy inside the original National Memorial African Bookstore location circa 1945. Courtesy of Vaunda Micheaux Nelson.

I was fourteen. The store was narrow and crowded with books and pamphlets and customers, and portraits of famous black people displayed high up on the walls. Uncle Lewis gave me two books—*The Masquerade*, a novel by Oscar Micheaux (no relation), and a copy of the King James Bible. This experience must have meant something to me because these books remain in my collection.

Fast-forward to the late 1980s and my time in library school at the University of Pittsburgh.

"Micheaux? Are you related to that Harlem bookseller?"

Time and again I was asked this by students and professors alike. Apparently, big things had occurred at the National Memorial African Bookstore. It made me want to learn what these people knew about my family that I didn't. And so began my research.

At first, I was simply compiling family history. A book was not in my plans. Later, the notion emerged. I had unearthed enough about Lewis to realize the bookstore was only the culmination, that the real story lay in his journey from lost soul to "the Professor."

The project started as a straight biography but, after completing a draft in this format, I felt it wasn't working. There were holes and discrepancies in the information about Lewis's life that I could not resolve. Sources were contradictory, unclear, and unreliable, and the people who might have been able to help were already in their graves. Nonfiction didn't give me the flexibility I needed to bring my great-uncle to life.

So, with some informed speculation and cautious fictionalization, I began telling the story of Lewis Michaux through the voices of those who surrounded him—family, friends, associates, and bookstore customers. Recordings and interviews with Lewis enabled me to replicate his voice. Census and court records, church documents, newspaper and magazine articles, even FBI files, all became parts of the story. My husband began calling the book "documentary fiction."

The more I worked to pull the pieces together, the greater my passion grew for Lewis and his story and the more compelled I became to tell it.

I lived with this project for years, putting it on the back burner when I had to. I was working full-time and writing other books, so I couldn't actively work on it every day. But Lewis was always hovering, enticing me back into his world, challenging me to finish.

In 2012, *No Crystal Stair* was born. The book contains the stories of those affected by Lewis, by his simply saying, "Here are some books about you." These vignettes, based on what I learned from and about actual patrons, are only those I could uncover—surely it's just the tip of the iceberg.

It seems wherever I go to speak about Lewis and the National Memorial African Bookstore, someone stands up and says, "I was in that bookstore!" Who knows how many more are out there?

Lewis Michaux spent most of his adult life working to provide books by and about black people and encouraging them to explore their history and culture, to give them a sense of pride, to empower them. Frequent bookstore visitor A. Peter Bailey put it this way: "When I'm there, I don't just read. I listen. I listen to Brother Michaux talking about the books and current events. He and his peers are like older brothers to the rest of us. They discuss issues and argue. I just stand around and get free history lessons."

Lewis was a self-defined man, and he wanted black people to define themselves, not be defined by others. He believed books could provide the knowledge and language to do this. He never tired of stressing the power of learning. "You gotta know who you are before you can improve your condition," he said.

Lewis's words, his definitions, bored into me, turned me around and upside down, tripped me and flipped me.

He said, "I am not a so-called Negro. I say 'so-called' because a Negro is a thing, not a person. The word is an invention. A Negro is a thing to be used, abused, accused, and refused. That's his role in this stroll. And blacks who continue to accept this ain't going nowhere."

He took my breath away.

I hope those who learn Lewis's story will be left with a deeper desire to know more, to learn more, to question, and to be informed enough to avoid allowing others to decide who they become.

Lewis said, "Knowledge is the thing today that is needed among the young people." He cautioned, "You can't protect yourself if you don't know something." I love what he's saying here. *You can't protect yourself if you don't know something.* I wish all young people could take this to heart.

Lewis determined that reading was good for him, and it would be good for other striving African Americans. He believed who we become depends a great deal on our desire to be educated, our efforts to know our history and ourselves, and our resolve to contribute.

One quote of his I keep going back to is this:

```
I listen to everybody, but I don't hear
everybody. It's all right to listen, but
you don't hear everybody because if you
do, you cease to be yourself and become
the fellow you hear. It's an intelligent
thing to do, to entertain the man who's
trying to tell you something, but never
           lose your individuality.
```

This is not a new idea—thinking for yourself—but I'd never heard it expressed quite *his* way.

As essayist Christopher de Vinck observed, "Reading aloud to my children every day gives them the widest entry to that place we call freedom."

As a former children's librarian and a believer in the power of books, the power of knowledge, I found this resonates with me. In a broader sense I'd add that *literacy,* too, is a part of "the widest entry to that place we call freedom." Frederick Douglass (whom Lewis Michaux admired) understood and lived it. And Lewis surely believed this was the way to freedom for black Americans. "Knowledge is power," indeed, but only if it leads to independent thinking.

Lewis used books as a compass in his search for self. Books saved him, and he went on to save many others who were fortunate enough to enter the National Memorial African Bookstore.

A Reading People Is a Rising People

# FREDERICK DOUGLASS BOOK CENTER

"Think free! Act free! Be free!" Richard Benjamin Moore, activist and owner of Harlem's Frederick Douglass Book Center, urged Harlemites.

Moore and his wife, Lodie Biggs, established the "small, but crammed with books" storefront around 1942, only a couple of years after founding the Frederick Douglass Historical and Cultural League. Moore and Biggs stated the goal of the Book Center and the Cultural League was "to spread the knowledge of our history, to keep alive the heroic traditions of such characters as Douglass, and to foster cultural advancement."

More than one hundred years before, Frederick Douglass and his wife, Anna, would find freedom at David Ruggles's Manhattan bookstore, where they were sheltered and married as runaways. At the Frederick Douglass Book Center, husband and wife duo Richard B. Moore and Lodie Biggs brought a new generation of Black New Yorkers freedom between the pages. Located at 141 West 125th Street between Lenox and Seventh Avenues, it became the place to realize their goal.

∗∗∗

Richard B. Moore frequented Young's Book Exchange as a customer, and like George Young, Moore's expansive personal book collection led to his business's formation. Unlike Young, Moore housed many of his personal books at the Book Center, confusing casual customers who couldn't understand why displayed books weren't for sale. Nevertheless, Moore welcomed all to learn from all of the books at the store.

Moore, a self-taught scholar, held lectures about African people's history and culture and published *The Name "Negro": Its Origins and Evil Use* in 1960, the written component to his campaign to promote the adoption of "Afro-American" as the race's preferred designation. He stated "this name 'Negro' is still loaded with contempt, derogation, and hostility. The logical conclusion . . . is that this harmful misnomer 'Negro' should

be eschewed once and for all and its use wholly abolished." Moore argued that language "has been used as an enslaving and oppressive device" and that "part of the liberation process must be a liberation of the language."

In a birthday dinner invitation celebrating Richard B. Moore, writer Cyril Briggs and Lodie Biggs praised Moore's "devotion to the cause of all the oppressed."

Unfortunately, the store fell into decline as Moore suffered from a stomach condition that caused him to default on debts owed to publishers and utility companies. Then, in 1968, the state of New York razed the Frederick Douglass Book Center to make way for the Adam Clayton Powell Jr. State Office Building.

Yet long after its closure, the store would be remembered as a historic landmark of Black intellectualism. From all around the world, researchers flocked to the 141 West 125th Street Book Center to study Moore's collection of old and rare volumes by and about the African diaspora, the Caribbean, and Afro-Americans. Fittingly, the Frederick Douglass Book Center even became something of a shrine to its namesake. Researchers journeyed to the store to read the abolitionist orator's out-of-circulation works. During Moore's time, Douglass's classic autobiography had remained out of print for forty years. Yet in 1941, thanks to Moore, the Pathway Press issued what Moore considered the most important book by an Afro-American:

*The Life and Times of Frederick Douglass, the Centenary Memorial Subscribers Edition.*

Embodying Douglass's intellectual courage and zeal, Moore ignited the fiery liberation of literacy in a generation of Black scholars, readers, and activists across the diaspora. Blending the admiration of literary figures with the dissemination of their works, the Frederick Douglass Book Center epitomized the bond between Black authors and Black booksellers and served as a forerunner to later bookshops molding their names, catalogs, and missions in the image of activists and authors like Marcus Garvey, James Baldwin, Ida B. Wells, and so many others.

Richard B. Moore papers, 1902–1978, Schomburg Center for Research in Black Culture, Manuscripts, Archives, and Rare Books.

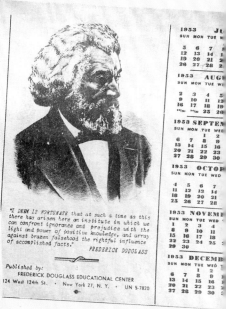

Specialty: African Culture — Afroamerican History — World Relations

# DOUGLASS BOOK CENTER

RICHARD B. MOORE
Phone: 534-6416

23 EAST 125th STREET
New York, N. Y. 10035

May 27, 1971

The Macmillan Company
Box 247 Church Street Station
New York, N. Y. 10008

Dear Sirs:

Because of serious and prolonged illness in my family, this bill could not be attended to until now. However, I am glad to be able to take care of it now. Thanks for your courtesy.

Enclosed please find check for $152.80 in settlement.

Very truly yours,

DOUGLASS BOOK CENTER

Richard B Moore

RBM:...

369

DOUGLASS BOOK CENTER
23 EAST 125TH STREET
NEW YORK, N. Y. 10035

May 27, 1971

1-315
260

OF The Macmillan Company $152 80/xx

hundred fifty-two 80/100 DOLLARS

Book Center

Specialty:
African Culture —
Afroamerican History —
World Relations

## DOUGLASS BOOK CENTER

Phone: 534-6416
RICHARD B. MOORE

23 EAST 125th STREET
New York, N. Y. 10035

# THE MARCH COMMUNITY BOOKSHOP

The March on Washington Movement of the early 1940s led to an executive order banning employment discrimination in defense industries, inspired the 1963 March on Washington where Martin Luther King Jr. declared "I have a dream," and paved the way for The March Community Bookshop.

The March Organization's national treasurer, Aldrich Turner, proposed a movement bookshop to help offset the coalition's administrative costs. Turner consulted with group officials, local business leaders, historians, and intellectuals like J.A. Rogers before opening the shop in 1943 with an initial investment of $1,000 of personal savings.

The March Community Bookshop organized out of a Hotel Theresa storefront on Seventh Avenue near 125th Street, joining the nearby National Memorial African Bookstore and the Frederick Douglass Book Center across the street.

While the shop lobbied support for and empowered Black civil rights organizations, its inventory didn't only assemble books on Black and African history and society. It championed all subjects, including psychology, sports, religion, music, philosophy, poetry, and drama.

In a review of Harlem-based bookstores, Langston Hughes hailed The March Community Bookshop as "spick and span, newly renovated and attractive, with a colorful and neatly arranged window display."

The bookshop's success allowed The March Organization to pay its rent and phone bills until the coalition dissolved in 1947. The store would run for another decade, until it closed in 1958. Today, its legacy lives on as a tribute to the enduring reciprocity between Black activism and Black literature. For decades before the iconic March on Washington would fuel countless Black books, The March Organization was fueled by a Black bookstore.

The March

Community

Book Shop

2086 Seventh Avenue
(Hotel Theresa)
New York 27, N. Y.

Tel.: MO 2-3350

The March Community Bookshop
brochure, index to the
Schomburg clipping file,
Schomburg Center for Research
in Black Culture, Jean
Blackwell Hutson General
Research and Reference
Division.

PROSE TO THE PEOPLE

# HAKIM'S BOOKSTORE

"I think he'd be happy. I think he'd be happy. Because he was taken before he could finish his mission. And I meant it when I told him I would try to continue what he started."

Yvonne Blake wipes away tears as she imagines how her dad would feel seeing her run Hakim's Bookstore today. In the fall of 2023, the decades-old shop received a state historical marker recognizing it "as the first Black-owned bookstore in Phila[delphia] specializing in Black history and titles by Black authors." Community members, customers, politicians, and news cameras gathered to commemorate the event.

But when Dawud Hakim started selling books out of his car trunk in 1959—and even when he moved into a brick-and-mortar location in the 1960s—customers barely dribbled in.

"Me and him would sit outside and play chess, waiting for customers," Yvonne Blake recalls.

Yet Hakim persisted while also working as an accountant to support his family.

"He was really energetic and optimistic about what he was doing and always trying to find ways to get these books in the hands of the people who needed to read them," Yvonne says, remembering multiple times when her dad gave away books like *The Autobiography of Malcolm X* to kids and quizzed them on it the next time he saw them. "He was a taskmaster like that," she chuckles.

Sharing Black radical texts, being Muslim, publishing books on Arabic and African names, and making Hakim's Bookstore "a civil rights and Black activism gathering space" attracted the ire of the FBI, Yvonne recalls. "[The FBI] would be across the street taking pictures and my dad said, 'Instead of trying to figure out that we're doing something wrong, they need to come in here and pick up a book and learn something.' He was never intimidated."

Hakim was so unintimidated, in fact, that he expanded his operations to Atlanta, employing future Medu Bookstore owner Nia Damali.

After her dad died of cancer in 1997, Yvonne suddenly helmed a business she hadn't planned on inheriting. She quickly learned she couldn't do business like her father did because it was a different time. She made the tough decision to close the Atlanta location but managed to keep active the store's prison mail-order program.

In 2014, history repeated itself: Hakim's had few customers and Yvonne had to get another job to support the store. The store's hours contracted to just one day a week, then finally, Yvonne put out the call that the longstanding business might have to fold. Once again, Hakim's endured, as new and old customers alike flooded the store with support, including volunteer Chris Arnold, who brought in younger customers and helped create a website so Hakim's could get online.

Now, Hakim's ships books all over the country and abroad, becoming a destination for tourists visiting Philadelphia.

Yvonne considers it all a fitting tribute to her father. "I think he'd be happy. I think he'd be happy."

Yvonne Blake is continuing what her father, Dawud Hakim, started.

e Case of Martin Sostre

*The Amazing, Untold Story of a Dedicated Black*
*Liberation Fighter Railroaded to Prison (or the*
*In 19*

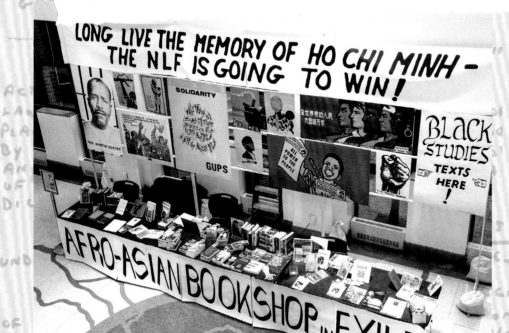

Jerry Gross, Geraldine Robinson, and Bob McCubbin
staff the Afro-Asian Bookshop-in-Exile, c. 1968,
William Worthy papers, MS.0524, Special Collections,
The Johns Hopkins University.

LONG LIVE THE MEMORY OF HO CHI MINH —
THE NLF IS GOING TO WIN!

SOLIDARITY

GUPS

BLACK STUDIES TEXTS HERE!

AFRO-ASIAN BOOKSHOP IN EXILE

BACKGROUND: *Workers
World*, "The Case
of Martin Sostre,"
December 27, 1968.
Excerpts from a legal
brief handwritten
by Martin Sostre
while in solitary
confinement at Green
Haven Prison in
Stormville, New York.

ABOVE: Afro-Asian Bookshop-in-Exile replica, "Sostre at 100," Schomburg
Center for Research in Black Culture, photo by Zachary Dean Norman.

# NOTHING DISAPPEARS IN THIS WORLD

## BY GARRETT FELBER

For nearly a week during the summer of 1967, Black residents in Buffalo took to the streets in response to organized abandonment and ongoing police violence in their neighborhoods. The city became one of nearly 160 to revolt during what became known as the "Long Hot Summer."[1] Although most store owners—Black and white—closed their businesses during the rebellion, one exception was Martin Sostre's Afro-Asian Bookshop at 1412 Jefferson Avenue. He kept the store open until 3 a.m., providing refuge from tear gas and police violence in the streets and giving rousing speeches to the crowds gathering inside. When a cop chased a Black teenager into the store after getting called a "pig," the police officer found himself outnumbered by twenty people. He shook his fist at Sostre and yelled, "I hope you're proud of this."[2] The bookstore was at the center of the rebellion, both physically and politically. Sostre later described the two weeks after the uprising as "the best I ever had."[3]

Law enforcement had surveilled and harassed Sostre since he'd opened his store in 1965.[4] Within weeks of the rebellion, they framed him. Using an informant with charges hanging over his head to pretend to purchase heroin from Sostre, police and the FBI raided the bookstore and arrested him and his girlfriend, Geraldine Robinson. Days before Sostre's appearance before the grand jury, Police Commissioner Frank Felicetta testified to the Senate Internal Security Committee in Washington, D.C., on the causes of the uprising in Buffalo. There, he described Sostre as a "prominent figure in the recent disorders in our city" and "the man who incited East Side riots."[5] He referred to Sostre as "Mr. X," a dog whistle meant to stoke white anxieties about militant Black Muslims.[6]

In 1968, Sostre was sentenced to thirty-one to forty-one years by an all-white jury. Like many narratives of Black bookstores from this era, the story of the Afro-Asian Bookshop often centers on state repression. Its life and afterlives offer a way to understand revolutionary Black bookstores outside this frame. Martin Sostre asserted

---

1   The Kerner Commission established by President Johnson to investigate these uprisings categorized Buffalo as one of eight major disorders that summer, at a scale equivalent to the better-known revolts in Newark and Detroit. Neil Kraus, *Race, Neighborhoods, and Community Power: Buffalo Politics, 1934-1997* (Albany: SUNY Press, 2000), 126.

2   Joe Shapiro, "In and Out of Prison: Revolutionary Politics in the 70s," *Introspect* 2, no. 1 (Spring 1976), 4.

3   Martin Sostre, "Report from Jail to My Revolutionary Friends," in *Letters from Prison* (Buffalo, NY: Martin Sostre Defense Committee, 1969), 21.

4   Martin Sostre FBI File (100-NY-154100).

5   "Fanatics Are Tied to June Violence," *Buffalo Courier-Express*, August 5, 1967, and "Lawyer Requests Disqualification of Grand Jurors," *Buffalo News*, August 4, 1967.

6   Quoted in "Sostre Defense Committee Answers HUAC and Felicetta," *Workers World*, July 5, 1968. Manuel Bernstein, "Man Held as Inciter of Trouble," *Buffalo Courier-Express*, July 15, 1967, and Frank Besag and Philip Cook, *The Anatomy of a Riot: Buffalo, 1967* (Buffalo: University Press, 1970), 46.

that "nothing disappears in this world. Either it lies dormant awaiting the propitious moment to manifest itself, or it manifests itself in different forms and manners. Once an act or thought is set in motion, nothing can stop it."[7] The elusiveness of his bookstores and what they represented—as well as their ability to contort and reshape themselves over time, space, and place—open possibilities for creating community spaces and political education that are beyond state capture.

∗∗∗

In his early life, Sostre, a second-generation Black Puerto Rican, was shaped by the protests, rebellions, street corner orators, and radical community spaces of East Harlem during the Great Depression. He was particularly inspired by Lewis Michaux's National Memorial African Bookstore, one of the first brick-and-mortar Black-owned bookstores in the United States since that of abolitionist David Ruggles a century earlier. In its early years, Michaux's included a spacious reading room in the back of the store. It was also billed as "Harlem's most complete lending library."[8] This commitment to bookstores as a community space, not unlike a public library, had a profound effect on Sostre.

Sostre had also been exposed to forms of communal study when he'd served an earlier prison sentence in the 1950s. Several years into his twelve-year sentence, he'd joined the Nation of Islam and led study groups in the prison yard with other incarcerated Muslims. He was the group's secretary and Spanish instructor. Information on Black history and Islam was limited and often considered contraband, so Muslims communalized their readings and kept books, pamphlets, and scrapbooks in a wooden locker they built and controlled autonomously. In 1959, amid a national panic about the Nation of Islam as a "Black supremacist" hate group following the television documentary *The Hate That Hate Produced*, prison officials raided their locker and Sostre and others were thrown in solitary confinement. He remained in isolation for five years, until his release in October 1964.

Upon his release, Sostre moved to Buffalo. After six months of work at Bethlehem Steel, he had saved enough to establish the city's first revolutionary Black bookstore—the first of three he opened over the next several years. From its very beginnings, the Afro-Asian Bookshop was an extension of other forms of Black community space and radical study, ones that were also targeted and disrupted by the state.

For the next six months, Sostre worked sixteen-hour days—one shift at the factory and a second at the bookstore. "I was continuously plagued by two main problems," he reflected. The first was making the store financially self-sufficient. The second

---

7 Excerpt from Martin Sostre letter, March 13, 1972, Box 13, Folder 13, Elwin H. Powell papers, University Archives, The State University of New York at Buffalo.
8 "National Memorial Book Store," *Amsterdam News*, May 4, 1946.

was "how to convert the shop into a political center for the Afro-American youth." Through experimentation with his inventory—literature, nonfiction, African statuettes, and eventually soul and R&B records—Sostre developed a community space and site of politicization, multiracial organizing, and self-affirmation for young people in Buffalo.

The Afro-Asian Bookshop's literature reflected the anti-colonial, internationalist perspective embodied in its name. Sostre carried the speeches of Fidel Castro and journals such as *African Opinion*, *Peking Review*, and *China Reconstructs*.[9] Mao's *Little Red Book* and the autobiography of Ho Chi Minh stood in the window to attract passersby.[10] Sostre also stocked books and pamphlets on the history, culture, and politics of the African diaspora—the novels of Richard Wright and James Baldwin, histories by Carter G. Woodson and Lerone Bennett Jr., and the autobiography and speeches of Malcolm X. Pamphlets, selling for as little as a quarter, served "as introductory manuals into revolutionary thought" and stimulated conversations.[11] A hand-drawn advertisement in one of the city's Black newspapers, the *Buffalo Criterion*, showed its eclectic range.[12]

Sostre described his bookshop as "a community center type of bookstore," with a reading room and lounge chairs where people could sit and read. He sat and talked at great length with anyone who came in. "His idea was to make the bookstore a hangout, especially for young people," said one patron. "It was more like a library," another remembered.[13] Karima Amin, a high school student who frequented the shop, remembered it as a "beautiful, warm, welcoming place, a place where I wanted to be, and where I felt I needed to be."[14]

✳ ✳ ✳

Although the state destroyed this community space upon Sostre's arrest in 1967, new forms emerged in its place. Within a year, the Martin Sostre Defense Committee established the Afro-Asian Bookshop-in-Exile (AABE) as its central hub on the University at Buffalo's (UB) campus. Sostre articulated the bookstore's goals in a letter to his committee: "Besides the income it brings in for our legal expenses, it is a sower of seeds in the struggle against the power structure."[15] He emphasized that it must be

---

9    "To the Black Community: Message from Jail, an Interview with Martin Sostre," August 1, 1967, Martin Sostre Defense Committee, Subject Vertical Files, Folder 2, Civil Liberties—Blacks—Black Nationalism—Sostre, Martin, Labadie Collection, University of Michigan, Special Collections. Also see Hearings Before the Committee on Un-American Activities, House of Representatives, Ninetieth Congress, Second Session (Washington: U.S. Government Printing Office, 1968), 2000.

10   Jerry Ross, interview with author, July 24, 2020.

11   "Report from Jail to My Revolutionary Friends."

12   "Afro-Asian Bookstore," *Buffalo Criterion*, June 22, 1966, Buffalo Public Library, Grosvenor Room.

13   Jerry Ross, interview with author, July 24, 2020, and Dan Bentivogli, interview with author, February 24, 2021.

14   Karima Amin, interview with author, November 30, 2021.

15   *Letters from Prison*, 69.

"action-oriented" and "not only . . . attract and train the active segment of the community but . . . spur to action the passive and fence sitters."[16]

The AABE at the UB campus lasted for nearly two years, spanning multiple tables in the student union and eventually featuring prominent backdrops of Sostre's profile, political posters, copies of the *Black Panther* newspaper with artwork by Emory Douglas, and a banner proclaiming "Long Live the Memory of Ho Chi Minh—The NLF is Going to Win."[17] For several of Sostre's comrades and defense committee members, running the AABE became a full-time job.[18] They even traveled to New York City to buy books from the basement of Lewis Michaux's bookstore. During her time out on bail, Robinson also helped staff the AABE. At the end of each day, the bookstore-in-exile was packed away in the small storage room that Black custodial workers secured for the committee.[19]

Like its predecessor, the bookstore-in-exile was targeted. In a "modern-day book burning," a maintenance worker incinerated two hundred-pound boxes of stored pamphlets and books, claiming he thought they were garbage.[20] In early 1969, the university also used bureaucratic tactics to push the AABE off campus. Citing a space shortage, the director of the student union stated that only one table could be used per organization. In response, the Black Student Union, the Philosophical Society, and Youth Against War and Fascism pushed together their single allotments to continue the AABE.[21]

Two years after Sostre's frame-up, comrades took the AABE on the road. At the pivotal Students for a Democratic Society Convention in Chicago, the AABE table gathered more than 250 signatures demanding Sostre's freedom.[22] The following month, they traveled to Oakland for the United Front Against Fascism conference organized by the Black Panther Party. Meanwhile, Sostre began a Black history lending library at Wallkill Prison under its auspices. He did so while facing ongoing political censorship, even of his own writings. He eventually won a landmark lawsuit against the state in *Sostre v. Otis,* which secured the right to due process and grievance proceedings for incarcerated people with regard to censored literature. By 1970, AABEs had emerged at universities in Boston, New York, Milwaukee, and Cleveland. A comrade Sostre mentored in prison opened the final Afro-Asian Bookshop-in-Exile on the Lower East Side of New York City in 1974.

16  Martin Sostre to Jeanette Merrill, June 24, 1968, in author's possession, courtesy of Ellie Dorritie and the Workers World Party (WWP). He also envisioned an AABE book club, capitalizing on the committee's extensive mailing list by sending a catalog of books and pamphlets with an order form at the end.

17  Claudia Dreifus, "The Crime of Martin Sostre, by Vincent Copeland," *The East Village Other,* 5, no. 34, July 21, 1970, 16.

18  Bob McCubbin, email message to author, December 15, 2020.

19  McCubbin oral history, January 13, 2021.

20  Jeanette Merrill to Mr. Williams, August 26, 1968, in Black Power Movement, Part 2: The Papers of Robert F. Williams, Group 1, Series 1: Correspondence, 1956–1979, Bentley Historical Library, University of Michigan—Ann Arbor. Also see "Books Destroyed, Representative of Afro-Asian Bookstore Calls Act Intentional," *The Spectrum,* August 9, 1968, and Worthy, "Sostre in Solitary," *Boston Sunday Globe,* September 8, 1968.

21  "Black-oriented Bookstore Opposes Norton Restriction," *The Spectrum,* January 29, 1969.

22  Petition in author's possession, courtesy of Dorritie and WWP.

TOP LEFT: *The Activist,*
October 5, 1969. |
TOP RIGHT: *Buffalo
Criterion*, June 22,
1966. | BOTTOM LEFT:
*Buffalo Challenger
News Weekly,*
September 9, 1965. |
BOTTOM RIGHT: *Buffalo
Challenger News Weekly,*
October 27, 1966.

✳ ✳ ✳

In March 2023, I partnered with the New York Public Library's Jail & Prison Services team to organize a centennial celebration of Martin Sostre's life. As part of the events held at the Schomburg Center for Research in Black Culture, we reconstructed a life-size replica of the AABE, featuring books and posters from the original, as well as some of Sostre's own materials loaned by his family, and zines and resources that attendees could take with them.

We donated the exhibit to Reclaim the Commons, a campaign at City College of New York to regain community control of the dining commons at the Graduate Center as part of the broader struggle against privatization and enclosure. Like so many iterations before it, the AABE was swiftly targeted by the administration and university officials, who ordered that custodial staff destroy it. Fortunately, staff and library workers rescued the exhibit by moving it safely to the library. Whether in the form of a wooden locker built by Muslims in the prison yard at Clinton Prison, the brick-and-mortar Afro-Asian Bookshop at 1412 Jefferson Avenue, or the tables of revolutionary literature on university campuses, autonomously organized radical community spaces remain targets beyond capture.

# LIBERATION BOOKSTORE

Most bookstore owners can't say they've managed two separate bookstores on two different continents, but Una Mulzac wasn't like most bookstore owners. Before owning Harlem's Liberation Bookstore, Mulzac managed the People's Progressive Party (PPP) bookstore in Guyana.

During Mulzac's second year as the PPP bookstore manager, a man firebombed the store, instantly killing PPP members Michael Force and Edward Griffin. The blast slammed Mulzac to the ground and sprayed her with shrapnel.

Despite the imminent danger, Mulzac continued to lead the bookstore for three more years, until she returned to the States to contribute to the burgeoning anti-war movement.

Upon Mulzac's return, she established Liberation Bookstore on Harlem's Lenox Avenue in 1967. The Black bookshop was as revolutionary as the Black activists roiling America. The red, black, and green storefront displayed large windows filled with book advertisements, Black heroes' portraits, slogans, articles from periodicals, and a hodgepodge of flyers announcing community events. Large painted letters proclaimed: IF YOU DON'T KNOW, LEARN. IF YOU KNOW, TEACH. Malcolm X speeches played from the store's loudspeakers onto the street, introducing many to his teachings.

By the thousands, books crowded the small store like a raucous rally, their spines reading like placards. Customers could peruse volumes on African and African American history, literary criticism, and various diasporic languages. One section of the store that Mulzac specially curated

was "Know Your Enemy." "We must not take our enemy lightly," Mulzac implored the crowd at the store's fifteenth-anniversary celebration. "This section is kept up-to-date!"

That directive amplified the store's mission, which was, in Mulzac's words, "to contribute to the fight for Black people's liberation by making available knowledge that would free our minds from that which keeps us oppressed."

Mulzac could hear the clanking chains linking Jim Crow and colonialism, the chains linking segregation and imperialism, the chains linking U.S. oppression and global oppression, thus she lobbied Black Americans to read about international liberation movements. With this goal in mind, she stocked newspapers, newsletters, pamphlets, periodicals, and books from progressive movements in Africa, South America, the Caribbean, Asia, and across the States.

Liberation Bookstore also allied with small, independent Black presses—Third World Press, Jihad Productions, Broadside Press, and Drum and Spear Press—and advocated for the expansion of the independent Black publishing industry.

As a former Random House secretary, Mulzac frequently noted that many large publishing companies are corporate multinational subsidiaries and that ownership gives those corporations the power to shape opinions and decide what information will and won't be made available to the public. Mulzac envisioned a world where Black people gained control over which books were published and reprinted. This concern haunted her in the 1980s as she found "the books

Tel.: 281-4615

IF YOU DON'T KNOW LEARN
IF YOU KNOW TEACH

# LIBERATION BOOK STORE

421 Lenox Ave. at 131st St. · Harlem. N.Y. 10037

ABOVE: Liberation Bookstore
in February 1992. Courtesy
of Alice Arnold.

LEFT: Liberation Bookstore
signage.

RIGHT: Una Mulzac standing
outside of Liberation
Bookstore with future
journalist Anoa Changa and
her brother, Djata, in
1985. Photo taken by Janet
Ehehosi, Anoa and Djata's
mother.

that were very important and were published in the sixties and early seventies during the Black book publishing boom are now out of print and difficult to get." She described these elusive books as "missing links of knowledge."

Despite declining sales and multiple threats of eviction, Liberation Bookstore operated until 2007. Mulzac died in 2012. And as she passed from elder to ancestor, Mulzac passed her inheritance to the next generation of Black booksellers, with her family donating Liberation's remaining inventory to Harlem's Hue-Man Bookstore and Café.

# TREE OF LIFE BOOKSTORE

On September 19, 1980, the roar of bulldozers silenced the hum of Harlem's Tree of Life Bookstore. According to Kanya Vashon McGhee, also known as Kanya KeKumbha, he "started the Tree of Life Bookstore of Harlem in 1969 with but seventy-five dollars initial capital as an experiment" in resolving the high school drop-out problem. He stocked the store to "awaken the sleeping giant" of untapped consciousness. Eleven years later, at the behest of Congressman Charles Rangel, the Harlem Urban Development Corporation bulldozed the Tree of Life to make way for a luxury hotel, International Trade Center, and a parking lot that it never built.

McGhee saw the proposed demolition as an indicator of a widespread attack. "The real dynamics behind this is the Carter Administration's plan for Black communities all over America. It's just another plan to move us all out of the cities and blunt our political power," he claimed in a *New York Times* interview. Before its demise, the Tree of Life gave life to Harlem, with Harlemites beholding the storefront's Floyd Sapp panoramic African history mural, perusing the store's metaphysical selections, attending "The Kanya Academy of the Occult" classes and seminars, and communing in the free reading room. In less than ten years, McGhee's "experiment" had won supporters from all denominations. In 1977, more than fifty people issued public comments in favor of saving the store:

The Tree of Life is life itself.

**—JEANETTE HARRIS, HARLEM STUDENT**

The dope addicts, drunkards, and everything be coming in there, you know, in their degradation, and they change, man, they really turn into beautiful jewels.

**—YUSEF OMFREE, HARLEM MUSICIAN**

I didn't know what living was about until I went to the Tree of Life.

**—JACQUELINE RIDDICK, HARLEM RESIDENT**

Our nation is sick. We are in agony, and we are looking for a new direction. We have the nucleus of a new direction at the Tree of Life, something that can spread and grow all over this country. The Tree of Life is a movement.

**—RUBY DEE, ACTOR**

But it took time for McGhee and the Tree of Life to earn their laurels. "I stood on the corner for four years next to Michaux's bookstore because Michaux's had cultural books, books written by Black authors. That's very important because it helps to enhance your analysis of your own background, your own history. But I wanted to open up a bookstore dealing with the other aspect of each person. That is the spirit. Ours was a metaphysical bookstore," McGhee said, chronicling the store's beginnings to Augusta Mann in the late 1970s. From his spot outside Michaux's, McGhee summoned passersby to learn about astrology, nutrition, metaphysics, Egyptology, philosophy, and African history. Sometimes he'd make only $3 in a day, but his consistency brought in regular customers and word spread throughout New York City.

"This is the only bookstore I know of that is specifically tailor-made to the consciousness of the Black person, and it's right here in Harlem, the spiritual capital," McGhee boasted.

From Michaux's corner to the corner of Lenox Avenue—a corner McGhee told the *Amsterdam News* "has the heavy vibrations of all the important Black leaders who came through Harlem"—it wasn't just Harlemites who witnessed "The Tree," as it was affectionately called. Dick Gregory, Muhammad Ali, pianist Ramsey Lewis, and the members of Earth, Wind, and Fire would all visit and leave the store with arms full of books and renewed spirits.

McGhee dreamed of the Tree of Life becoming a spiritual and healing center. He fought for the renovation of the building despite imminent demolition. True to his Virgo nature, McGhee had architects draft renderings of his vision. Plans included the bookstore, a juice bar, a plant store, a reading room, a prenatal clinic, a natural food restaurant by herbalist and Tree of Life instructor Dr. John Moore, and a school called the University at the Corner of Lenox Avenue (UCLA).

BELOW: A young demonstrator in front of the Tree of Life Bookstore.

THE TREE OF LIFE BOOKSTORE SAVED MY LIFE I WANT IT TO REMAIN ON 125th St & Lenox

News World

Jean Blackwell Hutson General Research and Reference Division, Schomburg Center for Research in Black Culture.

McGhee dreamed beyond Harlem, too. He dreamed of creating a hundred-acre commune of people of all races to live, work, study, and grow food in harmony. While divine intervention didn't save Harlem's Tree of Life, McGhee's spirit lives on, reminding us that the revolution starts in all of us.

"When we're able to recognize ourselves, really see who we are," McGhee once said, "that's when the revolution takes place, because it comes from within."

/Blæk/ /Bʊks/ /Plʌs/ n.

# BLACK BOOKS PLUS

1. A bookstore owned by former Schomburg
   librarian Glenderlyn Johnson that
   operated in New York's Upper West
   Side from 1989 to 1999

2. An establishment known for its emphasis on Black history and culture

3. The spot where Jesse Jackson pissed
   off a customer or two

"I knew nothing about business. I knew about books, and I knew about Black history and culture. I got a corner store in a very mixed neighborhood called the Upper West Side. The rest is history, I guess."

We're sitting in Glenderlyn Johnson's cramped Manhattan storage unit, a treasure trove. There are boxes of pristine first-edition novels. There are piles of nineties-era book displays. There are dozens of vintage posters advertising events I could only dream of attending. In the center of the unit is the reason I'm here—a meticulously organized filing cabinet dedicated to her store, Black Books Plus. X marks the spot. Glen, who insists I don't call her Ms. Johnson, opens the filing cabinet with the precision of a bank teller accessing a safe-deposit box. She's recently sold her Black Books Plus archive to the Schomburg and has invited me to take a look before she hands it over.

Most of Glen's files feature the names of authors who held events at her store, including Toni Morrison, Walter Mosley, and Terry McMillan. Inside folders, Glen stored handwritten notes detailing how many books she ordered, how

many customers attended each event, how much money she made, how much she lost, and how the authors interacted with her and her customers.

"Everything I wrote in those notes is true. And Jesse Jackson wasn't pleasant at all. I know he's a busy man, but he was talking on the phone when the customers were waiting [for him to sign their books]. A few of them called me the next day and said that he wasn't polite to them."

Glen speaks with the matter-of-factness of a seasoned elder who is used to telling it like it is. Wiping away the nonexistent wrinkles in her slacks, she recounts stories of a bygone era with clarity.

"My biggest event by far was Abyssinian Baptist Church with Toni Morrison. When I got out of the taxi, the street was blocked off. All I could see was

Glenderlyn Johnson gazes at Toni Morrison during her address at the Abyssinian Baptist Church. Courtesy of Marcia E. Wilson.

policemen and a line wrapped around the block. My knees started shaking. I said, 'Oh my God.'"

As Black Books Plus's owner, Glen did more than just interact with famous politicians and celebrated authors. She also sent books to incarcerated readers. She pulls out a letter from a man who benefited from reading books his cellmate's mom got from Black Books Plus and reads it to me:

```
Hey, Ms. Johnson. I'm writing to thank
you for the book. I love to read, but
I cannot afford to purchase books.
The prison library has nothing of real
interest. [My cellmate] noticed my
interest in reading and he began to
share his books with me.

He has opened up areas for me that I
didn't even know existed. He introduced
me to authors and ideas that I had
never heard of. Each day positive ideas
are created and through those ideas,
new life is born.
```

```
To understand how much that means to
me, you should be aware that I am
serving a life sentence with no real
possibility of parole. Yet, I know even
from this lonely prison cell, I can
make a difference.

As I learned, I can teach. I can live
through my thoughts, ideas, and newly
found ideals. My body may be impris-
oned, but my mind is free. Thank you
again for making this possible.
```

She sets down the letter. I'm transported from this man's prison cell back to the 4×7×8-foot storage unit. I feel tears welling up.

"I didn't make it possible. His friend's mother did," Glen says. Despite the stacks of memories, Glen is not sentimental. She remains mission-driven.

"I have no idea what these men did and don't want to know, but I know they have a brain. I want people to know that all prisoners aren't just what the average person thinks of them."

✳ ✳ ✳

Months after excavating the storage unit, Glen invites me to lunch at 702 Amsterdam Avenue, the same address where Black Books Plus once stood, now a Peruvian restaurant with a reasonably priced lunch special.

"That's where people lined up around the block to see Terry McMillan," Glen says, pointing over my shoulder. "And the guy who used to work across the street, he built my bookshelves by

hand." Her New York accent thickens as her mind drifts to the past. "The register was there," she says, gesturing toward the bar. "All these businesses had a terrible rodent problem." Glen chuckles. I put down my fork midbite.

"You know," she says, "what us Black booksellers did was important. It's important to tell the story, to teach the history."

My body may be imprisoned,
but my mind is free.

# THE BOOK BEAT

## BY HERB BOYD

If memory hasn't completely deserted me, one of the earliest encounters I had with a Black bookstore was in Detroit in the late fifties—Zampty's shop on Woodward Avenue and Seven Mile Road. His place wasn't exactly a bookstore, but it was an import and export store where you could purchase merchandise from Africa and the Caribbean.

A native of Trinidad, John Charles Zampty was a significant follower of Marcus Garvey, and he would regale customers with stories of his days traveling with the great leader as his auditor general. On some occasions, he would host meetings at the shop, where the discussions often centered on the books scattered around the place, particularly pamphlets and old issues of Garvey's publications. He was an engaging storyteller, and that made it impossible not to purchase a book he recommended, thus allowing you to take some of his memories with you.

In the sixties, I had similar encounters with Ed Vaughn, the owner of a bookstore on the west side of Detroit that featured books on African and African American history. Like Zampty, Vaughn was more of a political activist than a proprietor, and later he helmed a Pan-African organization. Along with a vast array of books, the store was stocked with African artifacts, posters, flyers, garments, and other items to expand one's cultural inclinations. There was no way you were going to get in and out of Vaughn's presence without an update on African affairs and the pertinent political issues in the city.

Mr. Zampty and Mr. Vaughn prepared me for the political activist meetings I would later attend in the 1980s, when I moved to New York City. Even earlier, when I lived in the city in the 1960s, there had been the educational visits to the "House of Common Sense and Home of Proper Propaganda," as Lewis Michaux often called his establishment, which was officially named the National Memorial African Bookstore. Festooned on the walls were huge depictions of African villages, famous Pan-African and Caribbean leaders, and contemporary images of Harlem, particularly the notable churches and schools. There were also several photographs of Michaux with Malcolm X and other prominent visitors, including several of him posing with Harlem's writers and politicians.

Malcolm X was a regular customer at the store and spent many hours getting Michaux's wise counseling, as many of us did. My visits there often included extensive discussions on the latest developments in Africa. He would quiz me on African history, challenging me on details of recent coups and the various leadership groups and their locations. After his store was demolished and the State Office Building occupied the spot, Una Mulzac's Liberation Bookstore continued Michaux's legacy.

Una's odyssey began in Guyana, where she was almost killed when an explosive device destroyed the store where she worked. Her Liberation Bookstore in Harlem was her successful effort to carry on the tradition and occupation she had in Guyana, and it soon became a venue for political activists from all over the African diaspora. Of central interest to her customers was the broad collection of pamphlets from the various political organizations then involved in the liberation movements in Africa.

Octavia E. Butler and Adelaide Miller at a signing for *Parable of the Talents* at Nkiru Books. Courtesy of Marcia E. Wilson.

From Eso Won in Los Angeles to Nkiru in Brooklyn, Black bookstores all over the country held signings for my publications and these stores provided ample opportunity to reach and develop my following. James Fugate, one of the owners of Eso Won, was originally from Detroit, so there was a special affinity whenever I had a signing there. Brenda Greene, the proprietor of Nkiru, a bookstore founded by Leothy Miller Owens and later run by Adelaide Miller, was a consummate intellectual who dispensed endless critiques of the most popular bestsellers. She possessed a scholarly regal bearing and was capable of discussing everything from Toni Morrison to Richard Wright.

When Clara Villarosa opened Hue-Man Bookstore and Café as an extension of her store the Hue-man Experience in Denver, I was among the first authors to have a signing there, and that would become a critical stop on my tour. One of my most unforgettable signings was a panel discussion with Dhoruba bin Wahad and T. J. English on English's recent publication *The Savage City*. Clara was always a gracious and knowledgeable host, and she would introduce her guests with a full understanding of their latest works.

When Clara retired from Hue-Man, what Marva Allen set in motion continued to appeal to the retinue of customers. Allen, later in partnership with Melvin Van Peebles and two other partners, expanded the activities at the store, most notably the readings and lecture series for children. Authors were always received by a sizable audience, and that was among the most memorable things about signings there.

Sisters Uptown Bookstore at 1942 Amsterdam Avenue, just beyond the borderline between Harlem and Washington Heights, is owned by mother-and-daughter team Janifer and Kori Wilson. I have done several signings at the store and covered the appearances of other writers. It was a wonderful moment to share the floor with Cinque Brathwaite when the selected writings and essays of his father were published. There were often weekly events at the store, and it housed a small café that served tea, soft drinks, and some pastries. Children's books are among the store's strong enticements as well as the warm greetings from the family.

In many ways, their place reminded me of Source Booksellers on Cass Avenue in Detroit, where Janet Webster Jones runs a precious book nook. A conversation with her about books is worth your trip there—she's a former librarian and educator with a reservoir of tidbits. There is a nice balance of old books and recent editions, as well as unique brochures and chapbooks about the city's history.

These book havens are among the most cherished, but there are others that should at least get a mention, even if they are not on the tip of my tongue, such as Tree of Life, once located in Harlem on 125th Street, or Earnest Hadley's store on 145th Street, not too far from my house. Much like the one that temporarily devastated Liberation Bookstore, a fire put Hadley out of business and put the records documenting the priceless moments I spent with him as he recounted his life and the history of Harlem out of reach. Memorable, too, was the friendship I established with Glenderlyn Johnson, the owner of Black Books Plus. She evinced a quiet, knowing demeanor, very much like the librarians I've known. I haven't seen her in quite a while but would relish an opportunity to resume our relationship.

Bookstores, for me, especially the small independent ones, have been a refuge. Whenever I journey to those faraway places, those strange new cities and towns, there are two places that I seek out immediately—the libraries and the bookstores. They provide a reliable resting place where I can get my bearings on how to navigate the next move. Many times, those moves are delayed by hours as I take full advantage of the store's bountiful resources and the remarkable reflections of the owners.

As an author and journalist, I have had ample opportunities to discuss literature and politics with the owners of bookstores. These moments have been particularly bountiful for me as a freelance reporter and columnist at the *Amsterdam News*. For nearly forty years, I have been in the catbird seat, so to speak, on some of the most eventful and exciting moments in Harlem's history. Whenever a noted author appeared at one of the local bookstores, that was usually my assignment. These occasions put me on very familiar terms with the owners, thereby making it easy for me to secure a signing when my own books hit the market. It's been a dream arrangement that I hope never ends.

# HUE-MAN BOOKSTORE AND CAFÉ

Harlem shined as Black literature's beacon during the early twentieth century. It swirled with the energy of its renaissance—the writers, the literary clubs, the Black bookstores all fueled Harlem's gleaming moniker as the "Black Mecca." But by the new millennium, the Harlem Renaissance had long ended, most literary clubs had shuttered, and many of the bookstores that left tourists and Harlemites aglow had flickered out.

So when noted bookseller Clara Villarosa moved to Harlem in 2000, she quickly commenced plans to open a bookstore with partners Rita Ewing and Celeste Johnson. But the trio didn't intend to open just any bookstore. They aimed for Hue-Man Bookstore and Café to be the largest Black bookstore in the country, the metaphorical phoenix rising from the ashes of the razed Black bookstores of Harlem's yesteryears.

Architect Alexander Zabasajja designed the 4,000-square-foot retail space located on Harlem's main thoroughfare, 125th Street. Harlem's Hue-Man boasted a coffee bar and a special children's area with direct access to the Magic Johnson Theater's lobby.

"I'm creating my dream store," Villarosa told *Publishers Weekly* weeks before the store's opening in 2002.

At Hue-Man's star-studded grand opening, Maya Angelou gave a special dedication. Stevie Wonder, Wesley Snipes, Ashford & Simpson, Jay-Z, Ruby Dee, and Ossie Davis were all Hue-Man day-ones. And the store continued to attract top talent, like Pearl Cleage, E. Lynn Harris, Omar Tyree, Toni Morrison, Alicia Keys, Bill Clinton, and Marva Allen.

Marva Allen joined Hue-Man around the time Villarosa, then in her seventies, retired. Allen worked her way to co-ownership along with Ewing and Johnson. And because she managed the store, kept book signings running smoothly, and spoke with beat reporters, Allen also became the face of Hue-Man.

"Harlem is the seat of culture that defines the African American experience," Allen tells me, remembering her time at Hue-Man's helm. "Hue-Man is sacred ground."

Despite gentrification, Amazon, and big-box bookstores threatening to encroach on that ground, Allen found creative ways to raise Hue-Man's profile and rally a steady stream of customers.

Hue-Man and fifty other Harlem-based Black-owned businesses participated in the Power of One Card program, where customers purchased a card for $1 and got discounts at all participating businesses.

"The whole idea, of course, is to keep the money within the community, circulating around small businesses," Allen explains.

And though many hesitated to embrace the internet and online shopping, "Hue-Man was one of the first Black bookstores with a website," she says.

Carrying the baton passed from Harlem bookstores of the past, Hue-Man made history. But that wasn't Allen's aim. "I didn't know that we were making history. I didn't even set out to do that. We are the keepers of history, but I didn't set out to make it."

The chapter of Hue-Man Bookstore and Café's time on 125th Street came to an end in 2012. In an email breaking the news to customers, Allen wrote in part: "We all know that there is a season for everything under heaven and the season of 'traditional book' selling has come to a close."

"I looked at the publishing industry, and I knew this was not sustainable. I didn't want to sign another ten-year lease. It was just a really sad, sad moment because the community didn't know we were leaving. We were a bedrock for that community," Allen recalls.

Nearly a decade after Hue-Man Bookstore and Café closed, Allen and Ewing launched Huemanbooks, a small pop-up featuring books by and about all races. Now, Hue-Man endures in independent coffee shops throughout Manhattan.

Photos courtesy of Clara and Linda Villarosa and Rita Ewing.

Rita Ewing and Marva Allen.

# FREE BLACK WOMEN'S LIBRARY

A stoop in Brooklyn served as the first site of the Free Black Women's Library. OlaRonke Akinmowo displayed one hundred books while playing music, dancing, and chatting with passersby about her collection. She invited folks to swap a book in their personal library with one of hers, as long as the book was written by a Black woman. The first person to take Akinmowo up on her offer was a seven- or eight-year-old girl. Akinmowo has been trading books ever since, inspiring Free Black Women's Libraries in Los Angeles, Detroit, Houston, Atlanta, and Urbana-Champaign to do the same. Together, they're turning the States into the stoop.

I spoke with Akinmowo from the Free Black Women's Library's brick-and-mortar location in Bed-Stuy.

**Was there anything from your childhood or teenage years that set the stage for the Free Black Women's Library?**

**OLARONKE AKINMOWO:** I used to cut school and spend the whole day in the library. The library has always been one of my favorite places to be. It's always been a place of refuge and a place of really good vibes all around. So when I think back to those days of sitting in the library for hours throughout the school day, just reading or writing or drawing, and then I think about how I have a reading room community space in Bed-Stuy that's a space for the community to come and read and write and just relax and chill . . . it all kind of makes sense.

**What is it about libraries in particular that make them a place of refuge?**

**OLARONKE AKINMOWO:** A lot of people talk about how they fall in love with reading at a young age then something happens when they go into the school setting. Either they lose that love or they forget that love. Something distances them from books.

I think that's pretty sad. The library is a space that helps people to fall in love with reading again. Books can provide inspiration, motivation, escape, representation, comfort, pleasure, excitement, joy. I wanted to do something to give people that kind of space.

**I'm struck by the selection at the Free Black Women's Library. It's vast, something for every interest. Was that intentional?**

**OLARONKE AKINMOWO:** Black people are not a monolith, and everybody has different interests. That's why I try to have a wide range of books on a wide range of subject matter. We have books on health and beauty, on fashion, on cooking, on travel. Books on urban planning, books on parenting, books on how to build an app, coding, and things like that.

I feel like that adds an element of that sense of community. We need different voices in this space. We need different minds. We need different perspectives. We need different ideas in this space.

It's very important to me to have an intergenerational space and a space where people come together. We have people who are atheists, people who are Muslim, people who are Christian coming together to have these really involved

THE FREE BLACK WOMEN'S LIBRARY
READING ROOM

The Reading Room is a literary hub, social site, creative community care space, cultural institution and Black Feminist archive.

All ages, races and genders are welcome to attend our events, take our workshops and use this space.

Follow us on social media:
@thefreeblackwomenslibrary

READ. WRITE. WORK. REST. DREAM.

men's
rary

OlaRonke
Akinmowo.

Marcus Garvey
Boulevard

WEL~
COM~
~TO~
THE
FREE
BLACK
WOMENS
LIBRARY

*Reading shouldn't be a closet practice... Everyone should have access to books.*

conversations about stuff like gentrification, police brutality, and reproductive justice. And it's great because people get to learn from each other.

I love that you've curated a space that allows for folks to have these conversations across different strata—be it race, class, religion, ability, or, even, reading interest.

**OLARONKE AKINMOWO:** Reading shouldn't be a classist practice. It shouldn't be a practice for specific types of people. Everyone should have access to books and not just books that are considered to be "the classics," like Shakespeare, but books like *Sister Soldier* and [authors like] Roxane Gay and Bernice McFadden and Beverly Jenkins or whomever—like Samantha Irby if you want to read something funny. There's no—there *shouldn't* be—parameters around who's considered a bibliophile, a good reader, etc.

So I'm just trying to make reading more of an accessible activity, more inclusive, and also take the pressure off. If it takes you six months to read a small collection of short stories, that's perfectly fine. You read graphic novels because you're not a fan of text, but you really love images? That's perfectly fine. If you only want to read nonfiction and you don't want to even go near Afrofuturism, that's perfectly fine.

People come to the library. They look through the collection. They pick what they want, and it's a personal journey. It could take them five minutes; it could take them hours. They're free to do that.

I wanted an inclusive space where people have a sense of ownership over their experience, and these ideas are developed out of Black feminist theory because I identify as a Black feminist.

I'm curious—when you were becoming a Black feminist and really identifying with that theory, were there any books that informed your thoughts on anti-capitalism and accessibility in the way that you run the library now?

**OLARONKE AKINMOWO:** Definitely bell hooks's *Sisters of the Yam* and *Ain't I a Woman?* Audre Lorde's *Sister Outsider* of course. There's the *Black Feminist Reader* by Joy James. There's this book by Toni Morrison called *Playing in the Dark: Whiteness and the Literary Imagination*.

And then there's *The Black Woman*, the anthology that Toni Bambara put together. But for me, mainly it's bell hooks, like bell hooks is the queen. A lot of what she has written informs my practice.

Are there any practices in your library that you can point to like "That's what I learned from bell hooks"?

**OLARONKE AKINMOWO:** One easy example is that all the events at the library are always free. All of our workshops, all of our film screenings, all of our presentations, all of our book talks are always free. So whether you're learning to write creative nonfiction or you're learning to sew or make a zine or tattoo or meditate or do yoga, it's free because we don't want anyone to have a barrier. That's specifically an idea I got from bell hooks. If you're doing something for the community, then you need to understand there are people in the community that don't have it [financially].

Also, before I had the reading room, when I was traveling with the collection, it was always important for me to have it in a space that was accessible to people of different body types. So if you are somebody who moves with a wheelchair or a walker, or if you are a parent or caregiver moving with somebody who's in a stroller, it's important to me that you're able to access that space easily and move through it and feel safe.

# HARRIETT'S BOOKSHOP AND IDA'S BOOKSHOP

Arguably, Jeannine Cook is the first Black woman to put hardbacks on horseback. I'm not talking *Black Beauty*, more *Black Is Beautiful*. Cook, the owner of Harriett's Bookshop in Philadelphia and Ida's Bookshop in Collingswood, New Jersey, galloped across North Philadelphia in 2021 delivering Black books to dazzled neighbors. More than a show-stopping stunt, Cook's pony show connected her to the city's young people, who had been learning about horseback riding through the Fletcher Street Urban Riding Club, a North Philly organization for youth. The year before, Cook's penchant for merging creativity and community compelled her to give out books for free.

When Philadelphians took to the streets to protest George Floyd's murder, so did Cook. Armed with dozens of copies of *The Autobiography of Malcolm X* and a biography of Harriet Tubman, she passed out free books to protesters with the help of her mom, son, and son's girlfriend. That same summer, she also traveled to Minneapolis to support protesters with free radical literature. Among the crowds, chants of "No justice, no peace, no racist police!" and "Whose streets? Our streets!" reverberated. Handwritten signs proclaimed, "Black lives matter!" and asked, "Am I next?"

The books Cook held up had powerful messages, too. Messages that spoke to why Harriett's and Ida's existed in the first place. As Malcolm X wrote, "The ability to read awoke inside of me some long dormant craving to be mentally alive."

From community to community, Cook shows that a bookstore isn't a building, it's a people. A people who love words and love others. A people who celebrate, who yearn for the life of the mind, who constantly and creatively feed that craving to be mentally alive, mentally free.

*a bookstore isn't a building, it's a people. A people who love words and love others.*

# UNCLE BOBBIE'S COFFEE & BOOKS

Marc Lamont Hill is a professor, television host, author, bookstore owner, and, perhaps most importantly, Uncle Bobbie's nephew.

Having grown up in West Philadelphia, Marc recalls seeing his Uncle Bobbie reading E. Franklin Frazier's *Black Bourgeoisie*. The book, which critiqued the Black middle class, lived among Uncle Bobbie's extensive collection of *Ebony* and *Jet* magazines and rare first editions.

"Seeing him read that helped me think differently about what my goal should be in life," Marc reflects years later. "I shouldn't be out here, just thinking about getting a good job or getting a fancy degree. Although those things might be important on a certain level. I should be thinking more deeply about the class position of my people, actually thinking more deeply about what freedom and liberation might really look like. His books gave me permission to imagine more robust forms of freedom."

Uncle Bobbie's library molded Marc at an early age—shaping him into an outspoken proponent of justice for oppressed people throughout the world. Today, that ethos refines the selections at Uncle Bobbie's Coffee & Books.

"We have a section on state violence with books on resistance. We have books on African political movements. Our children's book section is filled with Black and Brown faces," Marc says.

Just as Uncle Bobbie fashioned Marc's education through books, Uncle Bobbie's Coffee & Books sculpts today's youth, particularly those in the Germantown neighborhood of Philadelphia, where the store operates. "Part of the goal of the store is to be [. . .] building strong boys, rather than repairing broken men," Marc affirms.

One of the ways Uncle Bobbie's fortifies the youth is by emphasizing intergenerational bonding and conversation. "We recognize the value of listening to and learning from our elders. We also recognize the beauty and the power and the possibility of young people advancing our community forward and preparing us for the next wave of our struggle," Marc says.

"Unfortunately, we live in a society that wages generation wars. We're told anything that's old is not worthwhile. We destroy our ancient landmarks and ignore the past and erase history. At the same time, we're taught that young people are violent, dangerous, unserious, disengaged, and not worthy of taking on the mantle or carrying on the baton from us."

But the bookstore—named for the intergenerational bond between its owner and his uncle—pries apart those misconceptions. On any given day at Uncle Bobbie's, you'll find college students finishing up homework, retirees sipping lattes made by friendly baristas, young families searching for the latest picture book, and Marc holding court with all of them, bringing strangers together.

"Creating spaces for intergenerational dialogue is so important. I wanted to create a space where we could deeply engage with one another with books—something so rooted in tradition—at the center."

And the tradition of youth communing with elders, of grandchildren with grandparents, of nieces with great-aunts, of nephews with their uncle Bobbies now thrives at the center of the store, each day binding Philadelphia's generations together like the pages of a book.

*We recognize the value of listening to and learning from our elders.*

Marc Lamont Hill, Uncle Bobbie's nephew.

Darlene Okpo built Adanne for the Black girls.

ADANNE
BOOKS + GOODS

HOURS
...SDAY    12PM - 6PM
          12PM - 6PM
...Y       12PM - 6PM
          12PM - 6PM

"THE MORE YOU KNOW OF YOUR HISTORY THE MORE LIBERATED YOU ARE"
MAYA ANGELOU

# ADANNE BOOKSHOP

Adanne is for the girls.

"Adanne really is a love letter to Black women. When you walk in, it *gives* Black girl," owner Darlene Okpo opines as she waters the shop's mother-in-law tongue plants. She shoots me a playful smile. Her whole face—teeth, eyes, cheeks—beams, framed by shoulder-length locs. The small shop feels like it's smiling at me, too. Art, vintage vinyl, and of course books adorn every wall. A quote by Maya Angelou greets you as you enter: "The more you know of your history, the more liberated you are."

The large table in the center beckons strangers to become sisters. As I flip through Debrena Jackson Gandy's *Sacred Pampering Principles,* I overhear two shoppers swapping birth charts. "You're a Cancer moon, too? I could feel your nurturing energy when you walked in!"

The vintage rattan peacock chair and wood-grain love seat invite readers to crack open a good book and stay awhile. Adanne is a perfect balance of old and new, girlie and grown, with vintage Black literature stacks, merch designed by Okpo herself, sweetly scented candles, and records from Okpo's dad's extensive collection. The Bed-Stuy–based shop's name pays homage to Okpo's mom's childhood nickname. "*Adanne* means 'eldest daughter' in Igbo," Okpo shares.

A former educator, Okpo has found inspiration everywhere—in her parents, fashion, music, nature, and especially her students. "One of my students said, 'I want to read about Black girls,' so I gave her Tiffany D. Jackson's *Monday's Not Coming* and got to work on building Adanne . . . for the Black girls."

# BAILEY STREET BOOKS

Professor Anyabwile Love remembers not being able to pay for books.

When he was growing up in Northwest Philadelphia, the Scholastic Book Fair felt anything but fair.

"I'd get the Scholastic catalog like a week before and be circling books like 'That's mine! That's mine!' But then the day would come, and we just never had money to get that stuff."

"And you know"—Anyabwile smiles slyly—"I was tryin' to steal stuff."

"I couldn't take a book because, you know, those were high-priced items, but I'm getting an eraser, I'm getting a smelly marker, I'm getting a bookmark. Even if it's free, I don't care because I need to feel like I'm taking this."

Amid my laughter at this confession, Anyabwile breaks into his best Denzel Washington impersonation: "I'm leaving here with something! I'm from 'round the way. I'm leaving with something!"

From these humble beginnings, Anyabwile came to found Bailey Street Books, a bookstore and research hub that specializes in rare and vintage Black titles. His background informs the store's ethos. At Bailey Street Books, customers can sit and read—even if they don't make a purchase.

"Part of the reason why I opened Bailey Street was because folks who had the money, which was mainly white people, were buying this stuff up and then shooting the prices up," Anyabwile says.

"I don't like culture vultures. I don't like them at all. You can love Morrison and Walker, but I feel like if you have access to the money to buy those things, donate them somewhere Black where folks who those stories are being written for can have access to them as well. These are living things to me, not just something to hoard like a trophy."

The living tomes in the Bailey Street Books collection map onto Anyabwile's lived experience. His high school friend Bianca introduced him to Ntozake Shange's *Sassafrass, Cypress and Indigo*, traveling by bus to give it to him. Then there's Ralph Ellison's *Invisible Man*, which he first read at his English teacher's behest. *The Autobiography of Malcolm X* was a bestseller during the six months he volunteered for Nia Damali at Medu Bookstore in Atlanta. And *Dear John, Dear Coltrane* is a poetry collection about John Coltrane, Anyabwile's favorite jazz musician and the namesake of his son, Coltrane. Anyabwile says he couldn't have done Bailey Street without his wife, Shivon. "I told her I wanted to do this, and she was like, 'Okay, let's figure this out.'"

Anyabwile no longer has the urge to pocket books. Instead, he's democratizing access to vintage Black books for everyday Black folks in the city he grew up in. I'd say he's figured it out.

Professor Anyabwile Love remembers not being able to pay for books.

*These are living things to me, not just something to hoard like a trophy.*

# BEM | books & more

In New York City, America's literary haven, even the most voracious readers hunger for more than rich imagery and scrumptious scenes, so when the city's bookworms feel their bellies quivering and quaking, they know to slide down to the bookshop where readers can actually take a bite out of the pages—BEM | books & more, a bookstore focused solely on Black food writing.

In 2020, sisters Danielle and Gabrielle Davenport took their love of food, literature, and family and opened the store. In the interview that follows, Danielle and Gabrielle invite us to the table to chat about community, art, and their recipe for success.

**The name BEM is an homage to your grandmothers, Bernice and Marjorie. I've seen that books and food inspire intergenerational conversations and gatherings. How have you seen that manifest in your store?**

**DANIELLE:** There's so much all of us end up learning from someone who fed us, both literally and metaphorically. That sense of legacy and connection is absolutely at the heart of what we do.

We met a mother-daughter pair from New Orleans who were in their eighties or nineties and fifties or sixties. The mother was using a walker at our Black food exhibition with the

Museum of Food and Drink. Later that summer, we had a pop-up in Prospect Park, which is in a different borough, and they came and saw us again. The mother had wonderful memories to share about eating at Leah Chase's Dooky Chase Restaurant. It was nice to have that intergenerational connection to pass on those memories.

We're like, "Yes, dear elder, this is a place for you. Yes, dear baby, this is a place for you." We printed onesies at the same time that we printed t-shirts. It's all about welcoming in the fullest possible range of our community.

Gabrielle (*left*) and Danielle (*right*) took their love of food, literature, and family and opened BEM | books & more. Courtesy of Clay Williams.

**What about BEM is resonating with your community?**

**GABRIELLE:** We'll have chefs or authors walk in who are like, "All my friends' books are here together. I never see that." We get that a lot, and it's really gratifying because there's a really wide world of Black food writers who have been doing this work for a long time. Now, there's a national conversation happening and there's not necessarily a place where all that is living, so it's really exciting for the chefs and food writers, in particular, to come in and be like, "Oh, it's really lovely to have all of this in one place."

**You've spoken about how food relates to everything in our society. You say food is labor, economics, culture, and class. What's a connection that food has that we laypeople are overlooking?**

**DANIELLE:** Maybe it's intuitive, but I'm thinking about the ways food shapes so many milestones. The repast after the funeral, that first date with the love of your life, feeding your new baby. Food ties into all the most intimate human moments.

**What makes a good cookbook?**

**GABRIELLE:** The cookbooks I respond to the most are the ones that feel the most personal and where the writing is the strongest. There's history and there's memoir and there's all kinds of really great writing. The recipes should work, which I'm learning more and more is not always the case. There's a whole world of recipe testing, and it doesn't always come out like it's supposed to, so aside from the recipes actually working, the writing being of high quality makes a huge difference in people wanting to engage with it. Oh, and the photos. There has to be beautiful photography.

**Could you speak to the patterns you notice in the food writing of different cultures across the diaspora?**

**GABRIELLE:** A lot of people assume when we say we're a Black food bookstore, that it's only Black American food. Taking as wide a swath as we can of the diaspora has been essential to what we're doing from the beginning. The pattern I noticed is the grandmothers. People are learning so much from their grandmothers about how to be, how to eat, how to take care of themselves.

Courtesy of Clay Williams.

# THE ADVENTURES OF BOOK BOY

## BY MICHAEL A. GONZALES

*Dedicated to my writer homeboy and cool bookseller Brook Stephenson (1974–2015),
who worked for eleven years at McNally Jackson in SoHo*

I can't remember a time when I wasn't surrounded by books. Born to a bookworm
mother who always placed a paperback, magazine, or newspaper in my playpen, I
was looking at blocks of text before I could even read. Living in New York City, Mom
did most of her reading while commuting to midtown in the mornings and back to
Harlem at nightfall; she always carried bags containing various publications ranging
from *Ebony* to *Esquire* to *Essence* along with several bestsellers. Most nights, when it
was bedtime for me and baby brother, Perky, she read us stories, my favorite being
Roald Dahl's *Charlie and the Chocolate Factory*.

While my brother dismissed the written word and the magic it held, I grew up as one
of *those* kids. The ones who read everything, including cereal boxes, comics, and the
graffiti-covered train cars that roared into the 145th Street and Broadway subway
station.

A block away from the 145th Street stop and a few doors down from the unruly P.S. 186,
where I went to first grade, I found my sanctuary—an oasis of printed matter ripe for
reading—the Hamilton Grange Library. Though I don't remember the Black librarian's
name, I do recall the smile on her face as she handed six-year-old me my first library
card. I spent many years in that library, poring over fiction, art history, cultural criticism,
and sociology. For me, reading offered both education and an escape. While my interest
in books might've impressed my mom and the librarians, it didn't stop knuckleheads
from teasing me. In first grade, they taunted me with jeers of "Book Boy, Book Boy."
Despite the teasing, the Hamilton Grange Library became a second home, and as I got
older, I traveled to various parts of the city to visit other libraries and bookshops.

I also discovered the world of Black literature through my mom. In her bedroom were
books by Maya Angelou, Chester Himes, Ntozake Shange, various anthologies, and
the Toni Morrison–edited *Black Book*, one of the most fascinating nonfiction tomes
from the 1970s, containing historical documents, photographs, book excerpts, quotes,
poems, and so much more related to the history of Black folks in America.

It was during that period that I became aware of various Black bookstores in Harlem,
including the National Memorial African Bookstore on 125th Street, which I passed
when heading to my stepfather's place, and Liberation Bookstore on Lenox Avenue
and 131st Street, which I didn't enter until the early 1980s, when I was in college.
While I'm kicking myself for not getting to know the stores' respective owners, Lewis
Michaux and Una Mulzac, in 1992, I did make the acquaintance of Black Books Plus

owner Glenderlyn Johnson when me and my music publicist girlfriend, Lesley Pitts, moved to the Upper West Side.

Walking by Amsterdam Avenue and 94th Street one afternoon, I discovered Black Books Plus when I saw a line of Black women spilling out of the store. When I entered the store, I saw author Gloria Naylor signing her latest book, *Bailey's Café*. I bought a copy, waited in line, and got it signed. That was the first book event I ever attended.

Afterward, I talked to Glenderlyn about the hip-hop-themed record guide I'd recently co-written for Harmony Books. "You should do a book signing here," she kindly offered. Within weeks, me and my co-author, Havelock Nelson, were seated behind a table autographing copies of *Bring the Noise: A Guide to Rap Music and Hip-Hop Culture*. That was the extent of our book tour, but I'll never forget Glenderlyn's kindness and generosity.

While I haven't seen books being sold on the street in other American cities, in New York, it's a thriving market, and it happens all over town. Under the First Amendment, people who sell books on the street can do so without a vending license. From the 1980s all the way into the new millennium, the vendors on 125th Street specialized in Black books that were self-published or released by small publishing houses. Titles such as the controversial *The Blackman's Guide to Understanding the Blackwoman* by Shahrazad Ali (1989), *Countering the Conspiracy to Destroy Black Boys* by Jawanza Kunjufu (1985), and *The Isis Papers* by Dr. Frances Cress Welsing (1982) were sold alongside *The Autobiography of Malcolm X*, Islamic nutritional practices, *Manchild in the Promised Land*, conspiracy theories, and various volumes by Iceberg Slim, James Baldwin, and Donald Goines.

I became cool with a few Manhattan street vendors. There was a lanky African dude who sold coffee-table, art, and picture books on Fourth and Broadway, but my favorite was Hakim, who hawked near Sixth Avenue on Eighth Street. Featured in the sociological study *Sidewalk,* by Mitchell Duneier, Hakim was quite proud of this accomplishment and had the book on his table, where I began finding and buying out-of-print books by Black authors.

Among the textual jewels I discovered were *The Soul Brothers and Sister Lou* by Kristin Hunter (1968) and *Hog Butcher* by Ronald Fair (1966), a Chicago writer who fled to Europe and became a sculptor.

Both were young adult novels years before the YA category was created. Eleven years after it was published, *Hog Butcher* was adapted into the Blaxploitation classic *Cornbread, Earl and Me* starring Larry Fishburne. Years before, when I was a twelve-year-old brat going to see flicks at the local movie house, I'd seen and loved that movie that took on the hot topic of a young Black male slain by a white cop on the South Side of Chicago. Still, it wasn't until that day in 1996 that I discovered that *Cornbread, Earl and Me* began as a book that took on the heavy topics of race, brutality, and corruption.

I revisited *Hog Butcher* two decades later when, in 2016, I wrote about the book and author for *Sticking It to the Man: Revolution and Counterculture in Pulp and Popular Fiction, 1950 to 1980,* edited by Andrew Nette and Iain McIntyre. The "Hog Butcher" piece was my first essay about a neglected Black writer, but two years later, I began writing about out-of-print books and forgotten writers on the regular.

As a reader and fan of Black writers from years past, it was difficult for me to understand why so many brilliant Black scribes were merely blips on the literary radar while the same ol' white writers were constantly reprinted, reviewed, and taught in universities. In a small way, I wanted to rectify what I believed was an injustice.

When I pitched "The Blacklist" column to *Catapult* editor Mensah Demary, I was surprised when it was accepted but excited to wax poetic about Darius James (*Negrophobia*), Henry Dumas (*Jonoah and the Green Stone*), Kristin Hunter (*The Landlord*), Julian Mayfield (*The Long Night*), Charlotte Carter (*Rhode Island Red*), and Rosa Guy (*The Disappearance*). It became both a passion and a mission to highlight lesser-known Black writers. In a few cases, as with James and Carter, the writers were still alive and welcomed being interviewed.

Although "The Blacklist" only lasted a year at *Catapult,* I've continued the idea on other platforms including CrimeReads ("The Strange Story of Richard Wright's Lost Crime Novel, *Savage Holiday*"), Longreads ("Beautiful Women, Ugly Scenes: On Novelist Nettie Jones and the Madness of *Fish Tales*"), and *The Bitter Southerner* ("The Life and Short Stories of Diane Oliver").

Though I found many out-of-print books on the street, when I was looking for a copy of *Fish Tales* by Nettie Jones (and edited by Toni Morrison), I visited my favorite Black bookseller, Ben McFall, who worked at the Strand Bookstore in the East Village. Bald, soft-spoken, and wearing eyeglasses, he was always nattily dressed. (*Vibe* magazine book editor, friend, and the first person to let me write about Black authors and their books, Robert "Bob" Morales, introduced us.) Ben had worked at the Strand for decades and was very helpful in locating the book that I'd eventually write about in 2019. *Fish Tales* follows a Detroit party girl who relocates to New York City for wild times, including drunken antics, rough sex, and bizarre adventures. I'd learned about Jones's novel from Lesley, who had schooled me about *Fish Tales* early in our relationship, but I hadn't read it. However, ten years after Lesley's sudden passing from a brain aneurysm, I finally wanted to dive in.

$$* * *$$

A few blocks from the Strand, there once stood another one of my favorite bookstores, Shakespeare & Co. Formerly located at 217 Broadway, the store was named after the legendary Paris shop where expats Chester Himes, Richard Wright, and James Baldwin once hung out. Though not a Black bookstore, it carried many left-of-center Black novels by American and British authors, including imports that couldn't be bought anywhere else in the city, proudly presenting them in the ever-changing window displays.

There, I'd fallen in love with the new jacks in both Brit fiction and nonfiction when I stumbled onto the writings of Courttia Newland, Kodwo Eshun, Victor Headley, and Mike Phillips. My personal favorite find at Shakespeare & Co. was the writing duo Two Fingas and James T. Kirk (Andrew Green and Eddie Otchere), who wrote the 1995 book *Junglist*, a brilliant novel that documented Black rave culture in the lives of a London posse over a weekend in 1994. That book gave me a jolt as both a fan of the music and the electric energy in the writing.

One of my favorite out-of-print finds happened at Lexington Market in Baltimore. Every February for Black History Month, outside vendors were allowed to come to the market to sell their wares. I came across a guy selling old *Ebony* and *Jet* magazines along with a few boxes of paperbacks. Flipping through the books, not expecting to find anything special, I came across one of the holy grails of Holloway House Books crime fiction: *Poor, Black and in Real Trouble* by Jerome Dyson Wright.

The author was a Baltimorean who wrote about local hoods in the forties, fifties, and sixties, operating on the then-vibrant Pennsylvania Avenue. A semi-autobiographical tale that Wright wrote in prison, *Poor, Black and in Real Trouble* chronicled life on "The Ave," as most locals called it, where the action was—be it shooting loaded dice, buying stolen clothes from the booster girls, making sweet love in some hooker's hideaway, or hearing Billie Holiday swoon from the stage of the Royal Theater.

I'd been looking for that book for twenty years, and finding it for $20 was a treat. Granted, the seller tried to hustle me for more cash when he saw how excited I was, but when I explained that he was standing in the way of the world learning about the brilliance of that B'more writer, he relented. He then told me that Wright was his friend, proving it by showing me the writer's autograph in the book. A few months later, I wrote "Poor, Black and in Real Trouble: The Baltimore Noir of Jerome Dyson Wright" for CrimeReads.

From when I was a novice reader to when I became a literary essayist, booksellers have played a role in my development. Be they brick-and-mortar stores or street guys with hidden treasures buried beneath last month's *Vogue*, the memories of those merchants are as important as the books themselves. Today, many of my favorite bookstores are closed, and in the city where I currently dwell, street vendors don't sell out-of-print novels. These days when I need a certain text, I'll usually order it online, but I miss those personal relationships—the smell of ink in the air, the conversations with merchants and other customers, and the thrill of finding a book that the majority of the literate world has never heard of or read.

Book Boy forever, baby.

# CHAPTER 2

# THE DMV

Caribbean Festival goers in front of Sankofa Video Books & Café. Courtesy of Melketsadek, Sankofa Video & Books.

Courtesy of Jennifer Lawson.

Courtesy of Jennifer Lawson.

Courtesy of Jennifer Lawson.

LITERATURE

DRUM & SPEAR BOOK STORE

CATALOG.

2701-A 14TH STREET, N.W.
WASHINGTON, D.C.
(202)234-2883   234-2884

# DRUM AND SPEAR BOOKSTORE

Mere months after the Holy Week Uprising—rebellions following the assassination of Martin Luther King Jr.—rocked the nation's capital, a group of former Student Nonviolent Coordinating Committee (SNCC) activists founded Drum and Spear Bookstore. The smell of tear gas from the rebellions lingered in the books as the staff prepped for their June 1, 1968, opening. And though the destruction from the uprisings depressed much of the district, Chocolate City residents of all stripes endorsed the shop that symbolized "communications within the diaspora" (drum) and "whatever else might be necessary for the liberation of the people" (spear).

In the six years of its existence, Drum and Spear Bookstore and Press created an invaluable syllabus. From outlining the more mundane lessons in managing a popular bookstore day-to-day to sharing how they rebuffed the FBI's blatant surveillance attempts, the Drum and Spear workers testified to what it meant to be a part of a movement bookstore.

## Institution Building

Founder Charlie Cobb articulated it best: racism is built and maintained through institutions and can be combated only through counter-institutions. Thus, Cobb and other SNCC activists including Courtland Cox, Judy Richardson, Ivanhoe Donaldson, Ralph Featherstone, and Curtis Hayes established Afro-American Resources Inc., a nonprofit education corporation. Drum and Spear Bookstore became Afro-American Resources' first foray into institution building. And the bookstore ushered in other counter-institutions as well. There was the Center for Black Education and a children's radio program called *Sa Yaa Watoto*. There was Maelezo Bookstore, a satellite location in the federal government's Health, Education, and Welfare Building, and Drum and Spear Press. Whether publishing books, teaching community members, or acting out African folktales over the radio, the Drum and Spear team knew the importance of fostering understanding and inspiring action through media.

In 1994, Judy Richardson relayed Drum and Spear's ethos to Colin Beckles: "You can get these folks talking politics, and they don't do diddley, so our sense was towards some sort of action."

## Emphasis on Children's Literature

That bias toward action attracted more than fellow SNCC activists. Daphne Muse was a teacher who also worked at Brentano's. But when a fellow Black co-worker told her about a new Black bookstore near Howard University, she decided to investigate.

"I went up there and at the time, the manager was a man named Joe Gross," Ms. Muse remembers. "And we started talking as I was perusing this very small children's book section and he said, 'Why you working for the white people? Why don't you come up here and work for us?' And I said, 'Oh, okay!' So that's how I got to be a part of the Drum and Spear family." Along with Judy Richardson and Juadine Henderson, Ms. Muse went on to

DRUM AND SPEAR BOOK SHOP

Drum and Spear Bookstore pin. Courtesy of the Daphne Muse Collection.

expand the children's section she had seen the first time she entered the store.

"We wanted to make it one of the focal points of the store," Ms. Muse recalls. "We called it the Third World Children's Literature Section because it was not only Black books." Drum and Spear's children's section included books by Asian Americans, Latinos, and Native Americans. And because the imagery and messages children received could impact them for the rest of their lives, the Drum and Spear team read and vetted each book to make sure the kids' books espoused positive messages.

Daphne Muse poses inside Drum and Spear Bookstore. Courtesy of the Daphne Muse Collection.

In Drum and Spear Bookstore's 1971 catalog, they emphasized their reasoning:

We found that many of the new books being published on the "relevant-to-the-Black-community" bandwagon are either insipid and teach nothing, or are purposely designed to plant negative ideas in the child. We can't over-emphasize how important it is that adults carefully read any books which they intend giving to a child. We have found that a book whose title and story-line might seem to be beneficial often masks a kind of racism whose viciousness is even more dangerous because of its subtlety.

Decades later, Richardson echoes that 1971 catalog's message: "[We were] disgusted by the existing 'Black' or 'African' children's books, almost all of which were white-authored and showed Black folks as almost uniformly oppressed. The African books were almost entirely folktales or showed Africans in huts and barely clothed—no images of vibrant African cities or Africa's strong intellectual and political history."

Richardson also chronicles how Drum and Spear's children's section began: "The children's section began when Tony Gittens and I drove up to Bookazine in New York City in the spring of 1968. At Bookazine, I got taken by the children's book section shown to us by a Black stock manager who was delighted to hear we were starting a Black bookstore. It was the first time I'd seen so many books with Black children. We initially brought back a bunch of Black kids' books. Over time [between 1968 and 1970], we continued to order more. It was always a joy to host D.C.-based authors Lucille Clifton and Sharon Bell Mathis. And, of course, we organized a book party for Eloise Greenfield, once we published *Bubbles*."

Other sections in the store focused on African nationalism, social and economic thought, and keeping an eye on enemies of liberation. Like the children's section, the adult section included books about Third World people's struggles.

## Drum and Spear Press

While Drum and Spear Bookstore sold books, Drum and Spear Press published them under the direction of its first managing editor, Anne Forrester Holloway. Holloway's husband, Marvin, and Mildred "Mimi" Hayes were also instrumental in establishing the press. According to Drum and Spear Press's art director, Jennifer Lawson, the sentiment "We need our own books" drove the impetus behind starting a press. The press also aligned with the importance of being producers of media and culture and not just consumers, a value Courtland Cox held dear. Located in Washington, D.C., and Dar es Salaam, Tanzania, the press published *Enemy of the Sun: Poetry of Palestinian Resistance*, *Speaking Swahili/ Kusema Kiswahili*, *The Book of African Names*, and *A History of Pan-African Revolt* by C.L.R. James. The press quickly added children's books to its catalog: *Bubbles* by Eloise Greenfield and *Children of Africa: A Coloring Book*, for which Lawson drew the pictures.

## Relationships with Other Bookstores and Institutions

Before opening Drum and Spear, Charlie Cobb, Courtland Cox, and Tony Gittens visited Lewis Michaux's National Memorial African Bookstore to buy books and get advice from the veteran bookseller. Gittens described their visit and the advice Michaux gave him for the Library of Congress: "And when I talked to him . . . I said, 'Look, man, I'm trying to figure out how to do this.' And he gave me some advice. . . . 'Always remember that you've got to pay the sales tax every quarter. Never overbuy, overstock the bookstore. Don't take on too much credit.'"

Drum and Spear Bookstore supplied books published by the press to Black bookstores across the country, including Marcus Books (San Francisco), Hakim's Bookstore (Philadelphia), and Liberation Bookstore (Harlem).

Collegiate Black Studies programs and Black preschools alike leveraged the bookstore to teach students about Black history and Pan-Africanism. Sterling Allen Brown, the first professor of Black Literature Studies at Howard University, tailored his syllabus to the books available at Drum and Spear.

With Drum and Spear's emphasis on Pan-Africanism, it supplied *The African Writer Series* to other bookstores and was the only distributor of *Présence Africaine* magazine on the East Coast. Présence Africaine Bookstore in Paris had inspired Charlie Cobb to start Drum and Spear and, in turn, Drum and Spear inspired the creation of Bogle-L'Ouverture Bookshop in West London. The entire diaspora felt the vibration of Drum and Spear's impact, including Hodari Abdul-Ali, a customer who started Georgia Avenue's Pyramid Books "to carry on the tradition of Drum and Spear" after it closed.

"We were trying to build a sense of solidarity. . . . That's what these bookstores were about, they were revolutionizing the Black mind," Richardson asserted in the interview with Beckles.

That revolution of the Black mind led to Drum and Spear's satellite store, Maelezo Bookstore, in D.C.'s Health, Education, and Welfare Building. The Black workers in the building were offered a clothing store but instead demanded an offshoot of Drum and Spear. Richardson founded the store and asked Lawson for "a good Swahili name." Lawson suggested *Maelezo*, "which, she explained at the time, means 'causing someone to understand.'"

## Drum and Spear's Atmosphere

Former Drum and Spear employees remember the revolutionary bookstore fondly.

Gittens, Drum and Spear's first manager, emphasizes the hard work it took to organize the store. He and Richardson built the store's bookshelves after contractors only finished half of the job. As manager, he made sure to keep the door open to invite in the community.

Lawson remembers the space as cozy and intimate, like a clubhouse for the revolution, describing it as "cluttered with books, full of curious neighbors who became regulars, a gathering place." She used tile to create a silhouetted map of Africa on Drum and Spear's floor and designed the bookstore's interior.

Richardson called Drum and Spear her "second home" where she was "surrounded by [her] people, books, and art." She recounted the joy, the jazz, and the justice-seeking political discussions. In Colin Beckles's "Black Bookstores, Black Power, and the FBI: The Case of Drum and Spear," she described the store as a think tank for the anticolonial struggle in Africa and explains that the staff guided customers through political education. "It wasn't a dead store," she told Beckles, meaning Drum and Spear's staff witnessed customers changing and growing as they read.

But it wasn't just customers who were growing and changing thanks to Drum and Spear. Ms. Muse proudly asserts that she got her real education from the University of Drum and Spear. She admired Joe Gross, Charlie Cobb, Ivanhoe Donaldson, Courtland Cox, Don Brown, and Ralph Featherstone's intellectualism and willingness to teach others.

This commitment to political education attracted a motley assortment of customers.

"You had Pookie coming in Drum and Spear," Ms. Muse recalls, transporting herself back to 1371 Fairmont Street Northwest. "You had ambassadors coming in Drum and Spear. You had people like Amílcar Cabral coming in Drum and Spear. Toni Morrison came in looking for books written by African women specifically. You had heated debates. You had vigorous discourse. You had a little romance thrown up in there too, you know."

## FBI and Police Surveillance

Drum and Spear Bookstore's unique ability to unite Black people across class and political leanings threatened the FBI, which added "black extremist bookstores" to its Counter Intelligence Program the same year Drum and Spear opened. "[J. Edgar] Hoover hated us," Ms. Muse states plainly, speaking of the longtime FBI director. FBI files indicate Drum and Spear came onto the Bureau's radar after visits from former SNCC chairman Stokely Carmichael (Kwame Ture). Being in the same city as FBI headquarters made Drum and Spear an easy target for surveillance. Ms. Muse thinks back to "the trauma of the FBI coming in the store on a regular basis and flipping books off the shelves."

Ms. Muse had her own FBI agent, Jim South, who followed her to and from the store. He even came to her apartment door, trying to get her to talk with him. When she didn't, he left a note under the door: "Please call the FBI, exchange 73100, extension 765. Thank you. Jim South." "I hope he's still waiting by the phone," Ms. Muse quips.

DRUM AND SPEAR BOOKSTORE, Washington, D. C. Investiga
November, 1968, as bookstore founded by former members
were close associates of black extremist leader Stokel
Case closed 5/16/72.

"The FBI was after us," confirms Gittens, who had his own FBI file. The agency's access to Drum and Spear's bank accounts and all their comings and goings surprised him.

But federal authorities weren't the only ones after Drum and Spear. Ms. Muse and Gittens speak about getting tear-gassed outside the store by the local police and the National Guard.

"The day Gwendolyn Brooks came to read, a pregnant young Black woman had been beaten by the police and we walked out of the store, and we saw what was happening," recalls Ms. Muse. "The police came charging at us and threw a tear gas canister and I fainted in Lerone Bennett's arms. At the time, I was pregnant and didn't know it, and I miscarried. And I'm convinced it's because of that tear gas that I lost that child."

"A guardsman lifted his gun and shot a canister of tear gas directly at me," Gittens told *Black Power Chronicles*. "The canister missed me and crashed through our glass door, spreading tear gas, which choked us and our customers. One woman fell to the ground; the store was uninhabitable for many days afterwards. It was the closest I've come to being killed."

## Ralph Featherstone's Assassination

FBI scrutiny only intensified after Drum and Spear Bookstore manager Ralph "Feather" Featherstone was killed by a car bomb in March of 1970. Featherstone, a SNCC activist, was building bookshelves in the store's new location the night before heading to Bel Air, Maryland, to support his friend and fellow SNCC activist H. Rap Brown (Jamil Al-Amin), who was on trial.

The Drum and Spear family mourned their brother. Courtland Cox, the eldest, identified Featherstone's body. "He was a hard worker and serious person," Cox says.

"What a formidable presence he was, what a brilliant, strategic thinker he was," Ms. Muse echoes.

Lawson made the hand-carved urn that carried Featherstone's ashes to Africa. "Had he lived, Drum and Spear might still exist," she remarks, pointing to Featherstone's focus on making the store financially viable.

## The End of an Era

The bookstore ultimately closed in 1974. Drum and Spear alumni cite Featherstone's assassination, intense government surveillance, IRS harassment, debt, and intimidation of customers as the reasons the store closed.

In an address to the Library of Congress, Gittens said, "Our success would help lead to our own demise. . . . Drum and Spear showed that there was a market for Black books, and the bigger bookstores like Brentano's and Barnes & Noble, they also saw that and they began to take our customers. . . . They did book parties and book signings for Black authors that they never would have bothered with until we showed that we had a line around the corner coming in to see Eloise Greenfield and . . . Julius Lester. . . . And like all good capitalists, they took from us and went on."

Drum and Spear poured all its profits back into the movement (not the store). As Charlie Cobb told Joshua Clark Davis in 2015, "We didn't run it very well as a business. It was a movement bookstore."

But being bad capitalists is excusable—preferable, even—when you're instead good book people, good liberation people, people who, as Cox puts it, fought the "mental and intellectual violence" imparted on Black people.

Drum and Spear: a bookstore, a press, an education center, a movement.

# ELOISE GREENFIELD
# AND DRUM AND SPEAR

## BY CHAR ADAMS

The rejection stung. A fresh wound of disappointment erupted from each publisher who turned down Eloise Greenfield's manuscript. Eloise shed a few tears,[1] but she believed deeply in *Bubbles,* a story about a little Black boy, James Edward, learning to read. He rushes home to share his new skill with his mother, but only his baby sister, Deedee, has time to listen. Each line conjures images of childhood excitement and insists on its characters' Blackness.

```
"I can read," he whispered. Deedee giggled at
  his good news even though she didn't know what it
meant. She patted his head with both hands. When she
  laughed, her cheeks puffed out on each side, and she
  looked like a smooth, round piece of chocolate candy.
```

The story highlighted both the sweet bond between a young Black brother and sister and the joys of accessing another world through books. Any hope of publishing *Bubbles* was a long shot, though, at a time when mainstream publishing houses seldom cared about books with positive images of Black children.

It was the early 1970s and Eloise lived with her husband, Robert, and their two children, Monica and Steve, in a northeast Washington, D.C., row house full of books and music.[2] Eloise devoted herself to her short stories and poetry in between attending civil rights marches[3] and working as a clerk typist. She attended the March on Washington and regularly volunteered with the local Urban League, but she largely poured her pro-Black activism into her writing.[4] She'd devoured title after title from the local library as a child; her love for books ran deep. As an adult, the lack of trade books about Black children was disheartening. "Then and there, I decided to make that my mission,"[5] Eloise once said. "I wanted my books to enable Black children to realize how beautiful and smart they are. I wanted to write books that inspired and uplifted them, that made them laugh and be happy."

There was only one problem: no one would publish her books.

---

1   Eloise Greenfield, interview with Don Tate, *The Brown Bookshelf*, February 18, 2008, https://thebrownbookshelf .com/28days/eloise-greenfield.
2   Monica Greenfield, email to the author, November 29, 2022.
3   Monica Greenfield, telephone interview with the author, November 18, 2022.
4   Monica Greenfield, telephone interview with the author, September 8, 2023.
5   Emily Langer, "Eloise Greenfield, author whose picture books uplifted Black children, dies at 92," *Washington Post,* April 18, 2021.

Eloise had been writing for a decade before the *Hartford Times* in Connecticut published one of her poems, "To a Violin," in 1962, and *Negro Digest* published some of her short stories throughout the sixties. Eloise had endured ten rejections by the time she heard from Judy Richardson in 1971. Her heart raced as she tore open Judy's letter. It was good news: Drum and Spear Press wanted to publish *Bubbles*.

"I ran all the way downstairs to show it to everybody," Eloise said of the letter. "I was so excited!"

Judy was a young Black activist working the front desk at Drum and Spear Bookstore on Fairmont Street in D.C. and also serving as the children's book editor for the shop's press. Charlie Cobb had had authors like Eloise in mind when he started Drum and Spear, a passion project for veteran activists of the Student Nonviolent Coordinating Committee (SNCC).[6]

"We wanted a shop that warmly welcomed authors,"[7] he said of himself and the group of activists he put together to start the store. "We wanted a shop that a range of authors could feel comfortable reading in."

Eloise was more than happy to publish with such a press. Besides, she'd done her fair share of activism and these shared values endeared Judy and Eloise to each other. Before teaming up with Judy, Eloise had frequented Drum and Spear, taking her children to browse its shelves and even joining the store's writers' workshop. By the time Drum and Spear Press published *Bubbles* in 1972, Eloise had a deep and lasting connection with the shop.

After decades of writing, Drum and Spear's shelves would be the first place Eloise saw one of her books. She bounced down to the store with her children in tow and stared in awe at the dozens of copies of *Bubbles*, later retitled *Good News*, in the store's children's section. She clutched her handbag and smiled with excitement at the display. On the cover, little James Edward stood leaning on a table with the word *BUBBLES* written above his afro, the pink letters perched among his neighborhood's city buildings. A few other titles were on the shelves— *Children of Africa* and *The Book of African Names*—but *Bubbles* stole the show. Eloise inspected the books,

Eloise Greenfield looking at *Bubbles* on the shelves of Drum and Spear. Courtesy of Monica Greenfield.

---

6    Daniel Perlstein, "SNCC and the Creation of the Mississippi Freedom Schools," *History of Education Quarterly* 30, no. 3 (Autumn 1990).

7    Charlie Cobb, interview with Joshua Clark Davis, October 16, 2015.

thumbing through some of the copies and posing for photos in front of the display. Her joy and relief were palpable. A long-held dream had finally come true.

Judy eagerly courted neighborhood families into Drum and Spear to promote *Bubbles*. This didn't take much effort, though. Bubbly Black children piled into the store with their parents and hung on Eloise's words.

"She was very animated when she would read," Monica Greenfield recalled of her mother. "It was so important to her to have her words be rhythmic."

*"A smile was bubbling inside James Edward on his way home from school, and he opened his lips to let it out,"* Eloise read from the book. *"The three new words were printed on the sheet of paper that was folded and tucked in his pocket. James Edward felt like a lightning bug, warm and glowy, all the way from his inside self to his outside brownness."*

Smiles filled the room. Little ones hugged their parents, joyfully aware of their own "brownness." With just one story in a little Black-owned bookshop in Washington, D.C., Eloise exposed a room of Black kids to a world of possibility.

Judy pulled out all the stops for the *Bubbles* release party. After all, this was as much a victory for her as it was for Eloise. Charlie Cobb's aunt Charlotte excitedly volunteered her home for the event, and Judy set her heart on having a bubble machine at the party. Teachers, friends, and family all filled the home and gushed over the new book. Decades later, Eloise and Judy would laugh as they recalled their guests slipping and sliding on the hardwood floors thanks to the soapy bubbles.[8] It was memories like this, of community and joy, that came to define the relationship between Black authors and the booksellers who supported them.

Eloise went on to revolutionize Black children's literature, with groundbreaking books that reflected the cultural experience of growing up Black, in stories about Rosa Parks and Harriet Tubman. She explored simple childhood pleasures in books such as *Honey, I Love* (1978) and taught Black children about Black midwives throughout history in *The Women Who Caught the Babies* (2019). She read to wide-eyed children in schools, libraries, and Black bookstores across the country up until her death in August 2021 at age ninety-two.[9] In her final years, Eloise still spoke with a smile when reflecting on Drum and Spear Bookstore and the press that helped to launch her career.

At an appearance in D.C., she gushed about *Bubbles* as book lovers held on to their elder's every word. "This was my first book," Eloise said, smiling at Judy Richardson, "and this was my first editor!"[10]

---

8    "In Memory: Eloise Greenfield: Groundbreaking Author of Children's Literature," Teaching for Change, last modified August 5, 2021, https://www.teachingforchange.org/eloise-greenfield.

9    Greenfield, telephone interview with the author, November 18, 2022; Patrice Gaines, "Eloise Greenfield, late children's book author, inspired generations of Black writers and readers," *NBC News*, August 11, 2021.

10    "In Memory: Eloise Greenfield: Groundbreaking Author of Children's Literature," Teaching for Change.

# THE BLACK BOOK

Writer Ta-Nehisi Coates describes growing up in his Baltimore home surrounded by his father's books—books that "were all over the house, books about black people, by black people, for black people spilling off shelves and out of the living room, boxed up in the basement"—books that belonged to Paul Coates, founder of The Black Book and Black Classic Press.

Shortly after leaving the Black Panther Party, the elder Coates established The Black Book, a bookstore with the mission of "providing books to the inside and jobs to the outside." Through the George Jackson Prison Movement, The Black Book sent books to people in jail and supported incarcerated Panthers. By the late 1970s, Coates closed the bookstore and focused on publishing "significant and obscure works by and about people of African descent" through Black Classic Press.

Paul Coates's tireless efforts to recover, discover, and publish essential works of Black literature were honored with the National Book Foundation's Literarian Award in 2024. I spoke with Paul about Black bookselling and Black publishing.

**From the outside looking in, it appears that Black publishers rely on Black bookstores to have somewhere to sell their books and to get them to the community, and Black bookstores rely on Black publishers to have the inventory. So I see it as a symbiotic relationship. Would you agree with that or do you see it differently as someone who's seen it from both sides?**

**PAUL COATES:** I think at one time it was probably closer to what you're saying, yes. By the late eighties or early nineties, that relationship waned because by then white publishers began to produce more and more Black books. And so it's not uncommon for you to go into a Black bookstore today and not find a book by a Black publisher.

**Can you describe the similarities and differences between working with the Black publishers and working with the white publishers as a bookstore owner?**

**PAUL COATES:** The Black publishers—for the most part—I knew them directly. They were all small, and they were in the business of bringing information to the Black community. That was their calling for the most part. Some Black publishers were in it as commercial publishers. They didn't last that long. They felt that they could compete with the large houses. Most of them didn't last. It's just no way they could compete. They didn't have any kind of money to lose money on books and keep going. With the white publishers, everything was transactional.

**With bookstores like Drum and Spear, The Black Book, and Marcus Books, it seems like the legacy bookstores would have some way to disseminate the information themselves through a press. And I don't see that as much with the newer stores. Have you noticed that shift or do you remember when that shift occurred?**

**PAUL COATES:** You'll notice that all the stores you named were movement stores. They were all part of the Black Power Movement and for us, it was important that we control things because we never expected white people to distribute our books. Every one of them was fueled by a consciousness.

When you're looking at Black bookstores today, the majority of them didn't come out of any type of empowerment movement. They're in the business largely of raising consciousness, but it isn't connected with their movement experience.

What you're talking about is a particular phase of the Black Power Movement expressing itself through book publishing and bookstores and other ways of getting the message out to Black people. So, you're not going to see that as much today in the stores. Not saying that's good or bad, just an observation.

**When we first spoke, we were discussing the definition of a Black bookstore. Would you say that part of that definition is having Black-published books as inventory?**

PAUL COATES: I don't think so at all. Booksellers and bookstore owners have different interests. They bring different things to the table. They bring different loves, different likes, different expertise. And that gets reflected in the bookstore.

Maybe some of the Black publishers have published books on Afrofuturism but none specialize in that. But you have stores that see that as an important thing to deal with. Well, if the Black publishers don't do it, then that person has every right to—and he must—go to somebody else and get those books if that's their calling.

Many of the Black booksellers don't even know about the Black publishers. And I'm not saying that's their fault. That's an opportunity for Black publishers to take advantage of. If a Black bookseller doesn't know about Black Classic Press, that ain't on them. That's on me.

**The last thing I wanted to touch on is Black publishers and Black bookstores as institutions. As you made the transition from the bookstore to publishing, was part of the consideration that Black Classic Press would have more institutional power than one bookstore?**

PAUL COATES: No, not necessarily. Remember, this was all a part of the same plan from day one. It was that we're going to do the bookstore, and we're going to do publishing, and we're going to do printing. So that was the institutional thought. The thing that became different is I never conceived of closing the bookstore when we first put this plan together.

But the bookstore was a failure in terms of generating income. It took a little while for that to sink in, but over time it became very clear that we could not sustain a bookstore.

The whole idea was all three of those parts working to make a contribution to our community. So, it wasn't so much moving from one to the other for the reason of power; it was a fulfillment of the plan. And when one part of the plan wasn't working, that part had to be jettisoned to make sure that we could still accomplish the overall goal.

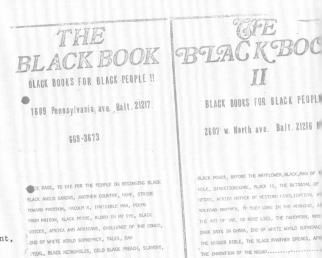

Black Book advertisement, reproduced in FBI file 157-BA-6828-3.

Paul Coates in his
Washington, D.C., home.

UNITED STATES GOVERNMENT

## *Memorandum*

TO : SAC, Albany

DATE: 10/9/68

FROM : Director, FBI (157-8415)

SUBJECT: BLACK NATIONALIST MOVEMENT IN THE UNITED STATES
RACIAL MATTERS
BUDED: 11/8/68

    The Bureau has noted an increase in the establishment
of black extremist bookstores which represent propaganda outlets
for revolutionary and hate publications and cultural centers for
extremism. Each office should locate and identify black
extremist and/or African-type bookstores in its territory and
open separate discreet investigations on each to determine if
it is extremist in nature. Advise under this caption by 11/8/68
of the investigations instituted in accordance with these
instructions.

    The investigation should determine the identities of
the owners; whether it is a front for any group or foreign
interest; whether individuals affiliated with the store engage
in extremist activities; the number, type, and source of books
and material on sale; the store's financial condition; its
clientele; and whether it is used as a headquarters or meeting
place. Submit results under individual caption in form suitable
for dissemination along with a recommendation as to whether
additional investigation is warranted.

    Investigations should be instituted on new stores
when opened and you should recognize the excellent target these
stores represent for penetration by racial sources.

2 - All Offices

*157-368-80*

SEARCHED............INDEXED
SERIALIZED.........FILED
OCT 11 1968
FBI — WASH. F. O.

SCREENED
By NS Date 8/9/16

*Buy U.S. Savings Bonds Regularly on the Payroll Savings Plan*

5010-108-01

Memo from FBI director J. Edgar Hoover ordering nationwide surveillance
of Black bookstores, October 9, 1968, FBI file 157-WFO-368.

# THE LIES—AND SURPRISING TRUTHS— OF SURVEILLANCE FILES ON BLACK BOOKSTORES

## BY JOSHUA CLARK DAVIS

In the summer of 2019, the National Archives notified me that they were releasing a large batch of FBI records on The Black Book, a store owned and operated by former Black Panther Party defense captain Paul Coates in Baltimore in the 1970s. Along with selling books, Coates operated the store as the "community/prison information center" of the George Jackson Prison Movement, an organization he cofounded to provide individuals incarcerated at the Maryland Penitentiary with free books, commissary payments, and legal advice.[1]

It had been so long since I had requested these records that I had forgotten even asking for them in the first place. But in the six years since my request, archivists had read through 974 pages of the Bureau's investigative file on The Black Book, releasing every page to me, most without redactions. What I found in those records was remarkable. I've requested too many FBI files to name over the years. Sometimes they're filled with newspaper clippings easily found online. Other times they contain records already publicly available in another individual's FBI file. But this, the largest FBI file that I had ever seen dedicated to a single Black bookseller, offered a fine-grained account of bookselling in the Black Power era and a window into Black community life and activism in Baltimore in the 1970s that I had not at all expected.

∗ ∗ ∗

Why did law enforcement officials—both the FBI and local police departments—spy on Black bookstores? I initially tackled this question in my first book, *From Head Shops to Whole Foods: The Rise and Fall of Activist Entrepreneurs*, and in a subsequent article I wrote for the *Atlantic*. Black booksellers promoted the literature and ideology of Black Power, often in open collaboration with movement organizers including the Panthers and various Black nationalist and Pan-Africanist groups. These stores were activist hotspots, the sites of strategy discussions, meetings, and sometimes even rallies. As the stores' numbers exploded—growing more than sixfold from the mid-1960s to the mid-'70s—so too did their prominence as purveyors of Black radical ideas.

---

1   George Jackson Prison Movement, "Brothers and Sisters," undated flyer, FBI file 157-BA-6828-3, National Archives and Records Administration (NARA), College Park, Maryland.

It's not surprising that the FBI was interested in Black bookstores, considering its fixation on African American literature. As author William Maxwell has chronicled, nearly half of the Black modernist authors featured in the second edition of *The Norton Anthology of African American Literature* were monitored by J. Edgar Hoover's FBI. As they scrutinized Black authors, scouring their literary output and investigating their political allegiances, agents produced more than 13,000 pages on the leading Black writers of Hoover's lifetime. In Maxwell's reading, "the FBI is perhaps the most dedicated and influential forgotten critic of African American literature."[2]

And yet, if Black bookstores caught the attention of the FBI by selling Black literature, the fact that they operated as social networks of Black intellectual exchange may have been even more suspect. Black bookstores were places where African American readers discussed, analyzed, debated, and celebrated the written word, where books were displayed on walls and in plate-glass windows, and where they were read aloud, by authors and audiences alike. Because American literature has been dominated by whites and disfigured by racism, Black bookstores played an outsized role in offering readers a critical alternative to the status quo of literary white supremacy.

In October 1968, when Hoover wrote to the Bureau's fifty-eight field offices ordering investigations on each Black bookstore in their local jurisdictions, he instructed agents to focus on seven areas of inquiry: "the identities of the owners; whether it is a front for any group or foreign interest; whether individuals affiliated with the store engage in extremist activities; the number, type, and source of books and material on sale; the store's financial condition; its clientele; and whether it is used as a headquarters or meeting place."[3]

Notably, only one of those seven investigative criteria pertained to books. Nearly all the rest concerned the people who gathered in these stores. The community that Black people forged at these shops, the coming together around literature and ideas and political writing: that was what most troubled Hoover.

The FBI director worried that Black bookstores could be covers for radical organizations. This suspicion sprang from the mind of a man who had spent decades of his life hunting communists who gave their organizational projects innocently non-Marxist names to ward off state persecution. Two of Baltimore's earlier communist bookstores, for instance, were the Free State Bookshop and the Frederick Douglass Book Center.[4] Hoover's invocation of the shadowy "front" here reveals his racist instincts, too, as though hidden political organizations, and not Black people's demand for relevant literature, explained Black bookstores' success.

---

2   William J. Maxwell, *F.B. Eyes: How J. Edgar Hoover's Ghostreaders Framed African American Literature* (Princeton, N.J.: Princeton University Press, 2015), 8–9, 18.

3   Memo, J. Edgar Hoover to Special-Agent-in-Charge, Albany, "Black Nationalist Movement in the United States—Racial Matters," October 9, 1968, FBI File 157-WFO-368, NARA; *FBI Annual Report: Fiscal Year 1968* (Washington, D.C.: Federal Bureau of Investigation, 1968), 2.

4   Joshua Clark Davis, "The Forgotten World of Communist Bookstores," *Jacobin*, August 11, 2017.

FBI agent Robert Wall offers us a rare insider's view of the surveillance of Black bookstores. An outspoken Bureau apostate who quit Hoover's agency in disgust after three years of service, Wall had been assigned to the FBI's Internal Security office in Washington in 1967. Among other cases, he worked on the office's "Racial Matters" caseload—an "absurdly and frighteningly broad" category of Bureau investigations, in Wall's words. "Clearly the Bureau had no rational criterion for opening these investigations," Wall charged in the *New York Review of Books* in January 1972. "The only consistent pattern that I found was that if an individual or group is Black and does something to gain attention it is likely to be investigated."

Wall recalled that one of his colleagues was tasked with monitoring the Drum and Spear Bookstore, operated by veterans of the Student Nonviolent Coordinating Committee in the Columbia Heights community just a few miles from the Bureau's Washington field office. After investigating the store, tracking its staff, and scouring its bank records for months, the agent failed to identify any evidence of criminal activity. With little to show for his efforts, the agent was ordered to visit the store and purchase a copy of *The Quotations of Chairman Mao Tse-tung*, presumably in the hopes that the sale would somehow implicate Drum and Spear in an international communist plot.

But Wall's colleague came up empty-handed when he tried to buy Mao's so-called "little red book" from the store. Not someone to let facts get in the way of doing his duty, the agent made his way to Brentano's, one of Washington's most popular white-owned bookstores. There he found a copy of the book and brought it back to his supervisor, who, none the wiser, gladly added a note to Drum and Spear's file that it sold Maoist propaganda.[5]

\*\*\*

Not long after I received the documents on The Black Book and the George Jackson Prison Movement from the National Archives, I wrote to Coates, whom I had gotten to know through researching for my first book and later through panel discussions we did on the history of Black bookselling. In 1978, after closing The Black Book, Coates launched Black Classic Press with the goal of republishing seminal out-of-print works on Black history and politics. More than forty-five years later, Black Classic Press is still going strong, and Coates is widely considered one of the deans of African American publishing.

BACKGROUND: Black Book advertisement, reproduced in FBI file 157-BA-6828-4.

---

5   Robert Wall, "Special Agent for the FBI," *New York Review of Books*, January 27, 1972.

After closing The Black Book, Paul Coates launched Black Classic Press. Courtesy of Paul Coates.

There's admittedly something strange about contacting someone to share surveillance documents a law enforcement agency compiled on them decades earlier. That person may well already know or at least suspect they were monitored by the authorities. In Coates's case, he had already seen some of his FBI records.

For anyone who ever gets the chance to read about themselves in surveillance files, such documents may stir up memories of violation, trauma, and betrayal. The records I shared with Coates, for instance, were filled with reports by an individual on familiar terms with The Black Book's staff who informed for the Bureau.

"Wow. There are some interesting things in here to say the least," Coates reflected after reading the pages I sent him, many for the first time ever. "Some I'd completely forgotten. Then there are some things that are just outright lies, perhaps manufactured to fill reports when they did not have information. I did learn that I had two more children that were fathered with women I knew. Pure, pure fiction."

Coates drove home a point that any discerning reader of law enforcement records knows well: you absolutely cannot believe everything in these files.

And yet, alongside the many misrepresentations and falsehoods, the FBI records surprisingly also preserve Coates's aspirations, his political objectives, his friendships, and, most significantly, his voice. There are flyers Coates created for Eddie Conway, his lifelong friend and Panther comrade who spent more than four decades in prison, a man he never stopped fighting for until he was released by authorities in 2014 in the wake of a groundbreaking Maryland court ruling that overturned the sentences of hundreds of people improperly convicted in the state prior to 1980.[6]

---

6    Justin Fenton, Ian Duncan, and Justin George, "Former Black Panther Freed," *Baltimore Sun*, March 5, 2014; Michael Millemann, Jennifer Elisa Chapman, and Samuel P. Feder, "Releasing Older Prisoners Convicted of Violent Crimes: The Unger Story," *University of Maryland Law Journal of Race, Religion, Gender and Class* 21 (2021): 185–247.

These files also contain a letter Coates sent to Ruchell Magee, a man incarcerated at San Quentin for his role in kidnapping a judge in an attempt to free George Jackson and the Soledad Brothers in 1970. The FBI pilfered the letter from the postal service and photocopied it, using a covert mail-opening technique practiced by the Bureau for years.[7] Many of these documents have likely survived nowhere else.

The FBI's files on The Black Book overflow with stories of community events designed to sate appetites and raise consciousnesses—chicken dinners, crab feasts, and even "the world's first de-gassed bean buffet."[8] And there are lots of comically mundane updates, the kind of pointless reports where an agent takes the trouble to relate that a prized source has "nothing to relate."[9]

Bookselling, like many retail businesses, can be slow at times. It demands a lot of waiting and grunt work. And when it's done right, it involves no shortage of public events, political engagement, and bringing people together to talk. This social dimension of Black bookstores alarmed the FBI and police intelligence units. For that reason, Black booksellers' record of forging fellowship among lovers of Black literature and history fills law enforcement's surveillance reports on their stores.

So yes, the files from the FBI and police on Coates and any number of Black booksellers did perpetuate countless falsehoods. But despite their best efforts to mislead, they inadvertently saved some truths for posterity, too.

*ement, 1609 Pennsylvania Av. Balto. Md. M.*

## : NOT GUILTY

ted out that Marshall Eddie Conway had been singled out
l Authorities to receive massive doses of Md.'s special
becomes more clear as we examine the circumstances of
railroad Eddie Conway.

now, Marshall Conway was convicted of killing one of
Baltimore's uniformed agents of repression (Baltimore
City Police), and attempting to kill two others. As a
result of the conviction he was sentenced to life plus
thirty years. At present this conviction is being appealed. It is our opinion as well as the opinion
of many other people that Eddie was railroaded to
jail not because of any crime he committed, but because of his Political beliefs and membership in the
Black Panther Party.

The latest attempt to railroad Eddie was based
on a confrontation that occurred in Baltimore City
Jail in Feb. 1971. Eddie had been accussed of strangling one of the Jail Guards with a piece of wire attached to newspaper. This device was supposedly made
and used by Eddie. All the attempts made by the State
Prosecution and the guard supposedly attacked by Eddie
to put Eddie in a position of strangling the guard
failed miserably. The jury of 12 men and women refused
to accept the story about Eddie Conway jumping out of
the blue and attacking the guard (part of the guard's
testimony was that Eddie jumped him for no known or apparent reason and attempted to strangle him.) The jury
preferred to believe Eddie's testimony. Yes, there had
been a confrontation with the guard but it was a result
programmatic insensitivity practiced by most guards in
nal institutions across America. And because of lack
nderstanding the guard provoked a situation in which
was forced to defend himself. The jury refused also
ter.

ed with attempted murder Eddie was also charged with
ult on the guard was based on the fact that even though
l struggled with the guard. The jury found Eddie
as been appealed by Eddie's attorney, Harold Buchman.

as wrongly imprisoned Marshall Conway and knowing this
s imprisonment by creating false charges against him
axpayers money trying to convict a man who has alrea
t of his natural life plus 30 yrs. in jail? We feel
of Eddie will surely be exposed to the people, who

e old and decaying. Time belongs to us. It is on o
life. We urge the community as a whole to join
J all Political Prisoners.

George Jackson Prison Movement
flyer for Eddie Conway, reproduced
in FBI file 157-BA-6828-1.

7    *Hearings before the Select Committee to Study Governmental Operations with Respect to Intelligence Activities of the United States Senate: Volume 4—Mail Opening*, Ninety-fourth Congress, First Session, October 21, 22, and 24, 1975 (Washington, D.C.: Government Printing Office, 1976).

8    Flyer, "The Black Book Presents a Book and Boogie Affair," August 1975, FBI file 157-BA-6828-4, NARA.

9    Report, received by SA Bryan E. Foy, September 26, 1973, FBI file 157-BA-6828-3, NARA.

# PYRAMID BOOKS

"We're proving that the old stereotype, 'If you want to hide something from a Black person, put it in a book' isn't true," Hodari Abdul-Ali told the *Baltimore Sun* in 1991, speaking of Pyramid Books, the D.C.-based chain he owned with his wife, Mayimuna Ali.

The first Pyramid Books—nicknamed the House of Knowledge—arrived near Howard University's campus in 1981. The gold-brick building beckoned curious minds with a bust of a pharaoh that sat more than 13 feet high, watching over Georgia Avenue.

"You'd walk in that joint and it was just Black power from the basement to the top floor," declares Sadiq Ali, Hodari and Mayimuna's son. When Sadiq's parents purchased 2849 Georgia Avenue NW, they invited other Black businesses into the House of Knowledge. "It became one of the first one-stop shops for all things Black culture in that area," Sadiq proclaims before launching into a list of the businesses he remembers: a health food store, the Nation of Islam's shop, and a Nation-run bakery in the basement that stuffed young Sadiq with "a wide assortment of bean pies."

The books, the bean pies, the bountiful Blackness were much needed. By 1991, Pyramid Books boasted five locations and sales exceeding $1 million, making it the first chain of independently Black-owned and -oriented bookstores in the country.

Hodari attributed much of the chain's success to the political climate. "I think the Reagan-Bush era jarred a lot of people, especially young people who found Black leaders not making enough noise. They found themselves rediscovering men like Martin Luther King and Malcolm X," he told the *Baltimore Sun* in late 1991.

But from Sadiq's vantage point, Pyramid's expansion revealed cracks in the business's infrastructure. "He had a good vision, but he didn't have great advisors around him. His first love was journalism, not business," Sadiq concludes of his father, who edited Howard University's student newspaper *The Hilltop* before running Liberation Information Distributing Company, a Black books and periodicals distributor.

Hodari's lack of formal business training coupled with a changing book industry proved to be more than Pyramid Books could weather. In 1995, Hodari told *Washington City Paper* that a B. Dalton employee visited his Prince George's Plaza location, wrote down book titles, and left. Soon after, those same titles appeared in B. Dalton's newly expanded African American section.

Hodari Abdul-Ali nicknamed the first Pyramid Books the House of Knowledge. Courtesy of the Ali Family.

"We didn't have the money to compete with their buying power," Hodari told the paper after the last Pyramid Books location closed.

But Pyramid wasn't Hodari's last foray into books. After successfully vending at the Million Man March, he opened Dar Es Salaam Book/Health Center, a hub for Black and Islamic texts and healthy food, in Mount Rainier, Maryland.

# EVERYONE'S PLACE

"We are in what they call . . . the 'hood,'" says Brother Nati with a laugh.

When Brother Nati and his wife, Sister Tabia, opened Everyone's Place African Cultural Center in 1980s Baltimore, the next closest Black bookstore sat in Washington, D.C. Fresh out of an African Studies program at University of Maryland, Baltimore County, the couple saw a need in their neighborhood and began vending on Baltimore's streets. Now Brother Nati, Sister Tabia, and their daughter Olakekan Kamau-Nataki run Everyone's Place as a family.

Just as Olakekan grew up in the store, so did much of Baltimore.

"People will say, 'Man, I bought my children's board books here, my grandchildren's board books here,' or 'My grandfather, my grandmother used to shop here,' or 'We went to college around here. We came to Everyone's Place and got all our books,'" says Brother Nati, recalling the words of his longtime customers in his thick Trinidadian accent.

Ta-Nehisi Coates immortalized the bookstore in his National Book Award–winning memoir: "I would buy tapes of Malcolm's speeches—'Message to the Grassroots,' 'The Ballot or the Bullet'— down at Everyone's Place, a black bookstore on North Avenue, and play them on my Walkman," he wrote. Years after the Walkman became obsolete, Coates held the first book event for *Between the World and Me* at Everyone's Place.

Mere months before Coates's return to Everyone's Place in 2015, Baltimore erupted after Freddie Gray's murder. "Next to us is a pharmacy. Protesters looted it but they didn't set it on fire because they knew we're right next door. And many people in the community came out to protect the store," Brother Nati remembers. "We always knew the community had our back, but in that moment, it was clear that we were doing something right."

When asked if he recognizes himself as a part of history, Brother Nati is characteristically humble. "Maybe when I die, I'll recognize it, but no. I'm not sure if I'd say I'm a part of history now. We definitely were a part of the intellectual, social, cultural, and progressive development of our people and we know that because people tell us." The bookstore, along with Afrikan World Books, the wholesale book business Brother Nati also owns, are foundational to Baltimoreans, but Brother Nati doesn't let the compliments go to his head.

Olakekan chimes in, "My parents may be seen as a part of history, but for them, they're doing this work each day. So, what we would consider as historically significant is just their life."

Though the store is a family store, it's also truly *everyone's place*.

# KARIBU BOOKS

When Simba Sana and Brother Yao (Hoke S. Glover III) vended together for the first time on Black Friday 1992, they made $400 in four hours. The pair, along with Yao's wife, Karla Wilkerson-Glover, hustled across Howard University's campus selling books such as *Erotique Noire* and *Mis-Education of the Negro*.

Over fifteen years, Simba and Yao transformed a modest street-vending operation into the country's largest Black-owned bookstore chain, with locations throughout Washington, D.C., and Maryland, before closing in the late aughts. Like that of so many Black bookstores, Karibu's story is one of an epic rise, a tragic fall, and an immeasurable afterlife.

At Karibu's height, the store grossed millions of dollars, hosted more than four hundred events a year, and employed more than forty people. "Community, Pan-Africanism, institution building . . . the bookstore represented all of that," Simba asserts.

And Karibu served the community wholeheartedly. As Karla explains, "*Karibu* means 'welcome' in Kiswahili and that's exactly what it did—welcome people into our world." But by 2008, the community bid *kwaheri*—"goodbye" —to Karibu Books. "There's this idea that some outside white folks came in and destroyed the business, but that's not the case for Karibu. Internal dynamics created Karibu's failure," Yao tells me.

But did Karibu fail? The store fits squarely in Black bookstores' celebrated tradition. "There would be no Karibu without Pyramid Books. Hodari Ali—he showed me it was possible," Simba acknowledges. "And Tom from Eso Won Books took me under his wing, taught me a lot about researching and curating the inventory."

That tradition cannot be graded on a pass-fail basis. It's true: Karibu no longer exists, and its absence left a void for its community of readers, but to leave a void is to mean what you did mattered in the first place. Like seeds from a tree, workers from Karibu's branches carried its ethos on long after the chain fell. Former Karibu district manager Ramunda Young and her husband, Derrick (who also worked at Karibu), cofounded MahoganyBooks. Reginald Dwayne Betts, who founded Karibu's book club for Black boys, became a celebrated poet and MacArthur Genius. Jason Reynolds, the *New York Times* bestselling author, discovered Richard Wright's *Black Boy* while working at Karibu during college. Karla became a librarian. Simba wrote a memoir. And Yao became a professor at Bowie State University.

Just as Karibu stood on the shoulders of Black bookstores that came before it, it offered a foundation for the many bookish pursuits that would come after it. Yao summarizes Karibu's journey this way: "It was a good run . . . shit don't last forever."

Courtesy of American Booksellers Association.

# LEGACY BLACK BOOKSTORES IN D.C., OR THE REJECTED STRAIN

## BY JOSHUA MYERS

It felt like just a normal day at Howard. Classes, studying, the grind. It was my junior year. The year I began engaging with Black intellectual and political traditions in earnest. A year that found me auditing classes that had very little to do with my degree program and everything to do with my life now.

Yet, it really wasn't a normal day. I decided to stop by Greg Carr's Black Philosophy, Religion, and Ritual course, and when he entered with an enormous cardboard box filled with books, I was curious. "I just returned from Karibu Books. They're closing," he informed us. Then he pulled Ben Ratliff's *Coltrane: The Story of a Sound* from the box and proceeded to place it within the context of the universe of Coltrane biographies.

With urgency, I went hurtling to Pentagon City on that now not normal day. It wasn't just the urgency of knowing that the books would be 75 percent off—it was the fact that I had not spent as much time in Karibu as I'd hoped. A few months earlier, my personal library had grown from the few books that I had retained from freshman-year English—Toni Morrison's *Song of Solomon*, James Baldwin's *Blues for Mister Charlie,* and Octavia Butler's *Kindred*—to include works that I had acquired from Clarke's Bookshop in Cape Town during a study abroad trip led by Carr and Dana Williams. There, I acquired my first copy of Steve Biko's *I Write What I Like* and the important biography of Robert Sobukwe, *How Can Man Die Better*, by Benjamin Pogrund—both texts I could not help but devour. Thinking back on those moments, it was as if Carr's love for book collecting had been passed on to me, and had introduced me to an entire tradition of Black bibliophilism through its connection to the Black liberation struggle. Taking us to Clarke's on Long Street had been a bit of an initiation. So it was that spirit that sent me to Karibu's liquidation sale that day, neglecting the fact that I had a full day of classes ahead of me. A different school was about to be in session.

Founded in 1993, Karibu was one of the most successful Black bookstores of its time, and perhaps in the history of Black bookstores. The store in Pentagon City was one of its seven locations. Its cofounder was Yao Glover, a young entrepreneur who had begun the operation as a street vendor, selling "Black consciousness" literature to students at Bowie State University and Howard. Karibu combined its roots—providing titles for those seeking what Glover has called "the activist" route—with a model that brought along the general reader by including a range of titles accommodating Black people of multiple interests and tastes.

When I skipped my financial modeling class that day in 2008, however, I was clearly in search of the former. I can still remember my haul: the racist tome *The Rising Tide of Color* by Lothrop Stoddard; a combined edition of Martin Delany's *Condition, Elevation, Emigration and Destiny of the Colored Peoples of the United States* and *The Official Report of the Niger River Valley Exploring Party*, edited by the Yoruba scholar Toyin Falola; a copy of the Karnak House–published *Ancient Egypt and Black Africa* by prominent Congolese Egyptologist Theophile Obenga; and the classic *The Crisis of the Negro Intellectual* by Harold Cruse in a new edition introduced by the critic Stanley Crouch.

Today, I imagine that very few of the newly emergent Black bookstores would be expected to carry these titles on their shelves. The ones that do are increasingly part of what Harold Cruse once characterized as "the rejected strain," the nationalist impulse among Black folk. But the Pan African nationalist bookstore was *the norm* for most of the twentieth century. There was something about the type of bookstore that read generalist lit alongside the work of Harold Cruse, Theophile Obenga, and, of course, Martin Delany, whom Cruse remembered as part of this rejected strain. Delany was rejected in the social and political imagination of academia and corporate media's sense of who Black people are. This rejected strain is what shaped my consciousness—just as it did those earlier generations of Black bibliophiles and collectors, organizers and cultural workers, and some academics.

For us, it is impossible to imagine the intellectual thrust of Harlem without Lewis Michaux's National Memorial African Bookstore: the House of Common Sense and Home of Proper Propaganda, Malcolm X's home bookstore. Or Chicago without F.H. Hammurabi Robb's House of Knowledge. Or Alfred and Bernice Ligon's Aquarian Bookshop in Los Angeles. And in the next generation, Una Mulzac's Liberation Bookstore in New York, Hakim's in Philadelphia, Detroit's Shrine of the Black Madonna Bookstore, Marcus Books in Oakland, and D.C.'s Drum and Spear.

Founded in 1968 by a coterie of Pan Africanist veterans of the Student Nonviolent Coordinating Committee, Drum and Spear is considered one of the founding bookstores of the modern era of D.C.-based Black stores. Stocking titles that spoke directly to ongoing struggles on the continent, the operation grew to include study groups and even its own publishing operation. This of course invited suspicion and surveillance from the federal government. But it also continued a tradition and simultaneously bequeathed it to Pyramid Books, founded by Hodari Abdul-Ali in 1981.

Part of the Georgia Avenue corridor of Black businesses once known as "The Nile Valley," Pyramid carried an eclectic mix of titles that represented the dynamism of Black nationalist thought. It was a space for Black ideas as well as Black publishers—both self-published authors and major publishing houses then operating in the Black community. Chicago's Third World Press, a publishing house founded by Haki Madhubuti to advance the Black Arts movement and its "spiritual sister," the Black Power Movement, obtained an important and significant distribution network in stores like Pyramid.

By the late eighties and early nineties, Black Classic Press, founded by Paul Coates, would contribute mightily to this ecosystem. Coates began as a street vendor, selling titles on Howard University's campus. But he also worked in Howard's Moorland-Spingarn Research Center, where he would often find books cited by scholars such as John Henrik Clarke or Yosef ben-Jochannan, who would name one of his sons, Ta-Nehisi. His Black Classic Press would grow to include these long-out-of-print titles in new editions. This was how I was able to read a text like Hubert Henry Harrison's *When Africa Awakes.* And in the same semester that I found myself at Karibu, my Pan Africanism teacher Louis Wright assigned David Walker's *Appeal*, which he had asked the campus bookstore to stock (the Black Classic Press edition with an introduction by Africana Studies legend James Turner). So much of this tradition is intentional.

It was that context that helped explain the emergence of Karibu as the nineties beckoned. But so does the emergence of the hip-hop generation. I would first learn of these connections during the process of researching my book *We Are Worth Fighting For: A History of the Howard University Protest of 1989.* Among the many interesting contexts for that protest was that the organization centrally involved, Black Nia F.O.R.C.E., was dedicated to study. According to one of its founding members, Carlisle Sealy, it was Yao Glover who had helped generate this devotion. A poet and English literature scholar, Glover had created not just a book cart but a classroom. Sealy recounts that Glover introduced Black Nia F.O.R.C.E. to the ideas of everyone from Sonia Sanchez and Frances Cress Welsing to Maulana Karenga and Malcolm X. This commitment to study brought freshman Howard students together at a critical moment in time and launched a revolutionary transformation—first of Howard University and then of the larger African world. That protest would not have happened without it.

I did not know any of this when I visited Karibu. But perhaps I was being similarly prepared. Some of it is just ancestral. I took to reading Cruse's *Crisis* the ensuing summer, which was a time that was full of organizing for me. At Howard, we were attempting to create a weeklong summit on Pan Africanist movements for young people, which we eventually hosted in February 2009, soon and perhaps too soon, for some, after the inauguration of Barack Obama. I was drawn to Cruse just as I was being primed to listen to the voices of the rejected strain. Cruse, who seemed to be upset at everyone, resonated with me. Much more so than the people who were upset at Cruse. There was something about his insistence on cultural autonomy and his critique of external representations of Black culture that was felt.

This was before I even walked into Sankofa Video Books & Café and met Haile Gerima. There was no better person alive to reinforce those feelings and suspicions. As I was reading Cruse, Gerima approached me to talk about the youth conference we were planning. I am thankful for what happened next. At some point, he stopped listening and asked me plainly, "You haven't read Cabral?" I could not respond in any intelligent way, and that sent me searching. I am unsure if I left that day with a copy of Amílcar Cabral's *Return to the Source*, but it would not be long before I had one. Cabral's injunction has never left me.

But Sankofa was also a space for more intentional encounters. Every week through-out that summer a group of readers dedicated to working through George Jackson's *Soledad Brother* met upstairs in the store's conference room. So, I joined them. Sitting with that group helped me understand a great deal. None of the fascism of today surprises me, because in closely reading Jackson, we saw it and understood it then. Neither does another reality: the way liberal commentators evade and ignore that there is a Black anti-fascist thinking tradition.

Founded in 1998, Sankofa Video Books & Café was the creation of Gerima and Shirikiana Aina, both filmmakers. Their vision was to continue to provide a space for Black radical artmaking and writing that was rooted in Pan Africanist struggle and liberation movements. Much like Drum and Spear and Pyramid, Sankofa's location near Howard University has served to offer space to students and faculty as well as benefit from the often unacknowledged (on campus) role of Howard folk in radical and Pan Africanist movement building.

This is what Sankofa became for me. That early encounter with Gerima proved to be deeply significant for my thinking and organizing. But Sankofa is also where we met, hosted events and talks, built community, and thought together about Black life. It still is. It is not just a store.

Yet, Sankofa *is* one of the few remaining bookstores where you are guaranteed to find a copy of Martin Delany's *Condition* and the many significant texts of this tradition. So for me, it is the DMV's legacy bookstore, representing that rejected strain, the tradition of Black refusal of the status quo. It is where *we* get our books.

But this story would not be complete without acknowledging the role of Baba Nati and Everyone's Place, the store and institution right up the interstate in Baltimore. Nati's impact on the world of Black bookstore distribution cannot be overemphasized. There's simply nowhere else to get the works of Chinweizu or Jacob Carruthers's *Mdw Ntr*—or, in my case (when I was teaching a course on the Black family at Temple University), a class set of Niara Sudarkasa's *The Strength of Our Mothers*, published, of course, by legacy Black publisher Africa World Press.

We also must pay homage to the Black women readers who helped support Sisterspace and Books on U Street in D.C., the brainchild of Faye Williams and Cassandra Burton. And to the House of Khamit, founded by Mykiel Raufu Bey, the store where Chadwick Boseman worked as a Howard student and where I got my first copy of Kwame Nkrumah's *Neo-colonialism*. Those physical stores have transitioned. But Baba Raufu can still be seen vending on the streets. Along with Brother Kwasi, whom I first met before gentrification killed the 9th Street Flea Market. Kwasi *always* has some gem for me—and a story of his time organizing with the African Liberation Support Committee.

When it comes to the world of books, these are the relationships that sustain me as a writer, teacher, and thinker. It is movement and cultural work more than it is entre-preneurialism. And maybe we are seeing a new model emerge. But there is a tradition.

**PROSE TO THE PEOPLE**

# SANKOFA VIDEO BOOKS & CAFÉ

Over a decade ago, I interned on The Hill, *click-clacking* around the Rayburn Office Building, and the rest of Washington, D.C., in my Cole Haan kitten heels.

Some Sundays, I'd venture from the claustrophobic one-bedroom apartment I shared with three other interns and attend Howard Chapel. After the service, the swell of the choir's sopranos rang in my ears as I walked across the street to Sankofa Video Books & Café to grab a Peach Pleasure smoothie, a book, and a few more hours of privacy.

Returning to my old stomping (*click-clacking*) grounds, I'm struck by how much the city has changed. Black Lives Matter posters hang in the windows of now million-dollar homes in once-majority-Black neighborhoods. Blonde and brunette ponytails bounce from upscale Pilates studios. The luxury condos gleaming near splashy murals depicting the Black people they've displaced add insult to injury. Everything feels different. Well, almost everything.

Sankofa Video Books & Café remains defiantly present, like the last unrenovated brick house among its HGTV-ified neighbors. Owned by filmmakers Haile Gerima and Shirikiana Aina, Sankofa has been Georgia Avenue's "sanctuary for Pan-African culture" since 1998. As a Howard University student in the 1970s, Shirikiana documented the displacement of poor Black D.C. residents in her film *Brick by Brick*. "That's why I made the movie—because the degree of displacement was just something you could not ignore. And the level of resistance to that displacement was great," Shirikiana tells me.

Sankofa's tan bricks and open patio act as a giant welcome sign for those interested in books and films by and about people of African descent. On the patio, old men squabble over chess while students scarf down Spike Lee–themed paninis. Store regulars swap book notes and tweeded professors pore over the semester's syllabi. A mishmash of languages—English, Somali, Spanish, French—envelops the outdoor space, blending with the aroma of the coffee and tea from the café like a diasporic melody.

Shirikiana first heard this melody at Vaughn's Bookstore as a high school student in Detroit. "Vaughn's was a central place for feeling like you were in the midst of Black Change. It was a place where Black people felt like there was real scholarship and thinking available to us on the shelves. Places like Vaughn's helped normalize that a place like Sankofa was possible."

Vaughn's Bookstore's spirit lives on in Sankofa. Sankofa *feels* independent, beholden to no one but the

Courtesy of Melketsadek, Sankofa Video & Books.

Courtesy of Melketsadek, Sankofa Video & Books.

Courtesy of Melketsadek, Sankofa Video & Books.

Courtesy of Melketsadek, Sankofa Video & Books.

Yonathan chats with a regular.

Christina Joy checks out a customer.

community of readers it chooses to serve and the institutions it chooses to be in community with. From the interior aesthetics and inventory to the weekly events, Sankofa doesn't chase trends or corporate checks' allure. Yonathan, one of Sankofa's managers, recounts the time Nike offered Sankofa a large sum for the honor of hosting a party at the store. The only catch was that their logo would be plastered on and throughout the building. Haile and Shirikiana turned down the offer. "They're not selling out," Yonathan states. The couple has owned 2714 Georgia Avenue NW since opening, giving them the freedom to resist displacement and co-optation.

Courtesy of Melketsadek, Sankofa Video & Books.

Instead of having corporate partners, Haile and Shirikiana opt to work with other independent, community-oriented institutions. "The reason that we were able to do Sankofa Bookstore is because Afrikan World Books in Baltimore, a wholesaler of books, said, 'You know what? Come and choose the books you want and pay when you sell them.' Brother Nati, he's one of the quiet Black angels," Shirikiana says.

The books Haile and Shirikiana packed in the car from Afrikan World Books honor the owners' commitment to Pan-Africanism. Some of those same books still stand on the shelves today. The bright yellow cover of George Jackson's *Blood in My Eye*; the red, black, and green of Walter Rodney's *How Europe Underdeveloped Africa*; and the orange and blue of George G.M. James's *Stolen Legacy* blur and blend like colors on a painter's palette.

Films by Haile and Shirikiana live right beside the store's books, a synesthesia of images, text, and imagination—cinematic literature.

"I wanted to be a communicator—a Black communicator—because I realized that one of the reasons that Black people didn't organize better was because our stories were distorted by white media," Shirikiana says, describing her filmmaking and bookselling ethic. She speaks with the assuredness of someone completely grounded in their politics and sense of self.

When George Floyd was murdered in 2020, Sankofa offered a soft place for the community to land amid the racist portrayal of Black Americans. "We weren't starting from scratch in offering and trying to lift up books that help us find who we are—who we are, not only in identity, but where we place ourselves in a historical context," says Shirikiana. "And how do we use that to build a new future? So, when something like George Floyd happens, we know what to do." Her assessment echoes the meaning of her store's name. *Sankofa* is an Adinkra term for "going back to our past in order to go forward."

Despite the rapidly changing demographics of Washington, D.C., Shirikiana isn't fretting about Sankofa's future.

"[As long as] Black institutions [are] determined to make sure that this material is available, Black people who are committed to a wholesome future of the Black community are going to be here. It's a determination to survive. It's why we're here and why we're gonna be here when all the rest falls. Amazon's not gonna be here forever—*Sankofa* will."

# MAHOGANYBOOKS

Strong and beautiful like the mahogany tree, MahoganyBooks looms as a resplendent giant of its community, with branches stretching across D.C. and Maryland, and roots burrowed deep in the region's Black neighborhoods and history.

Founded by Derrick and Ramunda Young, MahoganyBooks sprouted as an online bookstore in 2007 and opened the doors to its first physical location in Southeast D.C. ten years after its online launch. Four years later, MahoganyBooks expanded to Maryland's National Harbor in the midst of the COVID-19 pandemic. And in 2023, the store's third location opened in D.C.'s National airport. MahoganyBooks has grown to be a force in the independent bookstore world.

I got a chance to catch up with the store's busy owners.

**You both worked at Karibu Books before creating MahoganyBooks. How did that experience impact how you run the store?**

**DERRICK:** Karibu was one of the best Black bookstores in the country at that time, so having [Brother Yao] as my direct manager taught me a lot. He has a lot of wisdom, a lot of strategy. I used my time at Karibu as a springboard to shift the paradigm because at a certain point, you have to be yourself and not an imitation. So, I had to ask myself, "Well, how do I do it my way?" I think that's what a good mentor does, they challenge you and affirm you.

**One of the things that stood out to me about Mahogany is your events. Often, Black authors are celebrated posthumously. Can you speak about the thought process behind celebrating Black authors while they're still here with us?**

**RAMUNDA:** It's really important for our communities to have sacred space to have these conversations and to allow our kids to be in front of some of these speakers to

learn their stories. A lot of our kids may not have even met a real-life author before. So, it's not so much about getting high-profile people to us. It's more centered around the conversation and the experience that the community can look back at for years to come.

**Yes, I noticed Mahogany's focus on children. Tell me more about Books for the Block. I read that you've given over a thousand books away to D.C. kids.**

RAMUNDA: Oh, it's fun! For some kids, it's the very first book that they get to keep themselves. To see the pride they have in picking out a book that has a little Brown or Black face on it—it's priceless. Money sometimes can be a barrier. Books are luxury items. When we have families that have to choose between food or a book, books can go on the back burner. So to have the opportunity to say, "Hey, this book is yours and there's one for your sister and your brother, too," I think it's just been rewarding to see their faces and the pride and the excitement that this is theirs to take home to keep. It's one thing to just be in business and to be an entrepreneur, but to give back to the community that supported you means a lot.

**What do you think Mahogany's legacy will be?**

DERRICK: I want MahoganyBooks to be [remembered as] a place where the next great idea was formulated. Whether it's a business. Whether it's an activist project. Whether it's a book. I want MahoganyBooks to be a place where these thoughts and ideas are coming together. So when people think back to some of those milestone moments in their life, they think about MahoganyBooks as one of those places that helped to provide them with that spark of inspiration, of creativity to do whatever it is that they want to do. That's what I want MahoganyBooks' legacy to be.

RAMUNDA: When people look at our bookstore, I want them to feel affirmed and seen. When people think about our space, I hope they can recall that time the music reflected them, that the sights reflected them, that the books on the shelves reflected their culture, their history, our journey, our culture, our experience. I want them to remember that and always go back to that place where they felt seen.

# LOYALTY BOOKSTORE

"I wanted to make a place where we are the main story."

In 2019, Hannah Oliver Depp did exactly what they set out to do—establish a place that puts Black and queer stories at the forefront: the first Loyalty Bookstore in Silver Spring, Maryland.

Speaking with Hannah, it's apparent that Loyalty represents a correction.

"We have a huge emphasis on kids. Yeah, I'm a little bit bitter about the books I didn't have when I was a kid, and I don't want that to be the case for kids now," Hannah shares, showing off the expanded kids' section at Loyalty's D.C. location. A young child flips through a picture book on the kid-sized furniture, while Hannah rests for a rare moment of stillness on a small desk that belonged to their grandfather.

But Loyalty isn't just correcting Hannah's childhood bookshelf, it's looking to correct an overwhelmingly

white industry Hannah knew well from their career as a bookseller and former academic.

While the tradition of Black bookselling often meant working outside and around the mainstream publishing system, Hannah opted to work within it. They cofounded the American Bookselling Association Committee on Diversity, Equity and Inclusion and serves on the boards of Bookshop.org and the New Atlantic Independent Booksellers' Association. In 2021, they won the Women's National Book Association Award for their "meritorious work in amplifying the efforts of social justice movements, particularly Black Lives Matter, while using [their] bookstores to create community spaces."

"I don't particularly love being the only one in the room. I don't trust being the only one in the room. But I also know that's not the only room I'm in," Hannah says of their too-frequent experience of being the lone voice representing underrepresented identities in publishing. "It's really important to me to be around. I'm going into it with an agenda. I'm going in with a plan and projects. I'm there for a reason and a purpose. I'm not kicking back in comfort."

Luckily for Maryland and D.C. book lovers, if they're Black and queer, they'll never have to worry about being the only one at Loyalty Bookstore—a vision, a proof of concept of what the book industry may one day be.

# THE 21ST-CENTURY BLACK AESTHETIC

## BY CHANDA PRESCOD-WEINSTEIN

In 1925, a Black gay professor at Howard University published an essay titled "Enter the New Negro" as part of an anthology that he edited, *The New Negro: An Interpretation*. Nearly one hundred years later, this collection is an extraordinary time capsule, containing writing from Black diasporic cultural workers such as Claude McKay, Anna Julia Cooper, Hubert Henry Harrison, and W.E.B. Du Bois. Because I am trained as a theoretical physicist and because he has not until recently been remembered as part of the African American mainstream, I did not hear Dr. Alain Locke's name until 2017. And because I am Black, when Dr. Jeffrey C. Stewart won the 2019 Pulitzer Prize for Biography for a nearly thousand-page account of Locke's life, I sat up and paid attention. Locke, I learned, was the godfather of the Harlem Renaissance—known at the time as the New Negro Movement.

It is fitting that as we arrive at the one-hundredth anniversary of the naming of the New Negro Movement, we find ourselves amid another transformative Black cultural renaissance. Even as we struggle against the ravages of late-stage capitalism, complete with its violent commitment to legalized slavery via mass incarceration and genocidal policing policies that serve and protect white supremacist hetero cis patriarchy, we are also living in a time of incredible cultural production, both in response to the violence and in spite of it. The 2010s and 2020s, like the 1920s, have witnessed the mainstreaming of a new generation of Black cultural thinkers who, like the New Negroes before us, are in conversation (and sometimes conflict) with one another. I am thinking of Kiese Laymon, of Imani Perry, of Airea D. Matthews, of Mahogany L. Browne, of Camonghne Felix, of Ruha Benjamin, of Katherine McKittrick, of Robert Jones, of Christina Sharpe. Of writers and editors like Aricka Foreman and Lee Oglesby. Of publishers like Lisa Lucas. Of book influencers and media personalities like Traci Thomas. And of Black bookstores like Loyalty Bookstore, Semicolon Bookstore, Café con Libros, and Reparations Club.

The new crop of Black-owned—and specifically Black woman–owned—bookstores arrived at a moment that has another significant parallel with Locke's era: a global pandemic. The 1918 Spanish flu pandemic significantly altered the world, and death toll estimates range from 25 million to 100 million globally. A century later, we are years into a global COVID-19 pandemic with a death toll of at least seven million, though many experts suspect this is a significant undercount. The coronavirus pandemic initially led to a near-total shutdown of small-business activities in the United States, and for the businesses that did manage to survive, extensive government support is the only reason many of them stayed afloat.

The implications for authors were also dire. My own book *The Disordered Cosmos: A Journey into Dark Matter, Spacetime, and Dreams Deferred* was set to release in March 2021. Initially, we held out hope that the pandemic would subside by then, envisioning a scenario where society could safely reopen, in person. As fall 2020 arrived, it became clear that there would be no in-person book tour. Independent bookstores had pivoted to virtual events and worried that this wouldn't translate into sales, since they were now competing nationally with anyone else who shipped books—which was *everyone*.

I was advised that, to make stores feel like it was worth it to host me, I could only do three publicity events for my book. A book that was the product of twenty years of thinking. This felt like a devastating blow to a work that had taken huge risks, both in trusting that Black audiences were hungry for a book about particle physics and that repeat consumers of science books would support a book that spoke openly and honestly about colonialism, race, gender, and queer futurities. I was terrified that my book would never reach its central audience: Black and queer readers who never felt like science writing was for them.

In the end, I negotiated my way to five initial bookstore events and ended up having six that year. Black bookstores agreed to additional events with me. Café con Libros chose *The Disordered Cosmos* for a book club, and Loyalty Bookstore incorporated donations to a nonprofit organization aligned with the author's values into every virtual event. At these virtual events, instead of an author talking to the audience with a reading and then a Q&A, many authors at independent bookstores were asked to pick out a conversation partner. Because the events were virtual, nearly every single one was recorded and made available to the general public.

The result is an incredible archive. During a devastating, destructive pandemic that hit Black, Indigenous, and Brown communities harder than others, accessible Black literary conversations flourished. Many of them were facilitated by Black bookstores that sought to champion Black books that were pushing boundaries, like my weird love note to the cosmos and what the practice of physics could be.

The Loyalty Bookstore event featured a deeply spiritual conversation between me and fellow Black Jewish writer Camonghne Felix, a National Book Award long-listed poet. The Café con Libros event featured a conversation between me and Ytasha Womack, one of our foremost living Afrofuturist griots. In addition, the feminist Atlanta-based bookstore Charis Book Circle hosted a wide-ranging conversation between me and Black feminist theorist and historian Imani Perry about *The Disordered Cosmos*. My book launch was also an interdisciplinary exchange on Black thought: Harvard Bookstore served as the venue for a Q&A led by Kiese Laymon, an extraordinary novelist, memoirist, and essayist who was also the first editor to pay me for my writing.

My experience with *The Disordered Cosmos* is a microcosm of how Black cultural workers—from writers to bookstore owners—took the worst years of many of our lives and made an archive of Black art as it unfolded. The permutations of conversations between artists and thinkers from the early years of the pandemic, many of them hosted on Crowdcast and YouTube channels of Black bookstores, will live on as a part of our cultural memory. A book festival conversation between poet Nikki Giovanni and Kiese Laymon about Giovanni's dreams of growing okra on Mars spurred me to rethink my allergy to building human communities beyond Earth. Watching Jordan Ifueko discuss her deeply Black *Raybearer* fantasy duology with Ytasha Womack helped me understand the pressures Black authors face when imagining and building other worlds for their readers. And the National Museum of African American History and Culture helped open my eyes to understanding Tulsa one hundred years after the massacre when it livestreamed a conversation between John Franklin and Victor Luckerson, author of *Built from the Fire: The Epic Story of Tulsa's Greenwood District, America's Black Wall Street*.

The New Black Movement of the twenty-first century—a renaissance that will be long remembered—is not contained within one city or nation. While our relations remain deeply local, they are now intensely global, facilitated by the use of technology in service of Black liberation. As our conversations unfolded, so did fights in the streets for justice. Like generations that came before us, these were battles in which we were personally invested, not merely as spectators but also as participants. Whether we were physically able to participate or not, many of us were part of networks that helped sustain the movement by facilitating information or directing some of our incomes to bail funds and other resources that helped keep protests alive.

Bookstores like Reparations Club in South Los Angeles are both notable products and facilitators of this moment, as we are discussing what the struggle for reparations means to the diaspora, both within and outside colonial borders. Rofhiwa Book Café in Durham, North Carolina (which once Instagrammed a photo of a large stack of copies of *The Disordered Cosmos* from a special order), articulates itself as a bookstore that "strives to reflect the expansiveness of the Black imagination. We value books as repositories for collective knowledge." Meanwhile, Washington, D.C.–area Loyalty Bookstore casts themselves openly as "community-oriented bookstores" on their website. Café con Libros defines itself as an "intersectional feminist bookstore."

These stores are community institutions that engage with the wider world not simply as small businesses that provide their owners and staff with a wage to live on but also as facilitators of what Robin D.G. Kelley has called "Black freedom dreaming." Black bookstores offer Black readers and writers a space-time where we are at the center of the conversation, where we are core to the mission, and where our cultures are reflected in the institutional practices. These are the places that we expect to feature a stack of a Black physics book like *The Disordered Cosmos* or a genius time travel book within a book like Kiese Laymon's *Long Division*. They are also where we can expect to find canonical classics that are often ignored by the mainstream, like Toni Cade Bambara's *The Salt Eaters*, which is incidentally the namesake of a Black-owned bookstore in Inglewood, California.

The Salt Eaters, like Loyalty, is part of the community resistance to the gentrification that damages the fabric of our communities—a phenomenon that has radically transformed both Inglewood and D.C. in just a couple of decades. Like libraries, these bookstores are for community members seeking to learn, a home that carries the books that can inform our efforts to hold together our community fabric.

The first half of the 2020s has been terrifying. Between the pandemic, the fires, the floods, the ice storms, and the overt colonialist white supremacy that governs the foundations of broader society, no one could be blamed for feeling like they are trying to live and breathe through an apocalypse. But as our Indigenous kin have taught me, we have survived apocalypses before. And each time, we have created community institutions and a record of how we did it and why. From the textiles that Black women handed down from generation to generation under slavery to Sojourner Truth repeatedly sitting for photographic portraits, we have always sought to tell our own stories and create memories of our journey. Today, Black bookstores are part of a powerful ecosystem that platforms and coproduces a new, decentralized Black renaissance. Like Elmer Imes, the Black physicist who was married to Harlem Renaissance writer Nella Larsen, I am privileged to be a Black scientist who is along for the journey, in the audience, reloading Black Bookstagram, waiting to see what Black books, conversations, and collaborations drop next.

## CHAPTER 3

THE S

# MARSHALL'S MUSIC AND BOOKSTORE

"Don't listen to the GPS! We're in a Black neighborhood. They don't know where we're at," Maati Jone Primm says, fielding calls from first-time customers navigating to her bookstore.

Primm, the charismatic shop owner, is looking forward to one hundred years—in business that is. Marshall's Music and Bookstore

Maati Jone Primm is looking forward to one hundred years in business. Photo by Katie Mitchell.

began as Wilcher's Music and Bookstore, a Christian bookstore founded by Pastor Louis Wilcher in 1938. In the decades since, the store has undergone two name changes, five ownership changes, and in 2020, an inventory expansion into secular Black books.

Located on Farish Street in Jackson, Mississippi, Marshall's remained a constant even as the once-thriving business corridor went from crowded to crowdless. From the Great Depression to the Civil Rights Movement, integration, divestment, and COVID-19, the squat brick building has

witnessed more history than a Mississippi magnolia.

And the walls of Marshall's reflect that history back to Jacksonians. Pictures of Black activists, artists, politicians, athletes, celebrities, and reverends envelop the space. Primm's handwritten descriptions give a special shout-out to folks from Mississippi— author Angie Thomas from Jackson, editor Lerone Bennett Jr. from Clarksdale, and activist Fannie Lou Hamer from Ruleville.

During an impromptu visit to Marshall's, I watch a preacher espouse the goodness of God's mercy and grace on the shop's television. Primm echoes that sentiment.

"We have been blessed and highly favored. We survived it all, and we survived it all by being Black."

# SHRINE OF THE BLACK MADONNA BOOKSTORE AND CULTURAL CENTER

The origin of the Shrine of the Black Madonna Bookstore and Cultural Center traces back to the wellspring of the Civil Rights Movement and the surge for Black liberation. Gurgling amid societal upheaval, these bookstores ran as more than mere commercial ventures—they coursed as epicenters of enlightenment, pouring life into the narratives that were overlooked, suppressed, or purposefully forgotten.

With the Black nationalist Pan-African Orthodox Christian Church as their fountainhead, the Shrine's bookstore and cultural center symbolized the fusion of spirituality and activism. They weren't just seeking cash, they were seeking consciousness, offering a haven where the Black community could explore its heritage, reclaim its narratives, and forge a path toward empowerment through books.

"We don't have a few books on a wall that says 'African American.' When you walk into the store, the whole store is African American," Ayele Bennett, the Detroit location's manager, told *Detroit Black Journal* in 1993.

Beginning in the 1970s, three Shrine of the Black Madonna Bookstores and Culture Centers served communities in Detroit, Atlanta, and Houston. Barbara (Cardinal Nandi) Martin founded and managed the Detroit bookstore and cultural center with church members' help, and the store's lively environment grew largely out of her contributions.

Encouraged by church founder Jaramogi Abebe Agyeman (born Albert B. Cleage Jr.), roughly forty members of the Detroit Shrine of the Black Madonna moved to Atlanta's West End neighborhood in 1975 to build a congregation

Photos Courtesy of Shrine of the Black Madonna Cultural Center and Bookstore.

and establish a bookstore and cultural center. The members recruited from local colleges like Morehouse, Spelman, and Clark Atlanta. And with the recent election of Atlanta's first Black mayor, the city rippled with hope and possibility.

"Here was this group of Black people talking about things that affirm who we are as African people. The community welcomed them," relayed Germain (Aminika) Covington, the current manager of the Atlanta bookstore and cultural center.

One of those young people who came to Atlanta was prolific playwright Pearl Cleage, the daughter of Jaramogi Abebe Agyeman and niece of Barbara (Cardinal Nandi) Martin.

Decades after her journey to Atlanta to expand the Shrine's congregation, I asked Cleage about the bookstore, her father, the FBI, and the Shrine's impact.

**What was the Shrine's Detroit bookstore like? Are there any specific memories that stick out to you?**

**PEARL CLEAGE:** The Shrine bookstore came about when our church went from being the Central United Church of Christ to the Shrine of the Black Madonna of the Pan-African Orthodox Christian Church. I was delighted to have such a great bookstore grow out of my father's work. My aunt Barbara, whose African name was Nandi, became the manager of the bookstore in Detroit and later the ones in Houston and Atlanta. The stores were always filled with all kinds of black books. Contemporary, history, children's and young adult history, and literature. There were also displays of African art, which made the environment inviting and Afrocentric. My father believed strongly that a free people had to be able to have a great bookstore to enhance their knowledge and to affirm a love of reading, research, and discovery. As a devoted reader and a young writer, the bookstores were a wonderful addition to my life.

**With the Shrine's storied history, it is no stranger to social movements, Civil Rights, Black Power, Pan-African, Black Arts, and Black Lives Matter to name a few. How did the Shrine support those movements and how did those movements support the Shrine?**

**PEARL CLEAGE:** The Shrine was a national meeting place for the exchange of ideas and strategies to support freedom struggles around the country and across the world. During the Black Arts Movement of the sixties, our church hosted many, many writers who wanted to reach a black audience. They would read at the Shrine and sell their books. I remember watching them pull up in the inevitably raggedy little cars they were driving, open the trunk, take out their books, and then come into our church to read and talk. After the bookstores opened, the readings would take place there and they were often standing room only. My father was a brilliant man who devoted his life to the struggles of Black people to be free. He welcomed other activists and thinkers to our church for a lively exchange of ideas. I heard Stokely Carmichael, John O. Killens, Bill Worthy, Clifton DeBerry, among many others. Their energy and passionate dedication shaped my own view of my role as a black writer.

**We know that FBI Director J. Edgar Hoover started focusing COINTELPRO on Black independent booksellers in 1968. How did that surveillance impact the Shrine?**

**PEARL CLEAGE:** The FBI had been spying on my father for decades. The surveillance was constant, but it did *nothing* to dampen the spirit of the work my father was doing and the work that the Shrine was undertaking. We knew there were agents, spies, and paid informants in our midst, but we were dedicated activists/revolutionaries. We expected our institutions to be watched and investigated. It came with the territory.

**How has the Shrine supported your writing career?**

**PEARL CLEAGE:** I always, always started my book tours at the Shrine. I welcomed an opportunity to read at these wonderful bookstores. The bookstores were a great way to reach my target audience of Black readers, and I had great responses to every reading I did at the Shrine bookstores in Detroit, Houston, and Atlanta. Being my father's daughter did not make my experience unique. My peers and other writers were always happy to be invited to have signings at the Shrine, including Bebe Moore Campbell, E. Lynn Harris, Sonia Sanchez, Nikki Giovanni, Don L. Lee (Haki Madhubuti), Ntozake Shange, and many more. We/they were always treated so well. Lots of publicity guaranteed a good crowd. The business was handled correctly so the books arrived on time and were sold in a professional manner. I remember being at the Shrine in Houston and I was in the middle of my talk when my father arrived. I was so happy to see him, I completely lost my train of thought. "Sorry," I said, "I have to say hello to my daddy!" And I did! It was a wonderful gift to a young writer to have the resource of those bookstores to support my career at such an early stage. I am grateful.

**Is there anything else you would like to share about your experience at the Shrine?**

**PEARL CLEAGE:** Black bookstores, of which the Shrine was an amazing example, were the backbone of the careers of many black writers of my generation. Vaughn's Bookstore in Detroit. Great black bookstores in Dallas, New York, Chicago, and Los Angeles all nurtured us and gave us a place to meet our audience and interact with them in spaces that encouraged dialogue and allowed us to see our work impact the people we were writing for. I am forever grateful that this network of bookstores embraced and supported me.

Shrine of the Black Madonna Bookstore booklet cover, Michael Lomax papers, Stuart A. Rose Manuscripts, Archives, and Rare Books Library, Emory University.

Reverend M. Abeo Brown and Germain (Aminika) Covington.

SHRINE CULTURAL CENTER

AFRO-MOD BOUTIQUE
KARAMU GALLERY
BOOKSTORE AND GIFT SHOP
JEWELRY

They came in chains but with culture

of the Black Madonna Book Store
BOOKS AND GIFTS
13535 LIVERNOIS AVENUE
DETROIT, MICHIGAN 48238
PHONE: 491-0778

# BLACK IMAGES BOOK BAZAAR

"If I had a tombstone, it would say, 'She believed in networking, getting people connected,'" Emma Rodgers jokes from her Dallas living room. I believe it. As Black Images Book Bazaar's co-owner, Emma connected little-known authors to new audiences, connected Black-owned book-stores to the American Booksellers Association, connected customers to Dallas's Black-owned businesses, and most importantly, connected Black readers back to themselves.

As Emma told Karibu Bookstore's Simba Sana in a 1998 interview, she and her co-owner, Ashira Tosihwe, "formed Black Images because my business partner and I could not find books for our children or ourselves from the Black perspective. We live in a culture that says everything Black is negative. I knew that was not true from the moment I was born."

In 1977, "back when Jesus was a boy," Ashira jokes, the pair started a mail-order business, which became the biggest Black-owned bookstore in the country—Black Images Book Bazaar.

"I went to Atlanta's Shrine of the Black Madonna in 1984, and I remember asking my friend James Tyler, 'Do you think we can do this?' And he said, 'Yes,'" Emma reminisces.

Later that year, the mail-order business transitioned to a flea market stand, and two years after that, Emma and Ashira moved into their first solo retail space.

The business partners paint a vivid picture of the space: Notes of frankincense, myrrh, and jazz hung in the air. Customers navigated sections named for Kwanzaa principles—they found self-help books in Kujichagulia (self-determination) and business books in Ujamaa (cooperative economics). Emma strategically placed Malcolm X's bestselling autobiography near the back of the store to encourage readers to spend more time shopping.

At first, Black Images didn't stock urban fiction, but Emma later realized that her customers traversed genres and were open to her suggestions. "I lost every time I didn't carry them," she says. "Because the same people who read Toni Morrison also read Iceberg Slim and Donald Goines. So I started giving the customers what they wanted because once they got through that door, they were mine. I could introduce them to other material."

Sometimes customers surprised Emma and Ashira. In preparation for a large Christian conference coming to town, the pair created a Christian fiction display for the conference-goers who would surely stop by the store. Church ladies did visit, but as Ashira recalls, "They didn't want the Christian fiction, they wanted the spicy books! They wanted to read Zane." Everyone could find something to read at Black Images—even church ladies looking to read erotica in between hymnals.

Ashira and Emma decided early to emphasize children's literature. Emma established a relationship with Dallas Public Schools to provide books for their libraries and classrooms. Helen Jackson, Black Images' children's book expert, helped

Ashira Tosihwe (left) and Emma Rodgers (right),
the owners of Black Images Book Bazaar.

customers make selections and reviewed all children's books at the store, including Rosa Parks's *Dear Mrs. Parks: A Dialogue with Today's Youth*.

When Rosa Parks chose Black Images for her book signing, the entire staff celebrated. "To have a civil rights icon at Black Images . . . ," Emma trails off, thinking back to November 24, 1996. Before receiving Ms. Parks, Emma noticed something amiss at the store. "Somebody had etched a swastika on our sign. Dogs came through and sniffed for bombs." There were no bombs, only a coward who couldn't stop Ms. Parks, Black Images, or the Dallas community.

Though Emma and Ashira closed shop on December 31, 2007, after twenty-nine years in business, Black Images Book Bazaar's impact on Black bookstores' legacy is eternal.

Photos courtesy of Emma Rodgers.

# COMMUNITY BOOK CENTER

"They love our food, our music, our culture, but they hate us," Vera Warren-Williams declares, her sweet, laid-back New Orleans drawl betraying the intensity of her words. "We have to be the guardians and gatekeepers of our culture."

Now an elder, Ms. Vera has been a cultural guardian and gatekeeper since she was a twenty-four-year-old substitute teacher in the Lower Ninth Ward. "There were no books reflective of Black kids in the school library or classroom, so I started bringing my personal books, and I saw the impact on the kids," she remembers. Such were Community Book Center's organic beginnings.

"My intention was to have a museum," Ms. Vera continues. She holds a master's in museum studies from Southern University and curates Community Book Center as a gallery for proper representation and preservation of Black people, Black history, and Black culture. "Until the lion tells the story, the hunter will always be the hero," she says, referencing the popular African proverb while gesturing at all the stories in her store.

The bookstore on Bayou Road is as New Orleans as trombones, étouffée, or Saints fans trumpeting "Who Dat?" through gold teeth. Books by New Orleanians and about New Orleans history greet customers as

they enter the purple and teal building. Mama Jennifer, CBC's manager since the late eighties, sits by the register gossiping with regulars while wearing a vintage Community Book Center t-shirt. The neighborhood cat, Yanni, lounges about the store, alternating between seeking out slivers of sunlight and playing hide-and-seek.

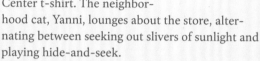

Being in business for over four decades, the store is a living artifact. Ms. Vera created Essence Fest's first book emporium in the mid-nineties, and the beloved neighborhood store was the only Black bookstore to survive Hurricane Katrina in 2005.

Mama Jennifer thinks back to the uncertainty surrounding the days, weeks, and months following the storm, remembering the sense of improvisation—of the community coming together in big and small ways. After the levees broke, Community Book Center hosted a pancake breakfast for the neighborhood, hoping to contribute to some sense of normalcy.

"The community is my biggest joy, seeing them walk through the door," Mama Jennifer says. "That's why it's important for us to have Black spaces so we can communicate what we gon' do and what we did."

Vera Warren-Williams, a cultural guardian and gatekeeper.

# FIRST WORLD BOOKSTORES

Navy sailor, newspaper deliverer, renowned photographer, bookstore owner: Jim Alexander has lived many lives.

When I visit him in his East Point, Georgia, studio, photographs from his decades-long career cover the walls. I step over boxes spilling out framed images from a Morehouse homecoming, Duke Ellington's funeral, and civil rights marches. For my visit, Alexander and his photography assistant, Renay Rajua Nailon, hung photographs from First World Bookstores. The pictures span from the five-store chain's grand opening in 1988 to when it closed in 1994.

Invoking his photography roots, Alexander tells his life story, and the story of First World Bookstores, in snapshots.

**I understand you spent time at Lewis Michaux's National Memorial African Bookstore while you were in New York. Can you tell me what you remember about the store?**

**JIM ALEXANDER:** I loved the atmosphere. I would always be there on Saturday morning. I would listen to the arguments that I knew nothing about. You know, that was the place where people came to argue. That was the forties and early fifties. [National Memorial African Bookstore] gave me politics. That's when I started reading different books about Black history and culture.

**What was the catalyst for starting First World Bookstores?**

**JIM ALEXANDER:** One day I go over to Hakim's [Bookstore] looking for a book, but I couldn't find it there. I couldn't find it a lot of places. So

I thought it might be great to have a bookstore where if people can't find a book, we provide a service of finding the book for them.

I wanted to see Black bookstores really prevail and be predominant in Black communities. I didn't just want to be a shopkeeper. I wanted to see Black bookstores in every Black community in the country.

**For those of us who never got to experience First World Bookstores, what was the atmosphere like?**

**JIM ALEXANDER:** Because I'm a photographer, we had my photographs up as big as 48 inches over the bookcases. We burned and sold incense. We sold other Black memorabilia, clothing, and kente cloth. We were the biggest sellers of kente graduation stoles.

Once a week I would have a Book Talk. We would either have a publisher or writer or someone in the community who I would give a book to and have them read it. We would have them present their idea about that particular book. That's how Book Talk started.

First World Bookstore
On Your 2nd Anniversary
May You Have Many More Blessings
Love Brendeema

I had Terry McMillan come in and do a talk. I was the photographer in residence at Clark [Atlanta University] at that time, so I was able to bring Terry over to Clark, where she got to talk to students.

**Sounds like a great time. Why did you decide to close up shop?**

**JIM ALEXANDER:** The big-box stores started pushing us independent stores all out of the way. Publishing companies started having stores also. They started discounting books at a rate that we couldn't compete with, so it got really, really rough to maintain and make a profit.

You had Amazon, you had other companies starting to sell books online. It all became a hassle. It got to the point that I'd have to go out and shoot a wedding to pay my employees. That's when I decided to call it a day. I went on with my life. I was doing so much at the time. Looking back on it, closing might have been a relief.

Courtesy of The Jim Alexander Collection.

beauty; can never learn to speak a language intelligible in all climes and for all ages, till this paralyzing grip of caste prejudice is loosened from its vitals, and the healthy sympathetic eye is taught to look out on the great universe as holding no favorites and no black beasts, but bearing in each plainest or loveliest feature the handwriting of its God.

And this is why, as it appears to me, woman in her lately acquired vantage ground for speaking an earnest helpful word, can do this country no deeper and truer and more lasting good than by bending all her energies to thus broadening, humanizing, and civilizing her native land.

116

Photos courtesy of Garbo and Auna Hearne.

**GARBO HEARNE (AMERICAN)**

*Pyramid Art, Books & Custom Framing, 1988*

*A Black cultural hub with an emphasis on children's literature and independent authors*

cil and which stands at the head of the chapter.

Miss Shaw is one of the most powerful of our leaders, and we feel her voice should give no uncertain note. Woman should not, even by inference, or for the sake of argument, seem to disparage what is weak. For woman's cause is the cause of the weak; and when all the weak shall have received their due consideration, then woman will have her "rights," and the Indian will have his rights, and the Negro will have his rights, and all the strong will have learned at last to deal justly, to love mercy, and to walk humbly; and our fair land will have been taught the secret of universal

# PYRAMID ART, BOOKS & CUSTOM FRAMING

Step into a collage of books, art, and events where imagination and reality intertwine. The Little Rock, Arkansas–based bookstore and gallery Pyramid Art, Books & Custom Framing was crafted and curated by visionaries Garbo and Archie Hearne. This long-standing establishment radiates a passion for educating customers about the beauty of our rich history. Pyramid invites readers to embark on a literary journey that includes art, Black studies, self-published works, and a mountain of children's literature.

A work of art itself, Pyramid envelops visitors in Black stories' endless possibilities. The store boasts towering bookshelves and comfy seating that welcomes readers to stay awhile. The children's section features a 3-D depiction of the baobab tree, known in Africa as the "tree of life." It's a marvel for young eyes to behold.

The store's emphasis on children's lit was inspired by its owners' four children. The Hearne kids grew up in Pyramid, helping with hundreds of book signings since the late eighties, including those with E. Lynn Harris, the Arkansan who changed the publishing industry by being one of the first Black authors to achieve mainstream success depicting Black men in gay and bisexual relationships.

Garbo remembers Harris's humble hustle: "He was selling out the back of his car. My brother was his college roommate, so when he came to me and asked if he could do a signing, I was like 'Yeah, sure.'"

Garbo doesn't limit her generosity to family friends. "Everybody has a book in them, so we do a lot of book signings for self-published authors," she says. "That's how we got our foothold in the community. Because we offer that opportunity."

Pyramid Art, Books & Custom Framing is more than a retailer; it's a storyteller. Whether you find solace in its coziness or inspiration in its storied history, this work of art testifies to Black creativity's limitless power.

Courtesy of Garbo and Auna Hearne.

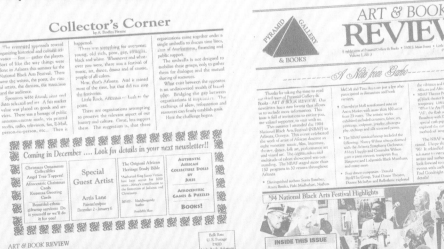

127

# MEDU BOOKSTORE

Nia Damali's journey to anchoring Atlanta's book scene started—in part—because of her afro. "I'd interview at corporate jobs, and they'd say, 'You're great, but what are you going to do about your hair?' After hearing that a few times, I realized corporate wasn't for me," Ms. Nia tells me, as we sit in Southwest Atlanta's Greenbriar Mall, the home of Medu Bookstore for over thirty years.

Ms. Nia—with her wide smile and fluffy 'fro—looks resplendent standing in the center of her creation. Notes of lemon pepper wet wings waft in from the nearby food court as I flip through old photo albums. Looking at the pictures, I see countless writers—Nathan McCall, Pearl Cleage, Nikki Giovanni—sitting in the same chair I'm in. The only difference is they're signing their latest release for masses of eager readers.

I linger, gazing at a photo of former *Essence* magazine editor in chief Susan Taylor. "Susan Taylor was amazing," Ms. Nia interjects. "When we had her, our community showed up! We had a line from one end of the mall when we used to be down by Macy's, past the food court. Susan was really, really pleased with us. She gave us accolades all through *Essence* for months to come."

Between stories of swoon-worthy book signings and butterfly effect hairdos, Ms. Nia recounts her store's early days and origins. *Medu*, she tells me, means "the power of the word," a name given by Dr. Asa Hilliard, the renowned historian of African Indigenous culture.

Before opening Medu, Ms. Nia worked and learned the book business at another respected Black bookstore—Hakim's on MLK Boulevard. After operating Hakim's Atlanta location for a few years, Ms. Nia decided to open her own store.

"[Dawud Hakim] wasn't too pleased, but he did not stop me. His whole thing was maybe we should partner and go into business together. I didn't want to. My vision was slightly different. I wanted to grow on my own without being restricted in any kind of way."

Ms. Nia envisioned a bookstore that "really tapped into the community" instead of catering solely to history buffs, politicians, and academics. "I wanted to be available to everybody, all levels of understanding," she says.

The community-focused bookstore Ms. Nia envisioned in the eighties is Medu present-day. The store's programming and inventory appeal to all readers—from the BookTok enthusiast to the well-read history scholar. She even carries books she published herself, *The Teachings of Ptahhotep* and *Golden Names for an African People*.

While some doubted Ms. Nia's ability to run her own store, Black women bookstore owners encouraged her, telling her, "We got you."

Notably, Emma Rodgers of Dallas's Black Images Book Bazaar and Clara Villarosa of Denver's Hueman Experience welcomed Ms. Nia into the Black bookselling club.

"Emma used to come in from time to time over at Hakim's. And when I told her what I was gonna do, she was one of the first people to give me encouragement. Emma would make sure that I was updated with all of my books and that I knew what was coming out. When Clara would come to town, she would check in on me and make sure I was good."

Raye and Julian Richardson of Marcus Books in California dispatched a box full of books to jumpstart her inventory.

"I was the baby of the group. They made sure I stayed afloat, and that I continued to be able to stand on their shoulders and grow. It was just amazing, so I give all appreciation to them."

Like the booksellers who came before her, Ms. Nia mentors younger booksellers and encourages them to do their own thing. Marcus Williams worked at Medu before opening Nubian Books in Morrow, Georgia, and Anyabwile Love volunteered at Medu before opening Bailey Street Books in Philadelphia.

"One of the things that we believe at Medu is we don't do it by ourselves. We do it as a collective. My joy comes from everybody else's assistance and work. We do it together."

Nia Damali with Third World Press founder Haki R. Madhubuti. Courtesy of Nia Damali.

Courtesy of Nia Damali.

Allyce Lee curates the "Flavor of
the Month" list, giving reading
suggestions tied to a theme.

Hope and Change in Black Tomes

# 44TH & 3RD BOOKSELLERS

For my inaugural visit to 44th & 3rd Booksellers, I arrived unannounced, figuring I'd poke around, get a feel for the place, and then casually say hi to Warren Lee, the store's co-owner, who I met the year before at an antiquarian books fellowship. But I was thwarted.

Warren, a retired lawyer and stalwart of Atlanta's historic West End, is far too keen and gregarious for such a clandestine plan.

As I open the door to 451 Lee Street, Warren greets me with a distinguished chuckle and bellows out, "Katie! Let me give you a tour." Just like that, away we whisk, around the store's handsome wooden bookshelves, for an overview that, like Warren, is polished yet friendly, thorough yet direct. (I've never seen him without a smile or a collared shirt.)

"The '44th' in 44th & 3rd represents the 44th president, Barack Obama," Warren explains, sweeping his arms toward a section filled with Obama-related memoirs, biographies, and photo books. "The '3rd' in 44th & 3rd stands for life, literature, and legacy."

As we bid farewell to the Obamas, Warren steers me to a cabinet filled with vintage Black titles. He hands me a first edition of Gwendolyn Brooks's *Riot,* which explores Chicago's response to the assassination of Martin Luther King Jr. The book is doubly relevant: we're in Atlanta, right down the street from King's alma mater, and Chicago inspired 44th & 3rd's founding. The store's inception drew heavy influence from the lack of Black representation in a Chicago big-box bookstore that Warren and his wife, Ms. Cheryl, visited during Obama's presidency.

I wonder if the connection was intentional, but before I can ask, Warren's showing me merch his nephew Lorin Brown designed. Next he is pointing out titles his niece Rachel Brown curated for the store.

It's a family affair at 44th & 3rd, and Warren is like a proud father showing off his baby. Warren and Ms. Cheryl take turns running the shop. Their daughter, Allyce, curates the "Flavor of the Month" list, giving reading suggestions tied to a theme.

We finish up near the Legacy section, and I ask Warren what he thinks 44th & 3rd's legacy will be. "A Black business that's focused on Black culture and the dissemination of the culture among Black people in particular," he replies. "Creating value for the community, that's our legacy."

As our tour wraps, Spelman, Clark Atlanta, and Morehouse students pour into the store for an open mic. They sing, recite original poetry, and rap, all while snacking on vegan ice cream. Warren smiles at the undergraduates, happy to have a space for them to gather.

From left to right: Allyce Lee, Warren Lee, Cheryl Lee, and Lorin Brown share a laugh.

Rosa Duffy's grandmother,
Josie Robinson Johnson, spends
Saturdays at For Keeps Books.

The Artist and the Archivist

# FOR KEEPS BOOKS

"Heyyyy, Cu-yatie!" Rosa Duffy exclaims as she glides over for a hug. She sports jorts, a crop top, and combat boots. Etta James's "A Sunday Kind of Love" croons out the speakers. Other times, the speakers pump out Future or an instrumental I can't quite place.

Rosa's always this enthusiastic whenever I pop in For Keeps Books, her bookstore on Atlanta's historic Auburn Avenue. I tell her about some dream I've had as I shuffle through the Polaroids on the reading table. She asks me to remind her of my zodiac sign. I feel like I'm among cousins in my grandma's house—the *Jet* magazines, the low hum of chatter and laughter. Whenever someone enters the store (a new cousin!), she gives them the same attention, introducing them to everyone browsing the store's books—some for sale, some for keeps.

My eyes fixate on *70 Soul Secrets of Sapphire* by Carolyn Jetter Greene. It's on a shelf along the exposed brick wall. That means it's for sale. The Polaroids and everything else on the reading table aren't for sale, but everyone is welcome to flip through them.

Inspired by her father's collection of *Soulbook: The Quarterly Journal of Revolutionary Afroamerica* and her grandmother's programs and schoolwork from Fisk University, Rosa began collecting Black books and ephemera over a decade before opening For Keeps in 2018.

And while most of For Keeps' customers weren't steeped in Black literature the same way Rosa was growing up, the Atlanta community has nuzzled the small shop like its kin. "That's why I

started For Keeps," chimes Rosa. "Because I felt like it was something that everybody should have access to."

I'm most taken by the mosaic made up of For Keeps regulars.

There's the unhoused trumpet player who shuffles in for a free sparkling water and a place to use the restroom. He updates Rosa about what's going on on the block, daps up everyone within an arm's distance, and then leaves, promising to return soon.

There's Rosa's grandmother Josie Robinson Johnson, a civil rights activist and sweet elder who spends Saturdays here, beaming whenever Rosa's friends call her "Grandma."

There's the film student typing up his final project, plopped down on the store's signature green couch.

There are the poets hosting weekly salons, workshops, and open mics in solidarity with the Stop Cop City Movement.

There's the MacArthur Genius discussing his latest novel.

There's the bookbinder, the sound bather, the tintype photographer, the former mayor, the socialist orator, the Freaknik collector.

And of course, there's Rosa—equal parts artist and archivist—who created the canvas that is For Keeps Books. Much of her collection could hang behind glass cases in museums or university libraries, but that's not the vibe at For Keeps. It's inviting and unpretentious.

"You don't have to have your library card or ID, you don't have to already know about Robert Hayden or James Baldwin. You don't have to know about Gwendolyn Brooks already, you don't have to know exactly what you're looking for," Rosa says, contrasting her approach with that of other rare book curators.

Rosa has received offers to buy the reading table's collection outright, but she turns them down. "It's not for sale," she says, shrugging.

Pristineness and prestige aren't Rosa's priorities; connection is. And the rare and vintage books she curates bind a new generation to generations past.

"There's been a boom in the need to know about yourself and the people who came before you, so For Keeps is really like a bridge," she says. "I want people to feel like folks have been through what you've already been through. They've written it down. They've explained it in a multitude of ways, and they've left you some kind of map, a mind map, to understand yourself when you're in the midst of these really traumatic, really tumultuous times."

Just as For Keeps' books blend the new and the nostalgic, so, too, does For Keeps itself. Mere steps away from the childhood home of Martin Luther King Jr., For Keeps Books reminds me of the bookstores I've accessed only through archives and oral histories, because they no longer exist. The ones with the charismatic shopkeeper who doesn't mind if you read an entire book in the store if you don't have the money to pay for it. The ones activists visited to learn, argue, and persuade. The ones whose impact stretches far beyond their tenure.

For Keeps Books forever.

W. J. Lofton reads a poem in For Keeps Books.
Courtesy of Andrew Daley.

# WHERE WE GATHER

### W. J. LOFTON

Do not enter
The poem here
But here
Through the ouija's planchette
Alongside Cashay
And Tortuguita
And our many gone
Even then
The bandana's knot
Did not come loose
From holding the hair
Of our glittering
Comrades
Must we always find our prophets
Kneeling under Georgia
Peach trees down the street
Where it is yet Spring
A boy sleeps close to traffic
Onassis
Durand
Maybe Bernard
Is his name
His mouth heavy
With empty
No one has told him what waits To
be opened
But now I will
Gayle Jones is what I read
Mari Evans is what I read
*Nappy Edges* is what was read To me
by my friends

The deep spirits
The Poets
The Griots
The Painters
The Photographers
The Dancers breaking
The wind with their limbs
The Archivists musing
Through both paper and digital
worlds No wonder
We children of domestic workers
And sometime-alcoholics gather
Like hands at the ends of the
world Around the reading table
Rosa placed Fanon there
For us
Uttering prayerful words
Before exiting
*Be safe*
Remember all of the faces
Who found yours
Searching for a blade of light
Count their names like nickels
Say this prayer aloud
I am truly a drop of sun
Under the earth

Lift Every Voice and Read

# LIBERATION STATION BOOKSTORE

Liberation Station Bookstore, a Black children's bookstore in Raleigh, North Carolina, is both niche and necessary. The founders, Victoria Scott-Miller and Duane Miller, drew inspiration from their oldest son, Langston. He sparked the idea to create a space that celebrated Black children through literature. The entire family—including Langston's little brother Emerson—began selling books out of their car trunk and at local pop-ups.

Here is Victoria describing Liberation Station's grand opening in 2023, in her own words:

> It was a three-day celebration. Our building is a historical building, and it's located on Fayetteville Street, which is where the [state] Capitol building is located. So if you go straight out of our door, you're facing the Capitol building, which is where all of the important decisions are being made. So the first day we invited Markel Williams, an incredible Black man who was a bass-baritone with the North Carolina Opera. We situated him at the top of the stairs during our grand opening. . . . So you walked into the building surrounded by all of this Black art that was saved from the George Floyd Movement. Phi Beta Sigma [Fraternity, Incorporated] linked arms and held the crowd back, forcing everyone to look at [Markel Williams] sing, "Lift Every Voice and Sing."
>
> A crowd of people were flooding onto the street, all looking up at this man singing. The hallways reverberated with his voice and the power of this moment. Elders were crying. Little kids looked around in wonder.
>
> My husband was upstairs at the register. We had a Black book signing and invited ten authors, including Derrick Barnes, Shelia P. Moses, Vanessa Brantley Newton, Tameka Fryer Brown, Kelly Starling Lyons. People came from all across the country, and we had them set up all across the space. That was glorious.
>
> Also, in our bookstore, we have a wall of affirmations that are made with braille mustard seed. We had a visually impaired child come in and he just came to touch the wall. And I think that was one of the most powerful moments for us, to be able to see this child reading these affirming words on the wall of the bookstore: "You are art. You are valuable. You are loved."

\* \* \*

Eight months after Liberation Station's grand opening, Victoria and her family vacated their downtown Raleigh location after reportedly receiving threats, but Victoria promises the move "won't mark the end of Liberation Station Bookstore. There is so much more work to be done."

# BALDWIN & CO.

"This shop isn't just a business venture; it is a testament to the power of faith and resilience," DJ Johnson proclaims in a 2024 Instagram post celebrating Baldwin & Co.'s third anniversary and his mother, whose illness beckoned the New Orleans native son home.

Named after American writer and civil rights activist James Baldwin, the store reflects DJ's fierce ambition and meticulous attention to detail. As we speak, he straightens in-store signage from 89 degrees to 90, returns books to their proper shelf location, and offers to throw away customers' empty coffee cups.

The modest square footage optimizes profit. The retail space leases out for both private and public events. The podcast studio rents hourly. The coffee shop underwrites the book business, and there's always a steady stream of espresso aficionados. And out-of-town customers can book a room in the Historic Baldwin & Co. Manor conveniently located right above the store.

DJ opened Baldwin & Co. in 2021 to give New Orleanians another cool Black-owned space to read, gather, and discuss ideas. To date, the Baldwin & Co. Foundation, the bookstore's nonprofit organization, has given away hundreds of books at its free book fairs. "We give all this away to the community for free to help individuals build home libraries," DJ states.

With help from program director Brittni Powell, Baldwin & Co. hosts literary giants in-store and right next door in its spacious courtyard. "Nikole Hannah-Jones has been here, Eddie Glaude Jr. has been here, Clint Smith has been here, Michael Eric Dyson, Imani Perry, Daniel Black. I mean, the list goes on and on. We bring these individuals in, and it's not just for a book signing, it's to engage in discussion so individuals gain this rapport, this relationship, with some of the most prominent thought leaders today," DJ notes proudly.

In a few short years, Baldwin & Co. has cemented itself as a force in the independent bookstore industry. "I've never been a person who believes that my destiny or life path is already designed," DJ tells me, "and even if it is—I'm arrogant enough to believe I can change it." With this belief, DJ, Baldwin & Co., and the city of New Orleans continue to cocreate the future of books in the Crescent City.

BALDWIN & CO

Coffee & Bookstore

1030

Program director Brittni Powell.

DJ Johnson opened
Baldwin & Co. in 2021.

Kin in the Community

# KINDRED STORIES

Bursting with books by Black authors, Kindred Stories welcomes Houston's Third Ward residents to dream and explore. Terri Hamm chose her location intentionally. "We deserve to have beautiful experiences *here*," Terri says, emphasizing the Black bookstore's importance in a rapidly gentrifying neighborhood.

Since opening in 2021, Kindred Stories has offered beautiful experiences. When the weather's right, authors hold events in the store's reading garden. Come by during story time and you'll find babies on blankets, a constant stream of bubbles, and surprisingly attentive toddlers. Kindred Stories exudes Black Southern hospitality. Terri greets customers with a chipper "Welcome in!" and an easy smile. "It's about showing Black people that their stories have value," she declares.

Indeed, Kindred Stories values stories from Black authors of all stations. Celebrated memoirist Kiese Laymon moderates author talks with debut novelists like Tyriek White (*We Are a Haunting*) and members of the Black literati, including Alice Walker. Store manager Chanecka Williams applies the same ethic to her curation practice, opting to showcase under-the-radar and local works alongside classic titles.

Before opening the bookstore, Terri was a stay-at-home mother of two looking to build community spaces. Houston, we have a solution: Kindred Stories.

BOTTOM PHOTO (*from left to right*): Chanecka Williams, Stevens Orozco, and Terri Hamm.

Photos courtesy of Troy Montes.

142

# YOU STILL NEED A BOOKSTORE

## BY KIESE LAYMON

By the time I moved to Houston in August 2022, I'd given away all 11,863 of my books.

In 2016, I donated most of the books in my office at Vassar College before leaving for a job at the University of Mississippi.

While in Mississippi, I judged the Kirkus Prize, the National Book Award, the *Los Angeles Times* Isherwood Prize, and maybe six other contests. This, and the fact that tons of authors were sending me books to blurb or promote, meant that it didn't take long to amass thousands and thousands of more books in Mississippi.

When I received an offer for a job at Rice University in 2021, I want to say my first concern was how to say bye to Mississippi, my home, and the place I'd worked so hard to get back to. But honestly, I was like, "How on earth am I going to move all these damn books?"

I didn't move those damn books.

I opened up my house, and all those bookshelves, to anyone in the community who wanted books. I felt incredibly happy to share them with people in need of stories. But I felt absolutely afraid of what it meant to not lean on my books in my new home of Houston.

✳ ✳ ✳

I moved to Luca Avenue in Houston in late August 2022. The night I pulled up to the house I was subletting, a bald-headed Black man with long jean shorts tapped the passenger side window.

"Keece?" he asked.

"Uh"—I was so confused—"hey, man."

He told me his name was Leroy and that he'd been living in that neighborhood for over fifty years. Leroy and I sat out there in that driveway, both of us sweating our asses off, talking about the history of the neighborhood I was moving into. The neighborhood was apparently once nearly completely white and Jewish, but eventually became nearly all Black and Mexican as more Black families moved to Houston from other parts of the South, and more Mexican families moved to the city. Leroy told me what my colleagues might call the neighborhood and what the actual residents called our home. We stood out there talking for hours about SWAC football, Texas Southern, Jackson State, maniacal Texas politicians, Mississippi casinos, and what he thought I should expect from my new job at Rice.

Before finally deciding I probably should see the inside of the house I was subletting, Leroy told me there was a bookstore I'd love.

"Kindred Stories?" I said.

"That's it," he said. "Swang by there and tell me what you thank."

There's this Mississippi custom of never telling friends you just met that something they think is new information actually isn't new information at all. So I didn't tell Leroy that one of the reasons I actually took the job at Rice was because of my experiences with Kindred Stories bookstore. Before coming to Houston, I hadn't touched base with anyone in the city except the incredible folks who run Kindred Stories.

The summer before my move, Terri, the visionary owner of Kindred Stories, connected me with her team member Chanecka, a brilliant book influencer I'd met on Instagram. Chanecka asked me if I wanted to be in conversation with Candice Carty-Williams, one of the most exciting and incredible young writers on earth.

The conversation happened a few weeks after I'd moved to the city, and it was my first actual holy book experience in Houston. Our conversation didn't take place in their beautiful store in Third Ward. It took place in a church/art museum. And it was love. The wonderful team at Kindred Stories made sure Candice and I were supported. They made us laugh. They took care of the folks who came to our reading with as much attention as they took care of us. That, to me, is the mark of redemptive Southern Black care. And maybe because this was the first time I'd ever moved west of Mississippi by myself, redemptive Southern Black care was exactly what I needed. I should have known that I'd find it in lovers of books.

In subsequent months, Terri and Chanecka would introduce me to the entire Kindred Stories team. I'd go on to do about six other events at the store, and most importantly, when I couldn't find the bookish spirit I'd felt in Mississippi, Kindred Stories restored me. Though I'd given away all my books, I came to understand that bookish Black communities are often equally as important as the books that anchor the community. Maybe even more important.

Now I am learning to love Houston. Kindred Stories was my portal of entry to this kind of love. It is not simply the greatest bookstore in my world; it is a rigorous, radical place of renewal for those of us who are Black, curious, and tired. And it, for me, as much as any place in Mississippi, is home.

For that, I am eternally thankful.

# yes, please books

The first event at yes, please books—a little pink house in Scottdale, Georgia—wasn't an author signing, poetry reading, or even a writing workshop. It was a home birth. That set the tone for the bookhouse and carespace. lauren jones, founder and steward of yes, please, couldn't plan out every detail of this space. Instead, she opened her heart to what and who wanted to come.

Below, lauren and I discuss community care, life insurance policies, anti-capitalism, nature, and what happens when you shoot your shot.

**You describe yes, please as a bookhouse and carespace. Can you describe what that means to you?**

**lauren jones:** It's literally a house filled with books that you can borrow, lend, or buy. Some people come to write books or share books.

It's a space to practice care for each other. I don't think that care and caretaking and even care receiving is something that you just can do. I think it is something that you have to learn and practice, being vulnerable enough to ask for and receive care.

**What do caretaking and care receiving look like at yes, please?**

**lauren jones:** We offer free acupuncture and low-cost body massages. We give people opportunities to come and volunteer and tend to the land here. A part of that tending is harvesting and turning herbs into different tinctures and teas that can be used for care. It evolves. It came from my desires and what I needed through my own grief work. It came from wanting to shift from a very interior,

individual self to more of a community, we-based self. And this space really gives me the opportunity to do that.

**How is this space related to your own grief, if you don't mind me asking?**

**lauren jones:** I love *A Raisin in the Sun* because it highlights the role of life insurance policies in Black families. We aren't able to build wealth in a lot of different ways, but we are able to put in $10 a month, $20 a month for a life insurance policy. So I was able to buy the bookhouse because I was the beneficiary of someone who passed.

And for me, it was not only being this person's beneficiary but also literally three or four days before they passed, they explicitly told me to do this.

**With the emphasis on care and the fact that folks can borrow books, your space feels anti-capitalist to me. I know you sell things, but was that intentional? Do you see yourself as an anti-capitalist?**

**lauren jones:** You know, I'm trying to get there because of the way that I was able to purchase this place. Being someone's beneficiary, I don't really feel like the owner but [rather] the steward of the space and the land. I own it in the way that I am doing it. I'm in charge of it. I got to pay the taxes. But it's not really *mine*.

I do feel comfortable with being a finder. I did find this place and I did spend two to three years finding all the books that are in the library. And I do take good care of finding the people who come to offer things here.

**What was the first iteration of what would become yes, please? Did you start with the bookhouse or did you have smaller pop-ups before?**

**lauren jones:** I started with Book Circle. I invited people I knew and people I didn't know and I was like, "Come to my house. I'm gonna feed you. We'll talk about a book." It helped me take a small step with support and encouragement from other people.

With Book Circle, I was just shooting my shot. I feel like grief makes you not care anymore. Like this is not real, being embarrassed is not real. Failures? Not fucking real. None of this shit is real.

*✳✳✳*

But yes, please *is* real—the books read, the conversations had, the naps taken. The intention lauren brings shows us what a bookstore is and can be—an answered prayer, a whisper of gratitude, a memory retrieved.

*It's a space to practice care for each other.*

lauren jones, founder and steward of yes, please books.

## CHAPTER 4

# THE MI

The Afrocentric Bookstore
INTRODUCING

Courtesy of Desiree Sanders.

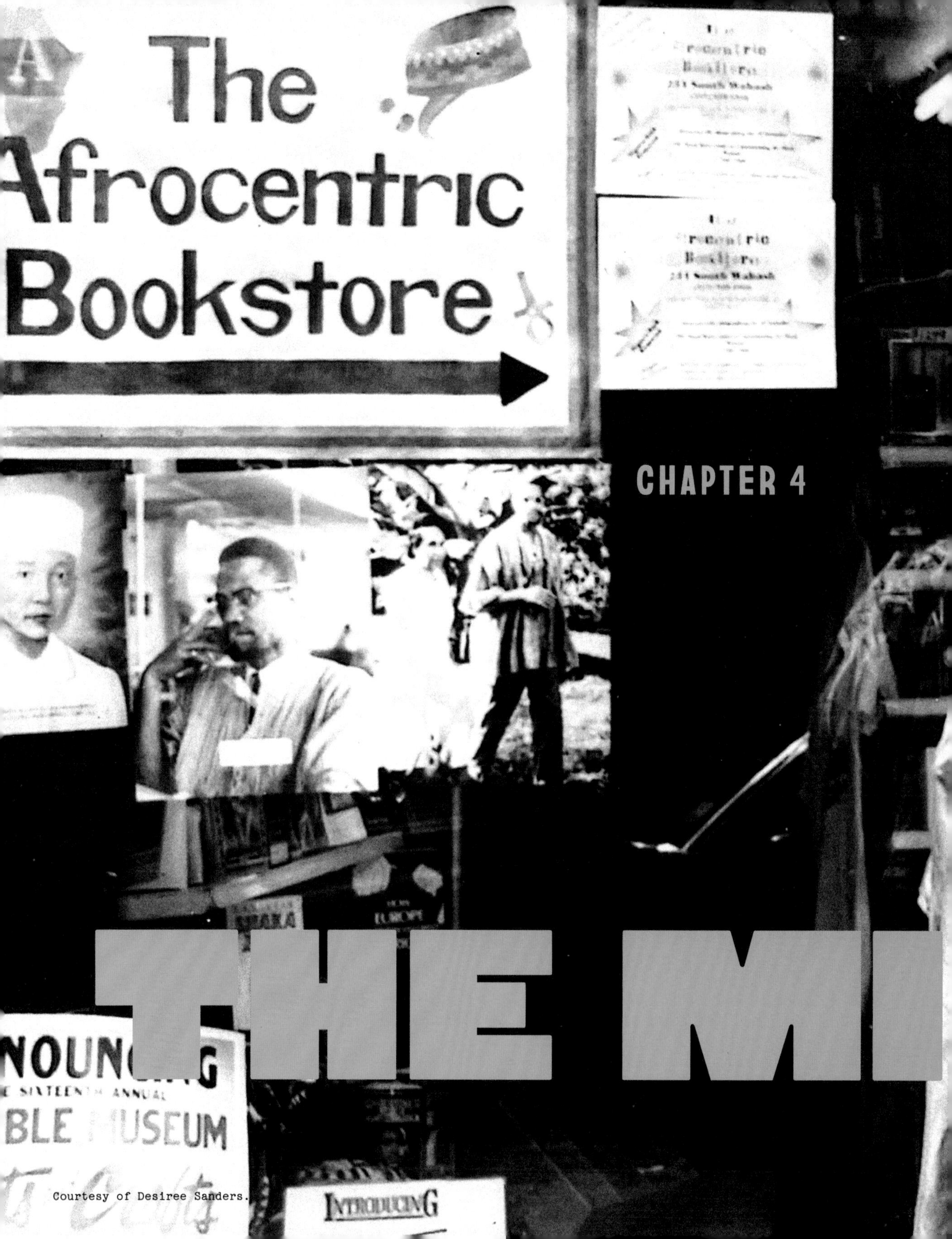

# VAUGHN'S BOOKSTORE

From selling books from his trunk to facing police officers' wrath, Edward Vaughn, the proprietor of Detroit's first Black bookstore, sold and made Black history. I dropped in on the then-octogenarian at his son's home in Atlanta in the spring of 2023.

The former bookstore owner, Michigan state rep, and theater owner recounted his story like an enthusiastic museum tour guide, carefully walking me through the exhibits of the past, stopping for questions, and emphasizing the salient points. Before I could ask any questions, Mr. Vaughn began reading from a handwritten statement he had prepared for our interview.

The statement traversed biographical information about Mr. Vaughn's life before the bookstore ("The post office was my first decent job in Detroit. Before that, I was washing dishes at Woolworth."), the approximate date Vaughn's Bookstore began ("I opened Vaughn's Bookstore between 1963 and 1965. I'm not totally sure of the exact date, but it was somewhere in that range."), and what his would-be business partner did with the start-up money for the bookstore ("He spent his portion of the partnership money on a brand-new Oldsmobile, so the partnership was off!").

Mr. Vaughn detailed how Dexter Avenue's white flight allowed him and his aunt, Ms. Polly Rawls, to not only purchase the building Vaughn's Bookstore occupied but also four other storefronts.

When Mr. Vaughn told neighboring businesses he planned to open a bookstore, they exclaimed, "A bookstore?! Don't you know these fools up in this neighborhood don't be readin' nothin'? Who's gon' read your books?" But Mr. Vaughn believed that if he opened a bookstore, there would be readers to support it. "I just had to open something to try to get to the Black community and let them know what time it was and what we should be about."

Mr. Vaughn built it, and the people came in droves. Books like Ralph Ginzburg's *100 Years of Lynchings* and the *Liberator* magazine attracted fellow Pan-Africanists, Black Nationalists, teachers, and schoolchildren alike. Vaughn's Bookstore hosted Forum '66, the group that organized Detroit's annual Black Arts Convention. The second annual Black Arts Convention crowded the store with notable guests: Stokely Carmichael (Kwame Ture), Betty Shabazz, LeRoi Jones (Amiri Baraka), and Dick Gregory, among others.

The consciousness-raising roused by Vaughn's Bookstore didn't go unnoticed by Black Detroit or local and national authorities.

"Vaughn's Bookstore at 12123 Dexter Avenue got to be a hot item, and I noticed that I was being monitored by the FBI and Detroit Police Department. They thought I was doing something that was illegal, selling dope, but I was only selling books. They couldn't understand that because they thought Black folks didn't read." Mr. Vaughn laughed at the absurdity.

Whether law enforcement actually thought respected business owner and activist Edward Vaughn was trafficking drugs out of a bookstore or they simply found the pro-Black rhetoric that Vaughn's Bookstore promoted too subversive, the store felt the state's ire. "The rebellion came in 1967, and that's when the Detroit police attacked my store," Mr. Vaughn noted.

On the first day of the 1967 Detroit Rebellion, Mr. Vaughn was traveling back from a Black Power Conference in Newark, New Jersey. Police barricades blocked the normal route to his store, so he steered to a back road to find his store unscathed besides the words "LONG LIVE THE BLACK REVOLUTION" painted on the building.

According to Mr. Vaughn, two days after the rebellion started, police officers broke in, firebombed Vaughn's, and smashed portraits of Martin Luther King Jr., Malcolm X, and Marcus Garvey. Mr. Vaughn placed the burned books on the sidewalk to show what the police had done. "The whole neighborhood came out to help me take out those burned-up books and salvage the books that had not caught fire," he recalled. The police denied involvement, blaming the destruction on the Black residents. "I know that Negroes did not do this," Mr. Vaughn told the *Michigan Chronicle* in 1967. "What Negro would chance his life just to steal a few books?"

What happened at Vaughn's during the summer of '67 made headlines across the globe, and the store received donations from as far away as China. With support swelling, the store expanded, but as the militancy of the Black Power era waned, so did sales. Vaughn's Bookstore moved around Detroit several times before eventually closing in the 1990s.

But the store's story doesn't end there. In 2023, Vaughn's Bookstore was added to the National Register of Historic Places, reminding us that preserving history is just as important as making it.

Edward Vaughn and Polly Rawls.

Photos courtesy of the Vaughn Family.

# AFROCENTRIC BOOKSTORE

Meeting Desiree Sanders made me wish I had a time machine so I could travel back to the 1990s and 2000s and just once, experience Chicago's first Black woman-owned bookstore, Afrocentric Bookstore. Cruising down Chicago's renowned Lake Shore Drive, enthralled by Desiree's tales, I yearned to travel back to 1996 on S. Wabash Avenue, to Afrocentric in all its glory.

Before the store closed permanently in 2008, Afrocentric Bookstore served the Black community for eighteen years. Thousands sat at book signings, partied at book festivals, browsed curated inventory, and soaked in the artful aesthetics that Afrocentric became known for—no time machine required.

Before Desiree built Afrocentric, she built her world out of books. As a bookish South Side kid, she fell in love with the worlds between the covers.

"I was the only child for a long time. I was a loner, too. I kind of stayed in the house and didn't go out, so books were my escape."

Desiree escaped into one book in particular: Maya Angelou's *I Know Why the Caged Bird Sings*.

"It really resonated with me how she experienced such severe trauma that she decided to be mute for several years and how she got out of that headspace. That was incredible to me. And then to go on and have these adventures in her life as a Black woman and be able to travel solo around the world and experience different cultures—it showed me what was possible."

In retrospect, it's easy to see how Maya Angelou's advice to "pursue the things you love doing, and then do them so well that people can't take their eyes off you" ran in the background of Desiree's life.

Desiree started Afrocentric Bookstore in 1990, at a time when the Black bookstore owners in Chicago skewed older and male. "I was extremely green and young when I started. I was in my early twenties when I opened up the bookstore. Wow." Desiree pauses, in awe of what she was able to accomplish at such a young age.

"The industry at the time was male-dominated. And not just being a young woman, but a young Black woman, there was, you know, certain"—Desiree waves her hands and rolls her eyes to conjure the right words—"machismo, misogynistic things I had to deal with from Black men."

But Desiree resolved to run Afrocentric Bookstore her way.

Desiree's way not only impressed local patrons—Desiree told *Essence* that the store grossed $207,000 in 1993, which would be over $400,000 today—but also literary giants.

"One day I get a phone call in the store on Wabash, and I'm like, 'Hello?' The person had an extremely distinguished voice, and she says, 'Hi, I'm calling to see if you have any copies of *I Know Why the Caged Bird Sings*?' I said, 'Yes, yes, I do.' And she says, 'Okay, where are you located?' And I give her my address. She tells me she and her driver will be there and asks me to put four copies on hold.

"That same day Maya Angelou walks in. There are no other customers in the store, and she just walks in and is like, 'Yes, dear, I'm here to pick up the four copies you put on hold for me.'"

Desiree had pursued what she loved and done it well. Now, it was Maya Angelou who couldn't take her eyes off her.

"I was like, 'Ms. Angelou, it's an honor for you to come in my store and get these books. You can just have them,' but she tells me, 'No, you have to make money. I'll be fine. I'll take these and one for my driver. He's been so good to me on this trip.'"

Maya Angelou's surprise drop-in eventually led to Afrocentric Bookstore hosting a packed book signing with the renowned poet—despite publishers' hesitancy to send Black literary stars to Black bookstores.

"The publishers didn't send the Black authors to us; they'd send them to the big white stores. Whenever I'd find out a Black book was coming out, I'd reach out to the publisher and request I be a stop on their book tour. They didn't send them at first, but I got Maya Angelou because she came to the store and was impressed."

It was easy to be impressed by the twenty-something electrifying the Chicago book scene.

Desiree saw a need for a Black book festival and brought the Book It Black To Bronzeville book fest—a full day of panel discussions and fun—to the South Side.

Afrocentric Bookstore's impact continues to reverberate. Desiree's daughter, Fatimah Warner (known professionally as the rapper Noname), also started a book venture, the Radical Hood Library in Los Angeles.

And Chicago shows love to the hometown hero, too. As we walked the streets of Hyde Park, we were stopped multiple times.

"Desiree! Is that you?"

"Heyyy, Desiree!"

Though Afrocentric no longer exists physically, the legacy of this vibrant Black institution transcends time and space, still rising in residents' hearts, still enchanting them like a swallow's song.

Desiree Sanders in the Carter G. Woodson Regional Library's YOUmedia room.

Verlean Singletary and Courtney Woods,
the mother-daughter duo of Da Book Joint.

# DA BOOK JOINT

Verlean Singletary's first book-related memory stings with the tinge of someone tearing a book right out of her hands.

"I was reading a Donald Goines book in the school cafeteria. The security guard came and snatched it from me and was like, 'What are you doing reading this book? You're not supposed to be reading this book!'"

Ten-year-old Verlean feared punishment for reading her mom's grown-up book, but it turned out Verlean's mother was happy to have her daughter reading.

Now, as the co-owner of Chicago's Da Book Joint, Verlean focuses on putting books *into* children's hands.

"I'll talk to kids and ask, 'What do you like to do? Oh, you like cheerleading? Well, we have this book about a girl who's a cheerleader.' Once you can get them reading something that interests them, it won't be difficult for them to transition to reading for school."

Da Book Joint's focus on Chicago youth stretches beyond book recommendations. The store's open mics have given local poets, rappers, and singers a space to perform. J. Ivy and Chance the Rapper graced the Da Book Joint stage years before taking the Grammy stage. Rapper Noname performed there, and now, Da Book Joint facilitates the Chicago chapter of the Noname Book Club.

So when Da Book Joint announced plans to close at the end of 2023, the community booked it to Da Book Joint, giving the store the support it needed to remain open.

"We decided to keep fighting," Courtney Woods, Verlean's daughter and Da Book Joint's co-owner, wrote, addressing their supporters. "We have a dream and most importantly—we have a mission. There is an extreme need for books on the South Side of Chicago, especially books that represent the very people who live and grow here. The South Side is already a book desert and finding books by black authors is almost impossible. We will continue to uplift these voices and showcase their stories."

# SEMICOLON BOOKSTORE & GALLERY

Semicolon Bookstore & Gallery in Chicago opened during the summer of 2019, less than a year before a global pandemic stopped the world and the protests against the killings of George Floyd, Breonna Taylor, and countless other Black people shook the world.

"I was walking and happened upon the retail space. I thought it was just going to be me and some random books and people coming in if they wanted to talk and it has turned into *this*"— Danielle Mullen, Semicolon's owner, gestures— "and I still don't know what's going on."

The *this* that Danielle gestures toward—national media attention, record-breaking sales, and accolades—flowed from the particular moment Semicolon happened to inhabit.

After George Floyd's murder, many Americans pledged to unlearn anti-Black racism by reading and "doing the work." Danielle told the *New York Times* that Semicolon

sold some 30,000 books on race and racism through Bookshop.org in just a few days in 2020. Corporate America promised billions to confront systemic racism. Semicolon's logo appeared in Google's 2021 #BlackOwnedFriday campaign.

Semicolon's meteoric rise elevated it in Chicago's flourishing book scene. "We've given away over a million dollars' worth of books, which is wild to me!" Danielle exclaims, referencing Semicolon's #ClearTheShelves initiative, which donates books to Chicago Public Schools students.

But as the news cycle and America panned away from racism and state-sanctioned violence, sales at most Black bookstores, including Semicolon, waned. "Last year, I found myself becoming increasingly disenchanted by the process of owning the shop because as times got harder, we couldn't give away as much as I'd become accustomed to. I had to choose what I wanted the future of bookselling in MY space to represent," Danielle wrote in an Instagram post announcing Semicolon's switch to a nonprofit model.

Now, Semicolon is the only Black woman–owned bookstore on Chicago's Magnificent Mile, and the significance of that isn't lost on Danielle. In another Instagram post she reflects, "People keep asking me how I feel . . . about opening the MagMile space. How I feel about making history. About getting back in the swing of the things with my team . . . and events . . . and everything else under the sun. My answer is always the same: Grateful. Tired."

Danielle Mullen, Semicolon's owner.

# READING IS A REVOLUTIONARY ACT

Nyshell Lawrence built the FUBU of Black woman—owned bookstores.

# SOCIALIGHT SOCIETY

Nyshell Lawrence admires Toni Morrison as a literary hero. So naturally, when Nyshell started Socialight Society in Lansing, Michigan, in 2021, she recalled the famous Toni Morrison quote: "If there's a book that you want to read, but it hasn't been written yet, then you must write it."

"That's how I look at Socialight Society," Nyshell explains. "This is a space that I hadn't seen yet, especially here in Lansing, so I really felt like I was the person who had to build it."

Nyshell built the FUBU of Black woman–owned bookstores in the Lansing Mall. Portraits of classic and contemporary writers dot the walls and bookshelves. Influential Black women—judges, politicians, authors—read books to Black children during a monthly story time.

With around 98 percent of the store's titles by Black women, Nyshell often fields the question, "What about us?" from folks who are either not Black or not women. "What's the issue with reading a book by a Black woman author?" Nyshell asks rhetorically. With Socialight Society, she posits, readers receive the particular and the universal through the Black woman's lens.

And the people of Lansing receive a Black bookstore that's exactly what Nyshell dreamed into being: woman-focused, eclectic, accessible, and sure-footed.

Photos courtesy of Laicee Thill.

# LITTLE BLACK PEARL

**BY MAYA MARSHALL**
**WITH LOVE TO MAYA ANGELOU**

She's her mama's
precious cargo
in tow to work
and every store.
Her hair
in the air
coils frankincense.
Her tongue
rolls against
the roof
of her mouth—
trapped.
Girl has
a little bit
to say,
a speck of *I Know!*
She sits
in the Cowrie
Corner
with books—
the brightest
pretty
quiet
girl
pressure
can make—
and plays
in the pages
that say
bitty black girl
play and say,
*Life Doesn't*
*Frighten Me.*

# BLACK GARNET BOOKS

Sometimes a tweet is just a tweet. But sometimes a tweet is the catalyst for a six-figure crowdfunding campaign for Minnesota's only Black-owned brick-and-mortar bookstore. This was the case in June of 2020, when Dionne Sims tweeted, "Minnesota doesn't have a black-owned bookstore. I think that's my new dream."

"When I made that tweet," Dionne shares, "about how Minnesota didn't have a Black-owned bookstore and that was my dream—to own a bookstore—I meant like when I was like sixty. But just the way that everything played out, the timing was right. The support was there. For me, the heart was there. So yeah, it just kind of all fell into place."

Minnesota, the United States, and the world were reeling after George Floyd's murder by the Minneapolis police the month before. With many staying at home due to the then-new pandemic and others taking to the streets in protest, Dionne quit her job as a user experience designer and started building Black Garnet.

Now Saint Paul's Midway neighborhood has a bookstore that's accessible for book lovers of all physical abilities, values pay transparency and healthcare, and rejects capitalism's reliance on punishment to control.

Dionne describes Black Garnet as leftist, adding an emphatic "Down with imperialism! Down with colonialism! Down with capitalism!"

Photos courtesy of Dionne Sims.

CHAPTER 5

THEY

Alfred and Bernice Ligon pose inside
Aquarian Bookstore, March 24, 1982.
*Los Angeles Times* Photographic Archive,
UCLA Library Special Collections.

## From Ashes It Came, to Ashes It Returned

# AQUARIAN BOOKSHOP

**UPRISINGS BOOKEND THE STORY OF
LOS ANGELES'S AQUARIAN BOOKSHOP.**

Despite opening in 1941, the astrology- and metaphysics-focused bookstore didn't become a fixture in Black Los Angeles until the mid-1960s.

"That's because Black people were not interested in reading Black material," founder Alfred Ligon told Ranford B. Hopkins in 1982, referencing a newfound Black pride and racial consciousness sweeping Black America in the 1960s. "It was only because of the [Watts] Uprising that they became interested in the Blacks, and they were establishing Black Studies and various other things of that kind that actually turned the Negroes into Blacks."

Ligon and his wife, Bernice, supplemented the bookstore with Alfred's wages as a waiter for the Southern Pacific Railroad, and later, with his pension. The couple described bookselling as a "starvation business" yet noted that although they didn't make a living, running the store made life worth living.

At its height, the Aquarian Bookshop hosted countless Black authors for signings—Maya Angelou, Alex Haley, Alice Walker—and counted Michael Jackson and his mother, Katherine, as customers. Rosa Parks visited the store in March of 1992, a mere month before the Los Angeles Uprising led to its destruction.

Amid the tumult, the store burned to the ground. By the time the last book lay as smoldering ash, the Aquarian Bookshop had operated for more than fifty years. Considering the uninsured losses including several thousand titles totaling hundreds of thousands of dollars, most business owners would have understandably bemoaned their misfortune, but the Ligons' spiritual background led them to more enlightened perspectives: "I understand that it is wrong to make attachments to material things," Alfred Ligon told the *New York Times* three months after the Aquarian Bookshop burned down. "Everything is for the better."

And Bernice Ligon—whom customers and friends described as more spunky and cheerful than her husband—simply told the *Los Angeles Times*, "This is the birthing of the Aquarian age and birthing ain't easy."

Independent booksellers and book lovers the world over came together and raised $70,000 to rebuild the store, but the comeback sputtered. The Aquarian Bookshop closed in 1994, when Bernice was diagnosed with liver cancer.

Decades later, as racial unrest continues to define Black politics, and as Black bookstores continue to make sense of the fallout, it remains clear that the Age of Aquarius and the legacy of the Aquarian Bookshop rage on.

# HUGH GORDON BOOKSHOP

"You got a book can teach me how to read?" asked the older, shabbily dressed man.

It was a question both heartening and heart-breaking. The shopkeeper, Frank J. Whitley, had spotted the man staring longingly into the Hugh Gordon Bookshop's windows and invited him in. Whitley had just handed the man a book whose pages dissected Black history when instead, the man asked Whitley if he could help decipher the black ink on the pages.

"I put the history aside and found a primer, and we sat down together at a table and right then and there I began to teach him the alphabet. It was the first time that man from Mississippi had ever had a chance to read a book," Whitley told the *Afro-American* in 1966.

This one-on-one community engagement embodies what Hugh Gordon had imagined his bookshop would mean to Los Angeles—the City of Angels, the city where his shop took on life after his death.

A child of the Great Migration, Hugh Gordon left the South, where his parents, James Gordon and Sarah Elizabeth Lewis, had toiled as slaves for former Georgia governor and U.S. senator John Brown Gordon. The janitor and avid book collector spent his free time studying Africa and Afro-America. The son of formerly enslaved people for whom reading was not only inaccessible but illegal wrote his last will and testament with the community as the beneficiary. Upon his death in 1946, Gordon bequeathed the entirety of his savings and his vast book collection to open a bookstore with the goal of "helping our children hold their heads up higher" so people like that man from Mississippi might have a chance to read a book.

Gordon named longtime friend Adele Young as the manager for the living memorial.

Young took on Gordon's vision along with volunteers Mary Foster and Frank J. Whitley. While corresponding with W.E.B. Du Bois, Young wrote, "Mr. Gordon left his estate with me for the purpose of opening this Book Shop and specialising in books about and by Negro people and their contributions to the building of America. We are the only Book Shop in the West with such a line in this field. The Shop is fast becoming the cultural outlet for the community."

But it wasn't just the community on Central Avenue that sought out Hugh Gordon Bookshop as a cultural outlet. "People from all over the world came because she was the only one who had a store like that," Carmen de Lavallade, Young's niece and a celebrated choreographer and dancer, tells me.

Hugh Gordon Bookshop advertisement, Schomburg clipping file, Schomburg Center for Research in Black Culture, Jean Blackwell Hutson General Research and Reference Division.

W.E.B. Du Bois Day at the Hugh Gordon Bookshop, undated photo, *Baltimore AFRO-American Newspaper.* Courtesy of the *AFRO-American Newspapers* Archives.

In that same letter to Du Bois, Young noted the challenges of "having to depend on a group who want to be informed but have little money to buy with." Foster, Young's colleague, recalled many times when they barely made the rent during her twelve-year tenure. The team threw "good old-fashion rent parties" to keep the bookstore's doors open.

After Young's death, Whitley (also the son of formerly enslaved parents) began managing the bookstore full-time. His interactions with customers like the man who couldn't read inspired him to not only sell books about history but to teach the community for free.

Curious students clambered into classes about "colored and African history," which ranged from college-level lectures to studying the photographs of "great colored personalities," such as Frederick Douglass, Harriet Tubman, Sojourner Truth, Lena Horne, and W.E.B. Du Bois.

In 1961, Langston Hughes inscribed his poem "The Negro Mother" to the Hugh Gordon Bookshop, which he affectionately referred to as "the House of Literary Curios." The poem artfully narrated the significance of Hugh Gordon's living memorial.

> God put a dream like steel in my soul.
> Now, through my children, I'm reaching
>   the goal.
> Now, through my children, I'm young and
>   free.
> I realize the blessings denied to
>   me. . . .
> I had only hope then, but now through
>   you,
> Dark ones of today, my dreams have come
>   true . . .

# MARCUS BOOKS

When the City of San Francisco inducted Marcus Books into its famed preservation registry, Dr. Jasmine Johnson considered it less of a historical marker than a historical erasure.

"All these historical landmarks are tombstones. It's the only way for the city to reconcile with itself," laments Jasmine, granddaughter of Marcus Books' founders, Julian and Raye Richardson. "It's shameful, or not even shameful, but an embarrassment—the history of Black and Brown out. All these signposts show all the ways Black folks are ghosts in the city."

Jasmine's hurt flows from the hypocrisy. Just as many other cities honor Black people as they remove them, San Francisco honored Marcus Books the same year the family was forced off the property. The cutting irony estranged Jasmine from her old Fillmore neighborhood, which she now describes as "gross," and from San Francisco, which she now describes as "a deeply beautiful and deeply inhospitable place."

"I have only been back to that house one time, and that was by accident," she recounts of seeing the former site of Marcus Books. "The building—the Victorian—that the store was in, there's big Victorian steps that go out. And every Fourth of July weekend there was a jazz festival. Those stairs used to be filled, and my mom would have her own . . . she'd just create her own band. Like, forget the formal festival schedule. She would just have the folks in the community who were musicians perform right there in front of the bookstore. There would always be people crowded on those steps. My sisters and I would play on those steps with friends.

"And that time I drove by . . . the people who had bought the house had put a gate on the stairs, and I just thought it was just so deeply antithetical to the previous lives of that house."

It was, in a word, gross.

\* \* \*

Before the gross gate, before the tombstone of a historical marker, before the flood of gentrification, buyouts, and evictions, Marcus Books brimmed as an epicenter of Black cultural life. Or as the city would note in its swan song Landmark Designation Report, Marcus Books' San Francisco location was "a center for Black intellectualism and idea exchange," "a community centerpiece for Black San Franciscans," "a space of Black community collectivity, empowerment, and action," and "a haven where Black people 'didn't have to apologize for their difference, their intellect, or their pain from racism.'"

Founded originally by the Richardsons as Success Printing in 1946, the bookstore began in 1960. "I began ordering so many Black books for Raye and myself, and for friends, that I had to hire a clerk. Before I knew it, the front of the printing shop had been transformed into the Success Bookstore," Julian Richardson explained in 1975. The couple changed the store's name to Marcus Books in 1964 after Marcus Garvey. Marcus Books is credited as the longest continuously operating Black bookstore in the United States. Throughout its tenure, the store has been family

owned, and is now run by Julian and Raye's daughter Blanche Richardson and granddaughter, Cherysse Calhoun. Their son Billy runs the print shop in the back. Julian and Raye's daughter Karen Johnson and Karen's daughter Tamiko and husband Greg ran the Marcus Books San Francisco location before it closed. Jasmine remembers growing up "quite literally in the bookstore," enveloped in a soaring symphony of Black discourse. As her grandfather told writer Gene Ulansky in the mid-1970s, "I'd rather rap about Black roots and uprootedness than sell you a book." "Conversations about Black folks, Black history, Black politics, Black wellness, Black maternity was kind of everybody's business, and everybody's voice was invited into that conversation, just by way of stepping into the door," Jasmine reminisces. "It was a certain kind of magic."

Part of the magic flowed from interacting with the stream of renowned artists, activists, and authors gracing the store. Jasmine recalls: Harry Belafonte "really profound," Rosa Parks "just power, this historical figure embodied," Toni Morrison "stunning—she's my favorite," B.B. King "my mom was freaking out," and so many more.

The intoxicating mix of the everyday and the extraordinary explains why locals fought so hard to save Marcus Books, and why the loss of the San Francisco location resounded with such pain for all those who relied on the bookshop as a home and a haven.

In so many ways, Marcus Books' story is Black San Francisco's story, is Black urban America's story. It is a story that scholar and poet Eve Ewing describes as "a pattern of Black post-industrialized cities that have large populations of Black people who are hanging on as the cities continue to be remade and evolved in ways that are not for us." As Ewing explains, "These cities are transforming themselves into the new iteration of what they want to be in the twenty-first century, [and] the presence of poor Black people is inconvenient for that plan."

Looking at those considered "inconvenient" in Baltimore, in Chicago, in Washington, D.C., in San Francisco, one cannot help but wonder what will happen to all of the vibrancy that the Black communities have built in these locales over all these decades. One cannot help but ask what James Baldwin asked, peering out at all of the hostility that the world aimed at his Harlem: "What will happen to all that beauty?" Where will all of that music, all of that discourse, all of that art, all of those schools, churches, and bookstores go?

\* \* \*

The question of displacement remains a thorny one for a people as nomadic as Black Americans, who, during the Great Migration, fled from Georgia to New York, from Mississippi to Chicago, from Louisiana to the California coast, and who now, in the age of gentrification, are fleeing once more.

In so many ways, that question, that central question of displacement, of removal, of a desire

for home, swirls at the very heart of the story of Marcus Books' namesake, Marcus Garvey, who, in an effort to preserve the Black mind, the Black body, the Black society, proposed returning us all the way back to the motherland. Embedded deep in Garvey's bold declarations, in his words and deeds, in his insistence on Black pageantry, was the elevation of Black beauty. In Garveyites' summoning of huge Black parades, the bustling Black band and choirs, the dressing of Black officers in

full regalia, one could see an answer to Baldwin's concerns about where Black beauty would go. It would go *with us.* Our Blackness casts beauty like a shadow, and it follows us from the South to the cities, from the cities to the suburbs, from the suburbs to wherever we might go.

Black beauty certainly followed Marcus Books in 2014, when it consolidated operations to its Oakland location, where the store's legacy and works live on, unfolding in both the past and present tense. This is what Jasmine describes as Marcus Books' "ongoingness," the fact that the store is "a museum in a sense, but it's a living one— that's still creating things."

Behind the bricks of its beautiful facade featuring Black books and authors of yesteryear, the store is still a hub of community, creating unchoreographed conversation, spaces to debate, spaces to convene, spaces to iterate on Black political thought, spaces, as Jasmine sees them, to honor the "deep regard for the rigor of Black literacy and Black intellect." Standing in that store, it becomes evident that the beauty of Marcus is more than an artifact, more than a history; it is right now, *still here.*

Julian Richardson. Courtesy of the Richardson and Johnson Family.

Karen Johnson and Billy Richardson at Marcus Books in Oakland, California.

Customer Nichelle Kitt browses.

Marcus Books

BOOKS ABOUT BLACK PEOPLE EVERYWHERE

OAKLAND
3900 M.L. King Jr. Way
Arthur BARTI

Billy Richardson with his son, also called Dilly, in the print shop.

# THE VILLAGE LIVES

## BY DR. JASMINE JOHNSON

I knew my grandmother to be equal parts deliberate, formidable, and intellectually agile. She was no-nonsense and playful, too, with a laugh like ringing chimes. I never heard her stutter, shrink, or use four words when three could do.

Her incisiveness, wit, and warmth organized her way about things. Whether she was holding court at Marcus Books, the oldest Black-owned bookstore in the nation, which she cofounded in San Francisco with my grandfather Julian Richardson, or engaging an author's work with scalpel-like exactness, or even conducting Thanksgiving dinner preparations while perched on her wooden dining room chair, her disposition was lucidity-meets-critique until the *thing* was done right. Raye's memory was shocking in its precision and sometimes emerged as an incantation—whether she was reciting poems or singing songs while inside a conversation or in the middle of quiet.

When we lived on Fillmore Street above Marcus Books, the faces of those who saw her on those Victorian steps brightened. "Sister Richardson," they would assert, holding their brown bag filled with newly purchased Black books. Hearing this call, she would pause, one hand on the stair rail—and during her later years the other on her cane (elbow hooked with the family member who was escorting her at that moment)—and melt out: "Hi, Babe." Her attention felt decadent and her caring for you, a luxury.

In my family, my grandmother began a lineage of women embodying intellectual precision and critical hospitality. It's impossible to measure Marcus Books' impact without accounting for the tireless work of Black women. Whether treadmilled by a kind of duty, passion, or force of inheritance, Raye's intellect, standard of engagement, and capacity to not simply sell books but also host robust intellectual dialogue taught me that Black women drive Black political thought.

A constellation of customers, writers, students, and neighbors respected, admired, and adored Raye. They knew her as her own institution. Fifteen years prior to Marcus Books' founding, Raye and Julian had established Success Printing, later renamed Richardson Publishers Co. The duo published canonical Black books that had gone out of print: texts by J.A. Rodgers, Carter G. Woodson, and Marcus Garvey, among others. They also printed collections by local poets, posters, pamphlets, artwork, and ephemera. Whatever the Black freedom movements needed.

After reading an out-of-print copy of Marcus Garvey's *Philosophy and Opinions,* my grandfather apparently said, "I can't call myself a success if I have to step over my brother on the way to the bank." Marcus Books, in title and ethics, pulled inspiration from Garvey's Black nationalist politics—an investment in the Black collective

Raye Richardson.
Courtesy of the
Richardson and
Johnson Family.

rather than the individual. Though the bookstore went through many iterations, what I remember most is an entire store organized categorically (history, fiction, picture books, poetry, sociology, and more), with the common denominator being Black life. I remember the sounds of music, debate, and children's laughter; the cakes we'd eat during book signings; the warmed apple cider and candy canes that were given out in the winter. The two words that I associate with Marcus Books are "warmth" and "rigor." Raye epitomized both.

Raye passed in February 2020 at ninety-nine years old. San Francisco lost her even earlier, in 2014, when Marcus Books closed its doors—our house and business foreclosed on. The eight family members who lived there at the time, including Raye, were set in new motion. Our story is no anomaly—it is a San Francisco classic.

The choreographic precision with which San Francisco exorcized much of the city's Black and Latinx communities is well documented.[1] Against this historical backdrop, the choice of staying or leaving San Francisco is a counterfeit ballot. I recall the 1964 KQED film report *Take This Hammer*, in which Orville Luster, executive director of Youth for Service, guides James Baldwin during the author's first trip to the city. In one scene Luster is amid a crowd of young Black men:

"The South ain't half as bad as San Francisco. . . . The white man, he's not taking advantage of you out in public like they doing down in Birmingham, but he's killing you with that pencil and paper, Brother."

---

1    See Ingrid Banks et al. *Black California Dreamin': The Crises of California's African-American Communities* (UCSB, Center for Black Studies Research, 2012); Albert S. Broussard, *Black San Francisco: The Struggle for Racial Equality in the West, 1900–1954* (Lawrence: University Press of Kansas, 1993); Rebecca Solnit, *Hollow City: The Siege of San Francisco and the Crisis of American Urbanism* (Verso: 2018); Jessica Trounstine, *Segregation by Design: Local Politics and Inequality in American Cities* (Cambridge, UK: Cambridge University Press, 2018).

In another scene, Luster and Baldwin ride in a car. With Baldwin in the passenger seat, Luster points out the Western Addition as they pass. Baldwin accurately recasts "urban renewal" as "Negro removal."

Ironically, the San Francisco store became a historical landmark the year it was pushed out of the city.

Still, Raye is a San Franciscan icon—a sinewed life of Black literary formation. Raye's life was a testament to Black intellectual thought, cooperation, community advancement, and grace. She practiced this through stewarding Marcus Books, chairing the country's first college Ethnic Studies Department (at San Francisco State University), her board work (for the Small Business Commission, the African American Disparity in Health Committee, the Black Nurses Association, and many others), and her under-celebrated work as a newspaper columnist.

I miss Raye's immediacy of thinking: always right there. The gymnastics of her intellect and the power of her throat. Sometimes I would see her standing behind the counter or in some corner of the store in conversation with an author. In other moments I would watch her in action in a way that I was meant to listen to, rather than ear-hustle: Raye in conversation with Toni Morrison or Harry Belafonte. Eventually, she would retire from both the in-store activities and the author events.

Her slow retirement as a public bookstore presence coincided with an increasingly growing family. She cared for a generation of grandchildren and great-grandchildren while being cared for by her own daughters and sons. Raye would watch the living room TV from her kitchen, studying the news, a sports game, or an afternoon judge show. An ironing board often flanked between her and the dining table held draft handwritten articles for her column, "Hi, Babe," in the *Sun Reporter* or the *Metro Reporter*—San Francisco's two Black news outlets.

"Hi, Babe" resounded as her signature greeting. It signaled both recognition and tenderness. In her hold, "babe" was not sexualized; it hailed belonging, not as possession but as care-work. Never patronizing, always delivered with rocking chair ease, "Hi, Babe" saw you and held you accountable to both yourself and a broader community.

Raye's "Hi, Babe" column spoke to the present through the lens of history and Black speculative futures. It covered topics like local electoral politics, voter suppression, morality and religion, homelessness, the history of the Black printing press, and the meaning of freedom. I am struck by the ease with which she drew on Roman history, Greek mythology, Indigenous histories, poetry, and Black political thought with such skill and boundlessness.

"Abolition," she wrote in the *Metro Reporter,* "was the primary goal of the Black Press."[2] Indeed, a guiding focus on abolition seemed to engine her life's work. Such a commitment ranged from the spectacular (she and Julian putting their house up as bail to get students who protested for the Third World Department out of jail) to the mundane (being trained at age five to offer book recommendations for other children; weekly afternoons during which my siblings, cousins, and I memorized and recited Black poetry and speeches with Black Power seriousness and precision, no cute kitsch; her giving me my first natural hairstyle. I was horrified and scared, but I developed a different, more prideful relationship with my hair). Abolition was not a single destination; it lived as an academic and familial practice through which I learned to love and think greatly of my Black self and those around me.

In a 2001 "Hi, Babe" column titled "Community Commitment," Raye wrote:

```
      Commitment allows a community to own, in
       celebration of the committed life, the
      dream that bottoms all existence. Though
       you make your statement in the individ-
      ual, solitary way, and though at times it
      appears that your commitment isolates you
       from the normative crowd, the isolation
       is not long-lived for it finds fellowship
       with the committed of all times and all
      places. [. . .] Though the body dies, the
       acts of love and justice and righteous-
      ness are planted like seeds into the very
        tissue and fiber of community. [. . .]
      The joy of this moment is that the people
       we come to honor have made such a state-
      ment of commitment that they are our best
       hope that a community will not be without
      guidance—that the unborn will be tutored
                 to the struggle.[3]
```

"The village lives." This is what she told us in "Hi, Babe" when her husband passed. This speaks to her own transition as well. Raye lives on in the Fillmore. She lives on in Marcus Books. Her tutelage is both crown and compass.

2   Raye G. Richardson, "Watchman, What of the Night?" *Metro Reporter,* August 26, 1997.
3   Raye G. Richardson, "Community Commitment," *Sun Reporter,* October 18, 2001.

# THIRD WORLD ETHNIC BOOKS

In the early 1970s, a West Adams, Los Angeles, garage housed one of the most impressive collections of rare African American books and ephemera on the West Coast. Mayme Clayton, a collector and former librarian of the University of Southern California and University of California, Los Angeles, had amassed the collection over four decades of scouring yard sales, used bookstores, estate sales, flea markets, attics and basements, even dumpsters—pretty much everywhere one might find books.

A signed copy of Phillis Wheatley's *Poems on Various Subjects, Religious and Moral*, published in 1773, anchored Clayton's collection, which also included signed first editions from Langston Hughes, W.E.B. Du Bois, Booker T. Washington, and Paul Laurence Dunbar.

Clayton retired early from UCLA after the university failed to invest in a more robust African American collection for the library. She later accepted a job at Universal Books, an L.A.-based bookstore with a large African American section, making $2 an hour to learn the bookstore business.

Two years later, Clayton partnered with Universal Books' owner, but her partner gambled away the store's money and the business shuttered. Clayton acquired the store's more than four thousand volumes related to Black society and culture. Combining those books with her personal collection, she opened Third World Ethnic Books out of her garage.

In a 1973 interview with the *Los Angeles Times*, Clayton described Third World Ethnic Books as

"a combination club, library, research center, and bookstore" and noted that she had yearned to own a bookstore since learning about Mary McLeod Bethune at age ten. "Her strength and dedication gave me strength," Clayton said. "I guess you can say it inspired me. That's what's important about Black history—it gives us direction, inspiration. For me it meant a bookstore, because I love to read and wanted to do something for my race."

Mayme A. Clayton, 1973 portrait by Art Rogers, *Los Angeles Times* Photographic Archive, UCLA Library Special Collections.

Because Third World Ethnic Books stored much more than a normal bookstore, Clayton's sons convinced her to change its name to Western States Black Research Center. The focus shifted from selling and educating to using the one-of-a-kind collection to educate community members about Black history, specifically Black West Coast history. After Clayton died in 2006 at the age of eighty-three, her son Avery worked to establish the Mayme A. Clayton Library and Museum in a former courthouse in Culver City, but sadly, the lease for the museum was canceled in 2019.

Mo' Betta Books

# OASIS IN THE DIASPORA

Ms. Daphne Muse is a walking museum. Explore her life and you'll discover a multitude of incredible experiences. She managed the Drum and Spear bookstore, secretaried for the Angela Davis Legal Defense Campaign, researched for Harlem Renaissance writer Arna Bontemps, and graciously hosted Rosa Parks. You'd struggle to find a person, place, or thing related to Black history that Ms. Muse hasn't impacted. Nowadays, Ms. Muse shares her vast knowledge of Black literature through Oasis in the Diaspora, an antiquarian bookstore nestled in Brentwood, California, and brimming with more than twelve thousand rare Black books and pieces of ephemera she's acquired since she began collecting in the 1960s. Originally housed in Oakland, Oasis in the Diaspora has spawned cultural and political events, hosted many out-of-town writers and artists, and even organized Alice Walker's first Bay Area book party.

Like Ms. Muse, Oasis's collection is one of a kind, including a signed first edition of *Beloved* with Toni Morrison proclaiming "And she was loved!"; pamphlets from Bill Clinton's inauguration featuring Maya Angelou's "On the Pulse of Morning"; a Gee's Bend Quilting Collective poster signed by all the artists; and books published by Drum and Spear Press that rested on the shelves of her former employer over fifty years ago. Each book sold comes with a provenance sheet printed on vintage letterhead that describes which collection the book comes from, which exhibits the book featured in, and how it came to be at Oasis.

Among the most priceless items at Oasis are the more than five thousand letters Ms. Muse has received from artists, activists, politicians, and

students. While sipping pomegranate tea at the kitchen table, she pores over letters from Afeni Shakur and Rosa Parks thanking her for her kind hospitality. She pulls out an invitation from Richard Pryor for a Hollywood soiree, which she had declined—the comedian felt touched after Ms. Muse reached out to him when he set himself on fire in 1980. "I'm not the Hollywood type, but I should've gone," she says, chuckling.

Ms. Muse sees Oasis in the Diaspora as a continuation of Drum and Spear Bookstore's legacy. "If you were to ask me, 'Would you do the Drum and Spear experience all over again?' In a heartbeat. In a heartbeat!" she says. "And Oasis is an extension of that experience, and being able to bring Grant and other people into it and carry the legacy forward just makes it even more powerful."

To Ms. Muse, Grant Williams-Yackel, who is Oasis's manager and chief curator, represents a new Black bookseller generation that is communicating and communing with those who came before. Through Oasis, Grant and Ms. Muse

Like Daphne Muse, Oasis in the Diaspora's collection is one of a kind.

## DAPHNE PATRICIA MUSE

Grant Williams-Yackel and Daphne Muse sort through inventory.

Reference is made to the memorandum dated
October 15, 1971, at Phoenix, Arizona, captioned, "Daphne
Muse." This memorandum concerned the activities of the

created an intergenerational conversation series called "Old School + New School = Mo' Betta School."

"The Mo' Betta School series came from what Ms. Muse would always say about the importance of ideas from multiple times and spaces coming together and coexisting in one space, which for me is the essence of what Oasis in the Diaspora is," Grant shares.

Going through Oasis's inventory illuminates diasporic writing's multiverse. First editions by Zora Neale Hurston, signed first editions by Octavia E.

Butler, and out-of-print African folktales stand side by side. "It's really intense to be in community with people who have already passed. That's something I take very seriously," Grant muses. "There's a community of Black thinkers, poets, artists, and creators who are so powerful that they literally don't respect time. They don't respect death. They're like, 'No, I will be here with you now and always.'"

Oasis has proven to be exactly this—fertile ground for discovering and strengthening our links to the past, present, and future.

OPPOSITE, BACKGROUND: FBI surveillance document, Daphne Muse papers, Stuart A. Rose Manuscripts, Archives, and Rare Books Library, Emory University.

Books at Oasis in the Diaspora.

ZORA NEALE HURSTON

Working the Spirit — Joseph M. Murphy

MY PLACE — SALLY MORGAN

PALEY — KWANZAA and Me — HARVARD

DEAD DAYS

DIOUF — DREAMS OF AFRICA IN ALABAMA — OXFORD

AFRO-AMERICAN ARTISTS

Ref. 759.1 C326a

An Autobiography of a Black Chicago — TRAVIS

AFENI SHAKUR: EVOLUTION OF A REVOLUTIONARY — JASMINE GUY — ATRIA

WOMEN, CULTURE & POLITICS · ANGELA Y. DAVIS — Random House

TOMORROW'S TOMORROW — Joyce A. Ladner — Doubleday

Jones — Big Star Fallin' Mama — Doris E. Saunders

I HOPE I LOOK THAT GOOD WHEN I'M THAT OLD

Dancing Up the Moon

remembered rapture — bell hooks — Henry Holt

Race Matters — Cornel West — VINTAGE

Raising RACISM — ROOKS — New Republic Books

HAIR RAISING

FREEDOM — Thursdays and Every Other Sunday Off — Anna Arnold Hedgeman — Doubleday

The Trumpet Sounds

GILLIAM · PAUL ROBESON

Jambalaya — Luisah Teish — Harper & Row

DAVID HILLIARD AND LEWIS COLE — THIS SIDE OF GLORY — LITTLE, BROWN

ZORA HURSTON — LIPPINCOTT

CHARLENE HATCHER POLITE — SOUL PLAY

FOUR WALLS EIGHT WINDOWS — E OF THE SOWER ● butler

BUTLER — kindred — bluestreak

M. MORRISON — ALFRED A. KNOPF

Petry — THE STREET — WORLD

Louise Meriwether — daddy was a number runner — Prentice Hall

KINDRED — Octavia E. Butler — Doubleday

JAZZ — TONI MORRISON

The Boar Hog Woman — Cleo Overstreet

JLA — TONI MORRISON — KNOPF

Country Place — Ann Petry — H. M. Co.

BrownGirl, Brownstones

TELL NO TALES — Monroe

The Upper R

HOPKINSON — whispers from the cotto

will make you BLACK

THE FISHER KING

I SAW THE SKY — T. OBINKARA

A DAY LATE and a DOLLAR SHORT — Terry M

# HUE-MAN EXPERIENCE

"I wanted the bookstore to be a lovely retail space. I wanted to look like a Barnes & Noble with modern software," Clara Villarosa, former owner of the Hue-man Experience bookstore, reminisces.

When Clara opened Hue-man in Denver in 1984 with business partners Louis and Yvonne Freeman, there hadn't been a Black bookstore in the area since Sundiata Bookstore closed in 1976.

With Black Denverites languishing for nearly a decade without a dedicated place to find books by and about them, Clara focused on the customer experience and marketing. "I wore Afrocentric clothing, earrings, and necklaces," she says. "Anything that helped me promote the Afrocentric. I wanted everything to go back to Hue-man. It was a brand."

And she even admits to exaggerating the Hue-man brand at times. "She was really good at promotion," Linda Villarosa, Clara's daughter, recalls. "She'd say, 'Oh, I have the largest Black bookstore in the country.' And finally, I'm like, 'How do you know that? Like, what is the metric?' And she'd say, 'Well, nobody else is saying it, so I said it!'"

"Yeah, I said it!" Clara echoes with a laugh, admitting that her fellow bookseller Emma Rodgers of Black Images Book Bazaar in Dallas probably ran a bigger store.

Quibbles over square footage or inventory size aside, Clara strived to serve Black book buyers and sellers across the country.

"Mom would come to stores and critique. She gave advice like the aunt who is harsh, but you know she's right, like, 'You should do this. I think you should do that. Why is this this way?'" Linda recalls. Clara adds with a shrug, "Some people appreciated my advice. The male bookstore owners appreciated it the least."

But Clara mentored Black booksellers through more formal channels, too. According to Clara, she was the first Black bookseller to join the American Booksellers Association (ABA), and she encouraged other Black booksellers to follow suit. "I attended the ABA's bookselling school and became one of the instructors. My specialty was marketing and finance."

Clara credits her experience in corporate America and living in predominantly white Denver for her willingness to leverage the all-white ABA. And when other Black booksellers joined the organization, Clara urged the ABA to create an African American segment to allow Black booksellers and authors to network with each other and publishers.

Like a Madison Avenue ad wiz, Clara enlisted her voice and vision to catapult Hue-man and Denver into the imagination of publishers and authors.

"I think the publishers didn't know about Black bookstores," Clara says. "It was often the authors telling them, 'You know, there's this lady who has a bookstore in Denver,' which wouldn't have naturally been a stop on a book tour because there are not so many Black people there."

There were even celebrity endorsements. Clara's good friend Maya Angelou hustled amid the many authors helping to hype the Hue-man Experience. "She'd tell people, 'You should go to my friend's bookstore in Denver because it's Black-owned, it's large, and you will get very good author care and professional treatment,'" Linda recounts.

Hue-man Experience's customer and author experience dazzled the likes of Colin Powell, Terry McMillan, and Black sororities and fraternities; Clara encouraged the latter to hold meetings at the store to broaden her customer base in the community.

But Clara wasn't a one-woman show. "Another interesting thing my mom did at the store was hire formerly incarcerated people," Linda shares. The hiring choices weren't particularly political. A group of incarcerated men bought books from the Hue-man Experience, then added them to the prison library. So naturally, when some of the men completed their sentence, they needed a job.

"Anyone working the floor had to be really knowledgeable. That was important to my mom," says Linda.

"And those men were well-read and good at hand-selling. And saying they worked at Hue-man helped them get their next job," Clara adds.

Clara's own affiliation with the Hue-man Experience helped her land her next gig—another bookstore called Hue-Man Bookstore and Café. After decades of growing Denver's Black book scene, Clara found herself in Harlem, close to her daughters and grandchildren.

Before leaving for Harlem, Clara sold the Hue-man Experience to Joi Afzal, Kim Martin, and Daryl Walker. The trio ran the store for three years, until it closed in 2003.

Photos Courtesy of Clara and Linda Villarosa.

# ESO WON BOOKS

James Fugate's reputation precedes him. The retired co-owner of Eso Won, Los Angeles's premier Black bookstore for more than thirty years, and his business partner Tom Hamilton have inspired many stories throughout their long careers and even during this book's reporting.

Simba Sana, the co-owner of the now-closed Karibu Books, recalls visiting Eso Won to write down book titles to stock in his stores back on the East Coast. Tom questioned why Simba didn't buy all the titles to show appreciation for Tom and James's research. Simba remembers feeling frustrated at the time but realizing Tom's point. "He got on to me, but I bought the books and he went on to mentor me. They're both real intellectuals. Real good dudes. Funny, too."

When I told an L.A.-based writer I'd be interviewing James, the writer warned me not to take it personally if James was a little grumpy, mentioning Eso Won's strictly enforced no-pictures policy that clashed with younger customers' desire to document their shopping trips through Instagram and TikTok.

Another former bookstore owner laughed about the time customers asked her to discount calendars like the big-box bookstores. She called James for advice. "He told me, 'I'll burn those calendars before I discount them!'" she recalled.

While going through the archives, I found articles about Tom and James banning a poet from their store after she gave a Maya Angelou book a harsh review.

With all this background knowledge, I nervously tiptoed into the interview. After a quick introduction and talk about the joys of retirement, James told me a story about a time when he was a customer at a Black bookstore in L.A. "I went over to Aquarian Bookshop to introduce myself, to tell them that I was running the Compton College bookstore and that I thought we could work together. Mrs. Ligon was wonderful. We were having the best conversation, but Dr. Ligon didn't want to hear it. He was very dismissive. At first, when he walked away, I almost put all the books back that I was going to buy, but then I thought, 'Oh, he's an old man, forget him.' I continued to talk with Mrs. Ligon and refer customers to them. This was the late eighties, so Dr. Ligon had been doing this for over forty years at the time. And as a bookseller, you get so many people that come in and they want to talk to you about how you could be running your business better or differently. And you just don't want to hear it at some point, and I think he was having one of those days."

James relayed this story unprompted, as if to say, "I know what they say about me. Don't pay it no mind."

Like Aquarian's Alfred Ligon, James lived the book business for decades. He, Tom, and Asamoah Nkwanta, a third partner who left the business early on, started Eso Won in the late eighties. James considered naming the store Black Books International, but Asamoah proposed a better idea.

"Asamoah and his wife had been to Aswan, Egypt, and they said the Africans called it Eso Won, and

James Fugate at home in Los Angeles.

one of us said, 'Water flows over rocks, so does knowledge flow through books.' So we ended up taking Eso Won as our name because it would take us back to Africa."

Over the years, Tom and James earned a reputation of being thoughtful book curators. They read and could hand-sell based on their own experience with the texts, whether they liked the books or not. *The Blackman's Guide to Understanding the Blackwoman* fell into the latter category. While other bookstores refused to carry the controversial book that encouraged Black women to submit to Black men, Eso Won did.

"We'd tell people if we thought they were nuts, you know, we'd tell them, 'I don't agree with this. This is foolishness.' But at least people had the opportunity to get [those books] and, you know, have access to them."

So when James and Tom announced their plans to close shop in 2022, the community responded as if a loved one had announced a terminal diagnosis. Leimert Park, surrounding

L.A. neighborhoods, and the rest of the country lamented the closing of another Black institution and the closing of the public's access to carefully curated Black knowledge.

And while I deeply regret not visiting Eso Won before Tom and James locked its doors for the last time, I love that they left on their own terms.

"Other people thought we should pass the store on to somebody. But the one thing that I don't see currently is people having the same perspective about books that Tom and I had. . . . It was special to us. And when we left, we just decided that, you know, that's it."

With Eso Won gone, there's one less place to discover Black revolutionaries' directives, one less place for a child to buy their first chapter book, and one less place to meet your favorite author and tell them how much their words mean to you.

But Eso Won endures. As water flows over rocks, the knowledge found at Eso Won flows through the minds and spirits of everyone it touched.

# CLOSED DOOR, OPEN WINDOW

## BY LYNELL GEORGE

Pulling up to 4327 Degnan Boulevard, in the heart of Leimert Park Village, I see that familiar front window. The one that's usually framed with stacks of tantalizing hardcovers and paperbacks, arranged around a set of bright red cubed letters spelling out *E-s-o-W-o-n B-o-o-k-s*. On this day, however, the glass is covered in heavy brown paper; so, too, are the front doors—a closed set of eyes.

Encountering this storefront shut tight with no hint of all it has been and means is beyond unmooring. The fine steady drizzle gathering on my windshield perfectly matches my mood.

Time moves faster in Los Angeles than it does in a lot of other places. Neighborhoods here don't just evolve, they transform: a different set, a new cast, then to now, a seamless jump cut. But this site has been a home base and emblem of perseverance and persistence. An anchor. The store's just a few months gone, and even the rest of the street, still with its own distinct pulse, flavor, and mission, already feels different without it.

Some traditions persist: two doors south of Eso Won's former entryway, two men in bright short-sleeve shirts and kufi caps tap out patterns on two tall drums. I see someone setting up at Sika's, the Village's master craftsman and jeweler's shop. In the nearby alley, I spy the sort of trucks, trailers, and canopies that signal a film shoot setup. Toward the north end of the street, someone is blasting bluesman Z. Z. Hill's "Open House at My House" and smoking herb—a crashing wave of sound and scent. Saturday night on Thursday morning.

Z. Z. Hill testifies: "Home just don't seem like home no doggone more . . ."

For so much of Black Los Angeles, 4327 Degnan had been a place to find your bearings. To buy books, yes, but also a place to discover your language. To strategize and commiserate. To celebrate and mobilize. To shoot the breeze. To reflect. When prominent figures—presidents and poets, athletes and activists, scientists and singers among them—landed in town, if even briefly, they knew the power move was a touchdown at Eso Won.

For thirty-plus years, at numerous locations around Southwest L.A., Eso Won, a Black neighborhood independent bookstore, connected people across the sprawling L.A. basin. Expanding the very definition of "neighborhood," store regulars drove far beyond the city's or county's limits to shop and attend readings there. Without Eso Won, the heart of Leimert Park Village beats a little differently.

*"Home just don't seem like home no doggone more."*

To flip back a few chapters for context, in June of 2022, I woke with a start at 7:00 a.m. My phone pulsed with texts and emails at an emergency-level pace. Gratefully, one friend sent along a clarifying link to a story in *Publishers Weekly* reporting that Eso Won's owners, James Fugate and Tom Hamilton, were planning to close Eso Won—our oldest and premier Black bookstore—by the end of the year. I read the story, slowly, in astonishment. Then read it again. Immediately, I posted on my socials: "I don't want to live in a Los Angeles without Eso Won. This is devastating news."

And many agreed with my sentiment. People from all parts of my life pinged me with questions, concerns, and strategies. As far as we were concerned, this was a family matter. Requests crowded my inbox. Invites to write op-eds or be interviewed on the radio and podcasts followed. Even though Tom and James had given us a generous window of time to say our goodbyes and browse the stacks, I was struck by the immediate outpouring of shock, of pure grief. It was clear: so many of us didn't want to imagine a Los Angeles without Eso Won.

I opted out of writing anything elegiac or past tense, largely out of a sense of denial wrapped up in hope. A large part of me wanted to believe that there might be some sort of eleventh-hour surprise and that Eso Won, as it often had when it landed in a precarious or narrow spot—be it finding a new space, weathering the book business's mercurial twists—would somehow steer its way to safety. There would be a reprieve, a plot twist. They'd gather themselves, catch their second wind. Turn a new page.

Albeit flimsy, it was hope. And so, when an email from the store landed in my inbox in late October, with the subject line "Eso Won is Closed," it took the wind out of me.

I could barely take in James Fugate's first paragraph, the tone and finality of it:

```
        Last Saturday, Eso Won Books closed. As
         so many of you know, Tom and I made a
         decision last November that 2022 would
          be our last year. Eso Won started some
        34-35 years ago to make sure that African
          Centered Books could be found in our
         community. We think that we were able to
          achieve that goal. We worked hard to stay
           in business and You our Supporters made
                      that possible . . .
```

I wasn't simply losing a store, I was losing a place that had played an essential role in my kinship circle, as well as in my formation as a reader, thinker, and eventually as a writer. For me, Eso Won helped to shape a path.

Not all bookstores—independent or otherwise—can claim this type of fervent loyalty and, consequently, inspire a commensurate swan song. The bookstores that stay with us, live within us, are the shops whose layouts we know as well as our own homes, whose phone numbers we've memorized, whose staff we've come to know on a first-name basis. Eso Won felt like an extension of ourselves.

✳✳✳

I started haunting Eso Won in my twenties, during its earliest years in Inglewood, when it was located on La Brea. I shadowed my mother, a teacher who sought out Black literature and Black bookstores throughout my childhood and beyond. She assembled ancillary libraries, not just for me and my brother at home but also for her students, to augment reading lists that excluded our stories, our very existence. Stores like Eso Won—along with former purveyors Aquarian Bookshop and Halls—invited us to explore broader visions of ourselves.

Within these sacred spaces, I came to know the echoing cadences of James Baldwin, the sparkling wit and gravitas of Zora Neale Hurston, the sumptuous simplicity of Gwendolyn Brooks. We browsed their vast selection of Black-themed and African-centered books, across genres—fiction, history, folktales, cookbooks, art and photography, biographies, memoir, and more. We also spoke to Tom and James about the books they had just finished, the ones they were looking forward to starting, what the tempo of city life felt like, and how that translated into what was popular on the page. They weren't just hand-selling books, they were reading us, reading the culture in the moment.

Perhaps, not surprisingly, Tom and James had met in a bookstore. Tom was browsing the shelves at Compton College's bookstore, where James worked at the time. They struck up a conversation, trading ideas, authors, and titles, which turned into the foundation of a partnership. Tom and a friend, Asamoah Nkwanta, had already been nurturing a plan to open a bookshop and invited James into the fold. It was Asamoah who floated the name "Eso Won" as a possibility: "It was a site he had visited along the Nile," Tom told me years ago. "He was struck by its quiet, its peacefulness. Almost like a library."

As I followed James and Tom from location to location over the decades, what struck me was that the store always felt familiar, warm—somehow unchanged: Tom had built the shelves with his own hands. Those shelves, along with the book-laden sales tables, could be moved quickly to create gathering space for discussions, meetings, meals, or readings that sometimes spilled out onto the sidewalk. I often bumped into old neighbors or childhood classmates as I filled my arms with books. We browsed amid the sales tables draped in mud cloth, alongside the textures of straight-ahead jazz pulsing over the speakers, and the paintings, quilts, and watercolors created by neighborhood artists who kept studios, just steps away, in the Village. A visit to Eso Won was more than a shopping trip; it was an infusion to the spirit.

Increasingly, ceaselessly, old territory here in Los Angeles rushes from below my feet, cedes like the tide rushing out. There are few places I could go that held on to that old feeling of what those neighborhoods truly meant—those past-times ways, those futures, hopes, and possibilities. As traditionally Black "legacy" neighborhoods in L.A. reconstitute demographically, driven by real estate spikes, development, and gentrification, Eso Won and its universe of ideas and possibility was a symbol of resilience. In a city that seemed determined to erase us—on syllabi and censuses alike—Black bookstores became our oases. Black bookstores allowed us to bloom in this indifferent desert.

Unique and intimate, it was ours. It was at Eso Won where I first heard the great writer and visionary Octavia E. Butler speak about her life and work, and my mother's North Star, Toni Morrison, read those sacred pages from her novels. It's where Black authors came to tell stories and answer specific, in-group questions, unlike those they might parse at chain stores. As James told me years ago, "Customers always say, the writers would be different here. They'd read longer. Seem more relaxed."

On those visits, my mother would fill her arms with books, greeting cards, and blank books and check in with James and Tom to see what more they had put away for her—because they knew her tastes and what leaps she might take. I knew early on that I wanted someone to know me that way, too.

Although my mother is now gone, she's alive in those books—in the margins and in the memories. I've inherited scores of her cherished volumes, many of them hand-sold by Tom or James, or by one of Tom's sons. I've also inherited the closeness. This is why, when I finally caught up with James after the *Publishers Weekly* announcement, I listened closely and quietly. I didn't ask reporter questions, rather I spoke to him as a friend might: "What do you need? Is there anything we can do to assist? You need to do what you both need to do. You've given us so much." His voice told the full weight and import of the decision: "It was time."

In the weeks between the *Publishers Weekly* item and the store's final day, Tom and James were inundated with bids, business schemes, and heartfelt overtures: people inquired about taking over their lease or purchasing the business and/or name, carrying it forward. Still others offered to hold rallies to raise money. Other booksellers and longtime customers brainstormed, wanting to find some way to pay formal tribute or, at the very least, host a thank-you dinner. Tom and James declined them all.

"People were under the impression that we were struggling," James explained. "'What can we do to keep it going?' Nothing. We want to retire."

They closed shop for the final time on a weekend afternoon. Tom returned to hang the brown paper in the windows while James sent out the farewell email. "We'd been having sales since the summer and didn't have a lot of inventory anymore," he told me. "It was very slow. We were only open from twelve to four. We just looked at one another and agreed, 'We're shutting down now.' We ended without any fanfare. Nobody knew except me and Tom."

They put punctuation on their own story. They'd done their work—laid a path, cleared space for others.

Anyone who really knows bookselling understands just how difficult it is. It's not just replenishing stock, hosting events, or passing books across the counter. It requires a sort of preternatural dexterity. James and Tom had been keeping us alert and informed through seven presidents, numerous waves of economic hardship, and bookselling's dramatic transformations. Add to it a pandemic and a dramatic uptick in sales in response to a media-fed "racial reckoning" that predictably petered out. But through it all, Eso Won was the shingle where we would go seeking what we'd come to know: The personalities and the tastes. The comfort of being and feeling at home.

✳ ✳ ✳

More than ever, I crave these alternative spaces, these sites that are more than shops but also networks that link us across time, interest, and distance. They are sanctuaries that connect kindred spirits.

Nikki High was one of those regulars who was part of the reading community that Eso Won so assiduously created and tended. Though she grew up as an avid reader in Northwest Pasadena, she would make the twenty-mile journey to Eso Won. "As soon as I got my driver's license at sixteen, I braved those curves on the 110 freeway," she recalls. "It was nothing like I had ever seen before. I felt [at] home and delighted. This was the late eighties. We didn't have that stuff, particularly in Pasadena. To be part of something that connected me. They were an important template for me."

In late 2022, about the time Tom and James shuttered their shop, Nikki responded to a Twitter thread about what dreams people were preparing to set in motion for the new year. Her response detailed her already-in-motion plan: She had quit her corporate marketing job and was opening a bookstore focused on BIPOC writers and readers. She was calling it Octavia's Bookshelf, named in honor of the late Octavia E. Butler, the Pasadena-born writer and visionary who was a hungry reader herself. That tweet went viral. A crush of press coverage followed. The flurry of interest under-scored the thirst: the need for safe spaces where Black writers and other writers of color could not only be featured but also understood. As a Black woman, Nikki knows how important context and safe spaces are for the free flow of ideas and conversation. "I truly did think that I needed customers, I needed people to be interested, but had told myself if my family and friends are interested and they told others, I would be fine," she recalls. "But when that tweet happened . . . it just blew up." People reached out from across the city, the state, and the country. "I even had people from Rwanda DM me. It all let me know that it was the right thing."

When Octavia's Bookshelf opened in the middle of Black History Month in 2023, lines wound around the block, one stretching north toward the picturesque backdrop of the San Gabriel Mountains. Television and newspaper reporters, cameras and digital recorders at the ready, interviewed Nikki, her staff, and her patrons. One visitor posted on Instagram that she had waited three hours in line *just* to be able to say that she bought something the first day, the giddiness rippling in her voice. I'd never seen anything quite like this, and I may not again. This was Black History in real time. Nikki's instinct had keyed in on something significant—people were there to celebrate a new Black venture and the spirit of Butler, who had relied on the power of literature to write herself, and us, into new worlds.

The name itself telegraphs an intimacy: the shop feels like an airy alcove, someone's dreamy reading hideaway, decorated with two plush matching sun-drenched chairs pushed together to make a loveseat and a tangle of thriving plants residing on bookcases labeled "You Think You Grown—Young Adult" and "The Black Card—Current Issues."

As serendipity would have it, the shop rests on the cusp of Butler's former working-class neighborhood in North Pasadena. And while the street coordinates would have been familiar to her, she would definitely make notes and calculations about the new businesses on the once sleepy block: the bustling greasy spoon, an acai bar, a Pilates studio, an elegant yet casual coffeehouse. In a certain way, as Eso Won had been, Octavia's Bookshelf is a flag planted in the soil that proclaims: "We belong here, too."

Butler read voraciously across genres and is best known for her speculative worlds. She frequently evangelized about the importance of libraries and bookstores in both shaping and broadening her, about what the feeling was when she bought her first book about stars, and the dream to build her own home library. Books were both pathways and destinations.

While Eso Won's papered front doors and windows were very much still on my mind and heart, I was comforted by the hand-stenciled message adorning Octavia's Bookshelf's front window: "Welcome, booklover. You are among friends"—its elegant serif script an open invitation.

That morning, I shopped alongside an avid flock of browsers. My purchases were as intentional as they were symbolic: a votive candle with the visage of a young James Baldwin to light my way, and a hardcover edition of Toni Morrison's short story "Recitatif" in honor of my mother's determination to keep our shelves filled with words that nourished and inspired. That first morning, as I took in the line of people dedicating their entire Saturday to stepping over the threshold of a bookstore—into a new beginning—I wondered who among them would pick up a title that would become a portal; the book they'd walk into that would permit them to not simply feel at home but to find themselves.

# MALIK BOOKS

If you've never been to a bookstore with its own theme song, you've clearly never been to Malik Books. Stroll into either of the store's locations, in Los Angeles's Baldwin Hills Crenshaw Mall or the Westfield Culver City shopping center, and you may be lucky enough to catch Malik Muhammad—the man himself—singing along as the tune plays over the store's speaker system.

> Malik Books!
> To feed your intellect and free your
>     mind and succeed at the same time,
> Malik Books is what you need!

When Malik decided to open a bookstore, he embarked on a journey of re-education, the type of re-education sparked only by Black books.

"I didn't have knowledge of self," Malik recalls. "I had a degree from USC and didn't know anything about my history, about Black history.

"We have a degree in white supremacy. We have a degree in white education. We grew up in white America, learning everything under the sun about them, but the minute you try to read something about yourself . . ." Malik trails off as if to say, "Well, you know the rest."

To bolster his own knowledge, Malik ventured to Eso Won Books, where he built his personal library with titles such as J.A. Rogers's *Africa's Gift to America* and George James's *Stolen Legacy* being the bricks in a new foundation.

> Malik Books! They carry all the rarest
>     books!
> Malik Books! You know it's hard to find
>     these!

Now, at both Malik Books locations and online, you can find the books that illuminated Malik's past and sparked the idea to open his own Black bookstore. He wanted others to unearth hidden truths, just as he did.

When the first Malik Books launched in 1990, Black bookshops were opening like flowers in spring.

"I call it the Black Bookstore Revolution. It happened in the 1990s. We were everywhere. We gave an outlet to a lot of books and independent authors. We made authors like J.A. Rogers very popular simply because he wrote a story that nobody knew about. Most of the major

The man himself, Malik Muhammad.

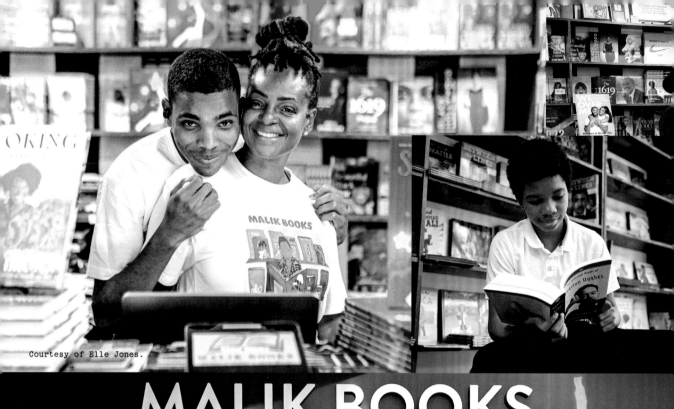

Courtesy of Elle Jones.

# MALIK BOOKS

Courtesy of Malik Muhammad.

Courtesy of Malik Muhammad.

Courtesy of Elle Jones.

Courtesy of Elle Jones.

Courtesy of Elle Jones.

Courtesy of Malik Muhammad.

bookstores didn't carry our books, and when they did, they only carried books that upheld the status quo. We were a space for people to find independent, self-published books. That's how the Revolution started."

The nineties' Black Bookstore Revolution paired with a political revolution—the 1992 L.A. Uprising, an eruption of Black Angelenos' rage toward the police's decades of unchecked brutality. The uprising claimed dozens of lives and hundreds of businesses. Los Angeles changed forever. Not even two years old, Malik Books stood tall amid the destruction.

"My first location was on Crenshaw and King, right across from the historic Baldwin Hills Crenshaw Mall. Macy's was robbed. All the stores on Crenshaw were broken into . . . except Malik Books. I was in my store, protecting it, making sure that it didn't get robbed or burned down, and it didn't."

After all the picketing and rallies, after the National Guard enforced curfews, after the TV town halls, megaphone monologues, and parking lot protests, Malik trudged through the trauma and triumph, and later, with the help of his wife and business partner, April Muhammad, he molded Malik Books into a community institution as iconic as Watts Towers.

"We do book drives and give out thousands of books to the kids, to the community," Malik says. "We give back to the community because the community gives to us, the community blesses us. We invest in our children because children are one hundred percent of our future."

```
And if you need a book for the kids to
   be inspired,
You know Malik Books is where the
   children's books reside!
```

Today, Malik Books touches people of all ages through its engaging programming and enthusiastic social media presence. Malik is camera-confident (the opposite of camera-shy). You can find short videos of him explaining the significance of Juneteenth; teaching kids about Mansa Musa; promoting the anthology *The Heart of a Black Man: Inspiring Stories of Triumph and Resilience* (which he contributed to); and sharing information about upcoming events. Spike Lee, Tabitha Brown, Omarion, and Terry Crews are a handful of the celebrities who come by Malik Books to sign copies of their latest books.

```
Malik has the books to help you with
   your wealth!
And if you're seeking guidance, books
   to help you find yourself!
```

Black books transformed Malik's life. Not only did they lead him to learn more about himself and his history—or give him a decades-long successful career and cement him as a fixture in Black Los Angeles—but they also bestowed him a new name.

You may assume Malik Books is named after Malik Muhammad, but Malik Muhammad is actually named after Malik Books.

"I no longer go by my birth name because I was reborn. I named the store Malik Books because *malik* means 'king' in Arabic. People would come into the store and say, 'Hey, Malik!' Everybody was calling me Malik and over the years, after decades, I realized that's my name. God wanted the people to give it to me. . . . The people baptized me in that name."

```
Malik Books!
```

# REPARATIONS CLUB

Jazzi McGilbert is an aptronym. Just as Usain Bolt sprints or Marijuana Pepsi Vandyck studies uncommon names, Jazzi radiates, well, jazz—the effortless cool, the improvisation, the creative freedom, the bluesy contemplation.

Though a bookish child who would rather read inside than play outside in her South Central L.A. neighborhood, owning a bookstore wasn't Jazzi's childhood dream. As a kid, Jazzi dreamed of working in fashion. Her mom gifted her Malorie Blackman's picture book *A New Dress for Maya* when she was little. The book, a story about fashion and mother-daughter relationships, foreshadowed Jazzi's early career in the fashion industry. But after her mom, Joyce, died, Jazzi was devastated. The loss repelled her from the fashion world's grind, where Jazzi felt uncredited for her contributions. She decided to dream differently.

"My priorities shifted in such a way that the only thing I could do was open the space. Or, you know, just fall into despair. Those were the options."

Nine months later, Reparations Club was born. "Rep Club was my grief baby," says Jazzi.

"[My mom] actually passed away from cancer, but I think the cancer was born of so much labor and so much stress. She didn't get to pursue anything she loved . . . community, creativity. She spent all her time in a cubicle and slaved away for a dream that wasn't her own. And so, the only thing that felt right was to not fall victim to that."

In her grief, Jazzi reflected on how her mother and countless other Black women give up their

dreams because they have to handle business and nurture family. She envisioned Rep Club as an avenue for escaping that pattern.

"A lot of people romanticize owning a bookstore, but there is a certain freedom in it," she says.

Freedom and reparations go hand in hand, so when Jazzi picked a name for her new venture, she made sure it was "very clear that this is a space that centers Black people and Black stories.

"You can't come here without having the idea of reparations on your mind, in your mouth. It was confrontational, and it did a lot of the initial legwork."

Entering Rep Club's imaginatively designed space feels like stepping onto a television set. Inside that unassuming gray building with the highlighter-yellow door lurks a spellbinding world of surprises.

Comfy U-shaped couches summon conversation and the occasional impromptu spades lesson. Waist-height custom-built bookshelves mesmerize customers with a mosaic of memoirs, graphic novels, poetry, and short stories. Pictures of beautiful Black faces conjure memories of days past.

"The magic is actually not the building itself," Jazzi insists. "It's the people, it's what we're pouring into any building."

Yet with Black people being squeezed out of Los Angeles, Jazzi and her team—Kayla and Tameka— know they might have to relocate the store due to L.A.'s gentrification.

"I think about us not being here, us in every sense of the word, like Rep Club, myself, the Black community in L.A. I want to make sure that the footprint is left behind," Jazzi says.

Borrowing from Toni Morrison, Jazzi sees Rep Club as a site of memory for the full range of Black L.A. Rapper Tyler, the Creator may remember bonding with Jazzi over the elusive *Black Ivy: A Revolt in Style*. Another regular may remember stopping in on his way to work to talk about adapting Donald Goines's urban fiction into screenplays. "Some houseless folks . . . know that they can come in and just sit and read a book, get a book for free," Jazzi says.

"I know that's the legacy. If we close tomorrow, people will be talking about the experiences they had at Rep Club, and that means a lot to me."

You can't come here without having the idea of reparations on your mind, in your mouth.

# A VOICE NOTE ABOUT MY EXPERIENCE
# AT REPARATIONS CLUB

## BY DEF SOUND

I find that some books find me, and what's been even more interesting is how close I've found myself with some of these authors.

So, I have this signed book by Fariha Róisín, and it started . . . actually wait—my name is Def Sound. That's my artist name. I'm from South Central L.A. From South Central to the world. I'm an artist, poet, MC, and educator, and this is my story about curiosity and appreciation and letting gratitude be your compass.

I was a student at University of California, Irvine, studying African American Studies with a focus on Black Critical Theory, and I was writing an essay on Afro-pessimism as a tool in the toolbox to explain specific suffering. The more specific you get with something, there's actually the possibility of more connectivity.

So, I'm in the back of the first Rep Club, Rep Club One, and I'm writing this essay, and there's so much ground to cover. I just had to be in my own zone. I was writing so ferociously that it was like the rest of the world disappeared. It was just me and this essay. As I'm in this essay, I don't know how late it's getting, so I get up and it's dark outside. And I'm like, "Yo, Jazzi, are y'all closed?" And she was like, "We're getting ready for a book club meeting. You can stay if you want." So I start setting up chairs. And then here comes Noname. Noname walks in the building. This is Noname's book club.

I sit in on the first session, and it's super generative. I have a good time, and I buy the book that they are reading for the next month, which is *How to Cure a Ghost* by Fariha Róisín. It's a book of poetry. It's beautiful and the design is so gorgeous. Their interior world is just as gorgeous and captivating. I underlined so many things in that book.

Fast-forward to the meetup and we were talking about Fariha and how vulnerable this work is. I used a lot of her pieces and applied them to my life. We were talking about moving through insecurity. I couldn't believe somebody who was this gifted had insecurities and then I looked them up, I followed Fariha online, and they started to reply to the things that I would say. I have a gift for appreciating people for the things that they would like to be appreciated for, and I think that's what resonated with Fariha. I became a paid subscriber on their Substack. So, I learned on one of their paid posts that they moved to L.A. I reach out and I'm like, "I would love to connect you with Rep Club." And at that time, I was just, like, an ambassador. I wasn't even working for Rep Club yet.

Fariha came to the space, signed some books. Then I'm talking with Fariha about what's next. And they have this forthcoming book called *Who Is Wellness For?* And they sent me an advanced copy. I was like, "Oh, my God, we are friends for real."

And I read the book as intently as I was writing that essay, which I got an A on, by the way. But I ended up really loving this book because it was also pretty academic. It was like if bell hooks had written it—and I don't say this lightly. Rest in Power, bell hooks. But it's this angle of personal and theoretical. Imagine if bell hooks had a critique for the modern-day wellness and Ayurvedic world. That's what this book is doing. And it's connecting it, of course, to white supremacy, patriarchy, capitalism, imperialism, that shit. So it's doing all the work of building bridges from ideas to theory to practice to lived experiences, because all theory is lived first.

Jazzi invites me to do the artist talk with Fariha at Rep Club. And it's very well-known that Fariha has IBS, so the first question I ask in the artist talk is, "Do you think that all great writers have IBS?" And it just opens her up for the rest of the night, like, we're able to really talk. And Fariha ends up telling me that was her favorite stop on the book tour. And it all began at Rep Club.

And then from there, Fariha is helping me edit my first book, called *Treat Me Like Water*. And so to go from staying a long time writing an essay at my favorite bookstore in L.A. to having this person edit my book . . . I mean . . . I'm speechless.

And it's a story that continues to write itself daily, but I am in deep thanks for the space that Rep Club is and remains. So, yeah, that's my story. I'm grateful to be a part of the anthology that is the space, the carrier bag, the container for so much culture at Rep Club. Much love to Jazzi and Tameka and Kayla and everybody—Sean too. That's it. That's my story. Oh, yeah, and Smalls— shout-out, Smalls.

Tameka (*left*) and Def Sound (*right*) play a jovial game of Connect Four.

ing parallel with the streams. There are
lso two bridges with gates, connecting
he inner and outer cities; two great gates
lso are near the mountain ranges, con-
ecting the outer city with the agricul-
ural lands outside the walls. The whole
rea is surrounded by extensive swamps,
rough which a passage known only to
he initiated runs, and forms an impa-
ble barrier to the ingress or egress of
rangers.

"But th...
he priests
he passag
eath the
irectly in
o the city.

"When
er hosts
hen did t
nning th
refuge,
ying with
thiopia's
s they tho
us mines

"Beneath
et of th
he rest is
n which
all gape
ght wher
ill living
y and m
hades wh
nd bewa
here abio
led crow
ble.

"This t
riest who
ird pyra
With th
art was
a to the
ear to Pr
The lette
as a hope

that gazed curiously at the straggling outlines.

"What do you make of it, Professor?"
asked Reuel, who with all his knowledge,
was at sea with the chart. "We have been
looking for mystery, and we seem to have
found it."

"What do I make of it? Why, that we
shall find the treasure and all return home
rich," replied the scholar testily.

"Rubbish!" snorted Charlie with fine
scorn.

"How about the sacred crocodile and
the serpents? My word, gentlemen, if
you find the back door key of the Sphinx'
head, there's a chance that a warm welcome is awaiting us."

Charlie's words met with approval
from the others, but the Professor and
Reuel said nothing. There was silence
for a time, each man drawing at his pipe
in silent meditation.

on the ruins of centuries. The weird
light increased, the shadows lengthened
and silence fell on the group, broken only
by the low tones of Professor Stone as he
told in broken sentences the story of ancient Ethiopia.

"For three thousand years the world
has been mainly indebted for its advancement to the Romans, Greeks, Hebrews,
Germans and Anglo-Saxons; but it was
otherwise in the first years. Babylon and
Egypt—Nimrod and Mizraim—both descendants of Ham—led the way, and

"We associate with the
the sciences of astronomy
and chronology. It was t
of the East to whom the
was revealed; they were
the Ethiopians. Eighty-
fore the birth of Abraham
known in history as 'Sh
subjugated the whole of
which they held in bon
three hundred years."

"It is said that Egyp

"What do you make of it, Profess
asked Reuel, who with all his knowledge
was at sea with the chart. "We have
looking for mystery, and we seem to
found it."

"What do I make of it? Why, that
shall find the treasure and all return hom
rich," replied the scholar testily.

"Rubbish!" snorted Charlie with fine

"How about the sacred crocodile and
the serpents? My word, gentlemen, if
you find the back door key of the Sphinx'
head, there's a chance that a warm welcome is awaiting us."

Charlie's words met with approval
from the others, but the Professor and
Reuel said nothing. There was silence
for a time, each man drawing at his pipe
in silent meditation.

ns he
an-

wor
Hebr
but
Bab
Mizraim
na kind in the
nowledge. The
Ethiopians, therefore, manifested great
superiority over all the nations among
whom they dwelt, and their name became
illustrious throughout Europe, Asia and
Africa.

"The father of this distinguished race
was Cush, the grandson of Noah, an Ethi-
opian.

"Old Chaldea, between the Euphrates

with the
ronomy
It was to
of the East to whom the
was revealed; they were
he Ethiopians. Eighty-
ore the birth of Abraham
known in history as 'Sh
subjugated the whole of
which they held in bond
three hundred years."

"It is said that Egyp
antedates that of Ethiopia,
el. "How do you say, Pr

"Nothing of the sort,
sort. I know that in co
with Ethiopia, one meets
ter denunciation from mos
ars. Science has done its
the race from Northern
evidence is with the Et
mistake not, the ruins of M
my words. Traditions

ng para
so two bridges with gates, connecting
e inner and outer cities; two great gates
so are near the mountain ranges, con-
cting the outer city with the agricul-
ural lands outside the walls. The whole
ea is surrounded by extensive swamps,
rough which a passage known only to
e initiated runs, and forms an impa-
ble barrier to the ingress or egress of
rangers.

"But there is another passage known to
e priests and used by them, and this is
e passage which the chart outlines be-
eath the third great pyramid, leading
rectly into the mines and giving access
e city.

"When Egypt rose in power and sent
er hosts against the mother country,
en did the priests close with skill and
nning this approach to the hidden city
refuge, where they finally retired, car-

# A MESSAGE FROM THE SISTAH SCIFI BOOK VENDING MACHINE

I could've sold anything—chips, soda, office supplies, heck, even pharmaceutical medicine, but Isis Asare chose me to distribute "a cauldron of all things Afrofuturism." I am the Sistah Scifi Book Vending Machine!

I bring a certain je ne sais quoi to the Black-owned coffee shops I call home. My magical blue and purple exterior summons curious readers to peek at the spellbinding stories I possess. Their eyes fix on Octavia E. Butler's *Patternmaster*, Janelle Monáe's *The Memory Librarian*, and Nalo Hopkinson's *Midnight Robber*. Little readers love me, too. *Mae Among the Stars* and *Sulwe* attract kids and kids at heart.

I feel like a celebrity. Every day, people dance up to me, fingers pressed on the glass, as they examine what I have to offer. "*Beep boop boop beep,*" I sing to them as they make their selections, some vlogging the entire experience. "I'm here at the Sistah Scifi Book Vending Machine in Oakland. A book vending machine! How cool is that?!"

I proudly pose for pictures with my adoring fans, wishing them well as they leave with a shiny new book in hand.

Some think of me as a mere contraption, but my mechanical innards do more than dispense literature. I'm helping Isis reach her goal of doubling the number of Black speculative fiction authors on the *New York Times* Best Seller list by 2030. I am the conduit to new and exciting worlds beyond the stars, yet on the page. Isis says my scifi reads open the humans up to different possibilities and ways of being. Explore your queerness through the *Lilith's Brood* trilogy. Discover your resolve to survive through N. K. Jemisin's *The Fifth Season*. Let these stories transform you.

You can always visit Sistah Scifi in cyberspace, but if you ever happen upon a bright blurple vending machine with Afrofuturism galore, stop by and say hi. For within me, there is a universe of imagination and wonder waiting to be explored.

# AN AFROFUTURIST COMING-OF-AGE STORY

## BY YTASHA L. WOMACK

My journey into Afrofuturism began at the union of the ethereal. When it wasn't in the form of dance and meter, it emerged as African philosophy and metaphysics—in the tangible hard matter of books. Books were my companions in my investigation of all things Black, global, and esoteric.

In my formative writing years, most of the raucous debates around what would be later dubbed as Afrofuturism took place with spirited men—us going toe to toe on a myriad of theories. However, the Black-owned bookstores that housed the works that prompted these discussions were, more often than not, manned, operated, or helmed by Black women. These stores cultivated community. As a result, I see reading less as a solo sojourn and more as a communal one.

Soul Source bookstore, located on James P. Brawley Drive, was my hall of wonder during my years at Clark Atlanta University. It was nestled on the same short block as a family-owned chicken spot. The bookstore also shared the block with a highly trafficked hair salon that stood across the street from the Atlanta University Center's Woodruff Library, a strip where students raced back and forth to class, flirted to no end, or yarned about Black people in times and spaces. The bookstore was one of the block's quieter offerings.

As I thought about African technologies, the realm of quantum theory as a cultural metaphor, and the relationship between antiquities and futures, I would often wander into Soul Source. The bookseller on site, a quiet woman who watched over us like a pleased godmother, also made the store's tasty sandwiches. My order? Chicken salad on a wheat roll with jalapeño peppers.

Today, as an Afrofuturist and consummate seeker, I believe the best bookstores are otherworldly paradoxes for scribes and wordsmiths. We run across underdiscussed histories and perspectives that enhance our worldviews, hopping from the physical world and the world within the page, forever reassembling ourselves. The process is sheer alchemy: a ritual of words, wonder, and transformation. Any bookstore worth its salt is a hovel of magic, each tome and pamphlet rich in spells of other times and the realm of subconscious matter. My favorite booksellers are, in fact, reincarnated lords of scrolls, shaped by duty, vision, and mission.

In the Afrofuturist play *stop. reset.* by Regina Taylor, the protagonist, a seasoned Black bookseller, argues with a youthful Elegba-like avatar about protecting Black books in a digital age. When I think of the heightened safeguards some booksellers apply to their collections, I think of those families tasked with protecting the ancient manuscripts from the Malian libraries of Timbuktu or those who risked life and limb to hide banned spiritual texts by the Gnostics. Much like the protector of Ethiopia's ark of the covenant, they are tasked with protecting knowledge. Yet even as they push back against possible threats to the texts under their stewardship, they are largely a welcoming bunch—ones whose enchanted engagement makes space for discovery. Such shamans of the scripted form take lesser-known knowledge and make it accessible to the masses, or at least those who are bold enough to wander into a room full of books. The best bookshops foster community. Such was the case with Soul Source.

Soul Source was an understated store, but it housed books like English translations of *The African Origin of Civilization: Myth or Reality* by Senegalese scholar Cheikh Anta Diop and *Signs and Symbols of Primordial Man: The Evolution of Religious Doctrines from the Eschatology of the Ancient Egyptians* by Albert Churchward.

Both books provided tools in making hard connections between how ancient ideas, when revealed and adopted, can shape new futures. Noted historian John Henrik Clarke would later write the foreword for *Signs and Symbols of Primordial Man*. Published in 1910 and written by a white author, this book was a rare find but was among the first in the twentieth-century Western world to respectfully write of ancient African, Indigenous, and Pacific Island cultures as sophisticated and aligned philosophically. It was my first deeper reading of Egyptian and Nubian iconography. Here, I first learned about the goddess Nut, the one who appeared in the downward-facing-dog yoga position, her body the curvature that contained the night sky.

"She must have fell off," my girlfriend, a fellow journalism major, said when I asked her if she'd ever heard of the Egyptian deity. "How does a goddess fall off?" I asked. This interaction sparked a deeper interest in what it meant when a diety's relationship to its populace changed, eventually giving rise to my graphic novel with Tanna Tucker, *Blak Kube*, which explored Egyptian deities of the night.

Shortly after college, I worked at Afrocentric Bookstore in downtown Chicago. Although I was married to Afrocentric's cash register, I found joy in their Black feminism section. Earlier, at Soul Source, I'd read my first works of Black feminist theory, including bell hooks's *Outlaw Culture: Resisting Representations* and Pearl Cleage's jaw-dropping *Mad at Miles: A Black Woman's Guide to Truth*. In Chicago, I purchased two books that anchored my relationship to being a Black woman writer: *Liliane* by Ntozake Shange and *Wounds of Passion* by bell hooks. These women were archivists of the heart and mind.

*Liliane* implored me to rethink literary form and how it could stretch time and space. Shange mixed dialogue between the main character and her therapist with the character's reflections in poetry and prose. In *Wounds of Passion*, hooks penned reflections that shaped her writing life, an undertaking she viewed as future-forward, etching herself into edicts of literary criticism.

My love of books and ideas eventually led me to work in a volunteer-run bookstore at Chicago's Christ Universal Temple, where I served on the board in the late aughts. It was one of the largest metaphysical bookstores in the region and reflected the incredible influence of Rev. Johnnie Colemon, whom I regard as an Afrofuturist. A modern-day mystic, metaphysician, and healer with a penchant for the bedazzled, she led the largest Black New Thought community in the nation, teaching the power of mind, positive thinking, and self-healing. She was once awarded for "guiding people into the twenty-first century." The store was managed by Rev. Gaylon McDowell with a staff of women volunteers, many of whom were retirees. The store sold thousands of Rev. Colemon's books, like *It Works if You Work It* and *Open Your Mind and Be Healed*, alongside an array of works in the Afrofuturist canon.

My experiences with Black bookstores are abundant. I spend much of my time perusing bookstores at large. When I launched *Black Panther: A Cultural Exploration*, a book on the Marvel comic phenom, I did so at The Silver Room, known as much for its stellar Black-authored book selection as for its culture fests and accessories. I taught my first screenwriting classes at Book Ink's bookstore, owned by bookseller Dr. Constance Shabazz in Chicago's Beverly neighborhood. I had some of my first book events at Azizi Books, owned by Kevin Roberts in Matteson, Illinois, and Hue-Man Bookstore in Harlem. I went to my first poetry reading at the Shrine of the Black Madonna in Atlanta and wielded the art of debate for entry when purchasing books from Underground Bookstore in Chicago. I've participated in events hosted by Sistah Scifi, who helms a hybrid Afrofuturism/Indigenous futures bookstore model. I can also find select works and banter at the Occult Bookstore, now under Black ownership.

Some of these bookstores are no longer standing, but like any hovel of spell-tingling words, their impact abounds—existing much like an Akashic record of the ether. When I wrote *Afrofuturism: The World of Black Sci Fi & Fantasy Culture*, I thought of it as a book that my spacetime debating friends in the Atlanta University Center would uncover as a hidden jewel, one with an array of deep readings and warmth, one much like Soul Source. While Soul Source is no longer in the physical, it remains an archive of heart and mind—one I can still envision plucking books from.

# THIRD EYE BOOKS AND GIFTS

*"It shall not be lawful for any Negro or mulatto to enter into, or reside" in Oregon.
It would be "highly dangerous to allow free Negroes and mulattoes to reside in the
Territory, or to intermix with Indians, instilling into their minds feelings of
hostility toward the white race." Former slaves who refused to leave Oregon would
be publicly flogged with "not less than 20 nor more than 39 stripes."*

—Oregon Black Exclusion Laws

With a Black population of less than 3 percent, Oregon's 1800s-era Black Exclusion Laws still haunt the state like a Confederate ghost. Michelle Lewis and Charles Hannah's Third Eye Books and Gifts in Portland is an anomaly that the state's antebellum settlers never saw coming.

Growing up in Oregon, Charles noticed that his white teachers mistaught Black literature. He recounts a high school English teacher explaining the moral of Toni Morrison's *The Bluest Eye* as "Blue eyes are the best, and that's what you should strive towards."

Now older and more conscious, Charles recognizes the teacher's ulterior motives. Charles and Michelle see Third Eye's offerings as a counterpoint to the negative narrative Black children and adults learn about themselves and their history.

Subverting the legacy of Oregon's white settlers, Third Eye represents elevated consciousness, and Michelle and Charles hope that the books their customers encounter at Third Eye Books and Gifts "elevate them for their highest purpose, their greatest good for themselves, their community, family, and humanity."

Courtesy of
Jason Hill.

Asha Grant, the owner of Inglewood's The Salt Eaters Bookshop.

# THE SALT EATERS BOOKSHOP

"Are you sure, sweetheart, that you want to be well?"

This sentence opens Toni Cade Bambara's novel *The Salt Eaters*. In it, Minnie Ransom poses this bold and courageous question, one that Asha Grant, the owner of Inglewood's The Salt Eaters Bookshop, set out to answer in the affirmative.

*The Salt Eaters* is a surging, ascendant novel that braids themes of healing, spirituality, and community into the story of Velma Henry, a Black woman seeking inner renewal and liberation after a failed suicide attempt. The store, like its narrative namesake, aims to whisk readers from hurt to revelation, from revelation to reinvention, and from reinvention to life anew.

"When you first start reading the book, Velma's in an incredibly vulnerable position and is literally being witnessed and held by members of her community," Asha tells me.

As beautiful as the novel is, *The Salt Eaters* is more than just a literary inspiration for Asha; it's her store's origin story.

This idea of "being witnessed and held by" animated Asha's vision of a true neighborhood bookstore from the beginning—and her community in Inglewood banded together to make it happen.

A commercial real estate broker helped negotiate the rent, reading through contracts and advocating for tenant protections. Volunteers came every day for two weeks straight to build, paint, and clean. A TV set designer sourced furniture and artwork. An interior designer optimized the store's flow. The store's inception was like listening to a Beyoncé track compelling each person to "get in formation."

"We would all eat lunch together every day in the store and literally talk about how exciting it's gonna be," Asha remembers.

But it wasn't just the locals who made sure The Salt Eaters Bookshop could serve as what Asha calls "a resting ground. A brave space. A Black place." Around 1,800 people donated over $85,000 for the shop's start-up costs.

The result? A loving and inviting bookshop dedicated to prioritizing books, comics, and zines by and about Black women, girls, femmes, and nonbinary folks. An altar honoring Asha's grandma greets visitors as they enter. The walls proudly display tapestries of Pam Grier and Beyoncé. Above the children's section lives a painting of Latasha Harlins, the Black teenager whose murder helped spark the 1992 L.A. Uprising. Latasha's steady gaze watches over the kids as they read about mermaids, natural hair, and family dinners.

The Salt Eaters' book collection includes the classics alongside books on spirituality, sexuality, and mother-daughter relationships, some of which are banned. Asha, a former teacher, takes pride in selling contraband literature.

"Book bans are just another reason why Black bookstores are so essential. We can't rely on systems to validate us or tell us that our stories are important. I feel even more empowered as a Black

Antwaun SARGENT

bookstore owner to be able to push narratives that others are trying to squash."

Like many L.A. natives, Asha is concerned about being pushed out of the city. "Gentrification is very real and it's very violent in Inglewood. I'm constantly thinking about and trying to figure out how we're going to stay afloat."

When the shop ran into financial issues, Asha hesitated to ask for help again. "It was like a rock-bottom moment. I felt like I couldn't ask for support two times."

But with big shop expenses and rent coming up, Asha and her team felt like they had no other choice, so they decided to throw a rent party. The community showed up and showed out, voguing, twerking, and two-stepping to sustain The Salt Eaters Bookshop and honor *The Salt Eaters* book.

OPPOSITE: A Beyoncé-themed rent party at The Salt Eaters Bookshop. Photos courtesy of Jordan Nakamura.

Book Club

HEADQUARTERS · RADICAL HOOD LIBRARY

Fatimah Warner outside of the
Radical Hood Library in Los Angeles.

An Ethic of Liberation

# RADICAL HOOD LIBRARY

Walking into the Radical Hood Library in Los Angeles feels like falling deep down a rabbit hole filled with secrets, solutions, and subversions. Black books and banned books trim the ample sloping shelves. Here, Dewey's decimal system has been overthrown. A new, more equitable division of readings reigns. Topics like family, labor, feminism, and disability justice order the stacks. This design deploys a gentle gravity. One step in teases. Two steps tug. Three steps, and the full sweep of literary liberation lining the walls whisks you away.

"We made it so you get progressively more radical as you come in," says Natalie Matos, the library's program manager. "The poetry and the novels are in the front and then memoirs. The kids' books are in the front and then books on gender, slavery, political prisoners. It gets a little bit more radical as you go."

It's a journey so many readers relate to.

Over the last decade, a generation has been prodded by more and more senseless arrests, more and more hung juries, and more and more live-streamed killings: *the less justice rendered, the more questions raised, and the more readers became revolutionaries*. The Radical Hood Library emerged from this reality.

In this Black Lives Matter era, patrons' prose has shifted along with their politics. They've swapped *Dreams from My Father* for *Freedom Dreams*, swapped interrogating the police for interrogating the society that enables them. The Radical Hood Library is built for a generation of writers, readers, thinkers, artists, and activists seeking answers, the Black radical tradition acting as their tutor.

The Library carries Noname Book Club's monthly picks. From Denver to Detroit, from Boston to Birmingham, book club members convene and converse about works such as Albert Woodfox's *Solitary*, Angela Davis's *Are Prisons Obsolete?*, Derecka Purnell's *Becoming Abolitionists*, and Mumia Abu-Jamal's *Live from Death Row*.

If this milieu is highly critical of the carceral state, it is in part because it was fostered inside of that state's vicious maw. "We operate in the legacy of Martin Sostre and other revolutionaries who have fought for access to radical text while incarcerated," the collective proclaims on its website. Intellectuals and activists like George Jackson, Malcolm X, and Martin Sostre serve as the intellectual forerunners to today's modern social justice movements and the Radical Hood Library itself. These are people whose political radicalization and education happened through prison reading and who have come to shape some of the most progressive and thought-provoking ideas driving Black publishing and politics today.

And while the namesake of Noname Book Club and Radical Hood Library collective member Fatimah Warner (aka Noname) has graced Coachella's stage and *Vanity Fair*'s pages, her presence is also felt by society's most marginalized—her incarcerated comrades.

"Incarcerated people have disappeared from our communities, so I think no matter how much of an abolitionist you see yourself as, you become even more of an abolitionist when you have regular conversations with [incarcerated] people," says Matos.

Since 2020, the prison program has sent books to incarcerated folks so they, too, can participate in the conversations happening on the outside. The Radical Hood Library extends these literary lifelines, helping the incarcerated understand the systems that oppress them. The library learns from political prisoners as political prisoners learn from the library.

Though decidedly *not* a bookstore, the Radical Hood Library expounds upon the Black literary tradition of Black bookstores past. Just as the National Memorial African Bookstore buoyed Malcolm X, just as Martin Sostre's Afro-Asian Bookshop taught Buffalo the language of resistance, just as Paul Coates's The Black Book brought progressive Afrocentric literature to those behind bars, the Radical Hood Library centers the community—all of the community—in an ethic of liberation.

# BODIES IN THE BOOKS

Black authors and booksellers finally got their piece of the pie just to find the pie was cut from pieces of them.

### BY AARON ROSS COLEMAN

Among the Black literati, perhaps no character ranks more loathsome than the Black sellout, the Afro-opportunist, those who, as the rapper J. Cole quipped, "profit off of racial stress" and get "so rich, they prolly wish we stay oppressed."

Nearly a hundred years ago, novelist George Schuyler sketched them this way: "They were never so happy and excited as when a Negro was barred from a theater or fried to a crisp. Then they would leap for telephones, grab telegraph pads, and yell for stenographers; smiling through their simulated indignation at the spectacle of another reason for their continued existence and appeals for funds." More recently, writer Paul Beatty fictionalized these hucksters through a Black mortician who travels to inner-city schools asking if the students "could kill a few more niggers this week because his twins were starting college in the fall."

Just as novelists amuse with sellouts, so do sellouts serve as scholars' muse. Liberal arts professor Eddie Glaude Jr. knocks them as the Black brokers "of guilt and shame." Historian Keeanga-Yamahtta Taylor pans them as "Black Faces in High Places." Sociologist Robert Allen lambastes them as the supplicants of "the white corporate elite." Yet for all the Black books that decry how people profiteer Black pain, perhaps the best-kept secret among the book writers is that we share in these profits as well. We, the scribblers and scribes, the collectors and critics, the book publishers and booksellers, know the same thing that the peddler hawking "Rest In Power" t-shirts the day after a lynching knows: that the streets will fill with righteous anger, that the police won't face accountability, and that we are about to sell a shit ton of merch.

One need not be an economist to see how Black murders move our markets, how the open caskets create the grand openings, how the blood brings the boom. In the Black Lives Matter era, lynchings feed our ravenous racial uplift. No-knock warrants have turned into opportunities knocking for Black vendors. Officers' shots sound the starting gun in the mad dash to print Black totes, pour Black candles, and bring the barge of Black businesses back into the black. And, bizarre as it is to watch these frenetic upstarts giddily plastering Black martyrs' faces on bank cards, soda bottles, and sweatshirts, it feels far stranger to see those of us who write and sell treatises against profiting off Black pain bundle our critiques and place them in the sales basket alongside the marked-up kente cloth and curling creams. How is it we claim righteousness when we, too, racketeer? How can we say we're gadflies when we, too, act like vultures? Our contradictions confound us. They call to mind the writing of the Black Arts Movement poet Etheridge Knight, whose 1973 "MEMO #9" ridicules a Black literary elite resembling its own parodies' punchlines:

```
doze o blk / capitalists
ain't shit
the blk / poet sung,
as he hustled his books
for 10.95.
```

Today, perhaps no writer unpacks the moral vertigo more honestly and nimbly than the *New York Times* best-selling author Mychal Denzel Smith. In *Harper's*, Smith wrote of the wrenching relationship between "Black suffering" and personal ambition, between Black life's fall and Black literature's rise. In his essay, Smith recounted how new murders pried open new markets, how after Trayvon Martin's killing, it became impossible to distinguish between death knells and Wall Street's opening bells.

"I found that each time there was a killing or a violent arrest caught on video, or a new report on police violence, white editors asked if I would be interested in writing about it for their publications with majority-white audiences," Smith explained, noting how the autopsy articles offered more than he had ever been paid. Reflecting on this exchange, he confessed that . . . "I feel as though I've built a career by capitalizing on Black pain—exploiting that of others and monetizing my own."

Soon, this guilt that plagued Black authors like Smith plagued Black booksellers. For after George Floyd was killed, Black bookstores made their own killing. The summer of 2020 was a season of lynchings, and the more the blood shed, the more the books sold. This morbid bull market prompted a series of articles tracing the divergence between Black literature and Black life. NPR and NBC's headlines dubbed the expansion as "bittersweet." Yet for bookstore owners, the taste flooded as something more surreal, more sordid. Shopkeepers recalled blood and money sloshing into a mind-warping, morality-bending cocktail. Their quotes lurched wildly, describing the experience at once as a holiday, as a blessing from above, and as a nightmare where raging screams turn to revenue streams. "I was first [thinking] it's like Christmas and we're not prepared," one bookseller told NPR. "And [then] I thought, no, I don't want to compare this to Christmas, because you hear [George Floyd] moaning and yelling on the ground." Talking to NBC, another book vendor echoed Smith's feeling of "capitalizing on Black pain," noting the way that "it can feel like you're profiting off of tragedy."

Yet profiting off of tragedy reigns as the blueprint far beyond the Black book business. Black tragedy is America's founding principle, our economic theory, our means of production. It is why Martin Luther King Jr. writes of New England's construction as an alchemy turning Black blood into cement, why Lerone Bennett Jr. writes of the Old South's rise as morphing Black screams into cotton, why Ta-Nehisi Coates writes of the suburbs' creation as transmuting Black bones into homes. Our writers reveal what our markets hide: that Black blood pumps as capitalism's lifeblood. And while this insight is benign enough as a subtext of American letters, it becomes dangerous when it is the text of American life. Thus during periods of intense Black protest, when consciousness rises, when America's painful profits become too apparent, when police killings over twenty-dollar bills become too visible, when segregation's revenues become too pronounced, the Black uprisings threaten to uproot our economic foundations. And that's when America responds, proffering its devil's bargain—a deal not to stop Black pain but to deal Blacks into the pain's profits, not to cease piling up our bodies but to cut us into their spoils, not to end our murders but to buy our memoirs, to feed us back to ourselves.

And sadly, so, so many of us are famished.

For those with rumbling stomachs, for us artists and sellers starved by Amazon, by consolidation, by shrinking attention spans, it's a struggle to not swallow the cured bodies to cure our hunger. Those bodies—beaten, battered, and marinated in blood money—seize our senses. It's the money that makes the mirage, that makes us confuse murder and moaning with Christmas morning. It's the money that salts the bitter until it becomes the "bittersweet." Money will make a writer salivate for Negroes "fried to a crisp," will bamboozle a bookseller into confusing a lynching for lunch.

But of course we, of all people, know exactly how all this works. We who sell Black books cannot purport to be ignorant of their truth. It is impossible to sell James Baldwin's memoirs, and Angela Davis's biographies, and Langston Hughes's stories, then pretend not to know *The Ways of White Folks*. It is untenable to market the histories of slavery, and segregation, and sharecropping, then purport not to know how America starves us to coerce us. How can we feign shock to the way they corrupt us when *Elite Capture* is on our shelves? How can we plead ignorance to the ways they consume us when *The Delectable Negro* is in our hands? Unless we purport to be illiterate bibliophiles, unless one claims to be more a "literary hustler than a literary scholar"—what novelist Mat Johnson calls a "book pimp"—it is impossible to trade in knowledge and ignorance at once. And it is our knowledge—Black knowledge—that eats away at us. For we know the game; our books teach us the rules.

We know the quid pro quo that white elites put on the table during times of racial upheaval. We know they promise our escape from poverty if we promise them escape from prosecution. We know that they'll admit us into their ranks if they don't have to admit to their crimes. We know that they will pay us to appease them. Yet we know perhaps more than anything else that their white guilt expires like a fruit fly, and their offers of fame, security, and escape last only as long as our protests do. Thus when officers fire shots, our race starts.

And we hustle like hell.

This is how trap artists get trapped into putting down Black protesters, how authors get turned into apologists, how bookstores become money launderers. This is how they wedge us into their pockets. And for those who have not yet been captured, they fear they will be, that they, too, will be swept up in the disaster-driven demands for cheap absolution and entertainment. They fear that they, too, will be swallowed up by the country that so eagerly swallows their Black kids, cousins, parents, and lovers. Arguably this is the most insidious part of the Faustian bargain offered to Black artists, thinkers, and entrepreneurs. For while white corporate America presents its partnership as a meal ticket, it is, in fact, yet another invitation to be eaten. It is the sap on a Venus flytrap, the nectar on a pitcher plant. It is an inverted buffet, where the more you consume, the more they consume you.

After publishing *Between the World and Me*, his searing memoir of police murder, Coates described being swallowed into this corrosive world—into a world eager to convert Black antagonists into allies. "I almost lost my mind," Coates recalled, writing for the *Atlantic*. "The incentives toward a grand ego were ever present," he mused. The "life of lectures, visiting-writer gigs, galas, prize committees" tugged at him like quicksand. The lure of "random swag, the green Air Force Ones, the blue joggers" assaulted his sense of "Baltimore ordinariness." The enticement of "movie stars, rappers, and ballplayers" threatened to erode his sense of resolve.

"The terrible thing about that small fame was how it undressed me," Coates recalled, "stripped me of self-illusion, and showed how easily I could be swept away, how part of me wanted to be swept away, and even if no one ever saw it, even if I never acted on it, I now knew it."

Pulling himself out of the thicket, trying to maintain integrity amid seduction, Coates framed his fight in existential terms. "Who are you if, even as you do good, you feel the desire to do evil?" he asked his readers. "How do you defy a power that insists on claiming you?" he beckoned in a later memoir. These questions on defying a power that insists on claiming you, on escaping a system that insists on consuming you, burn as the central queries for Black authors and Black booksellers today.

For we now stand at an impasse. Read our articles, our memoirs, our interviews, our group chats, and you will discover a palpable sense of guilt floats among us, among our generation of Black storytellers and storysellers. For while we have been rewarded for our books, we've also felt corrupted by them.

We rose to prominence reporting and publicizing racism's horrors. We followed the dominant strain in Black literary thinking that argued exposing the public to Black violence would stir it into compassion. Yet over a decade into the Movement for Black Lives, over a decade into the mass circulation of tales of Black slaughter, it remains an open question if it is possible to subvert our murderous nation with narratives of our murders, if it is possible to reform cannibals with tales of cannibalism. For while Americans do blanch at the notion of their nation nourished by eating flesh, Americans also proudly proclaim ours is "a dog-eat-dog world," that life is "eat or be eaten," and "that you are either at the table or on the menu." Under these circumstances, writing to subvert America with Black violence often feels like trying to subvert Willy Wonka with chocolate, like trying to subvert Heinz with ketchup.

Worse still, beyond the questions of persuasion loom concerns of our coercion. For if it is hard to see the substantive changes in society based on our literature, it is easier to see the change in lifestyles among the more lavish among us: the houses bought, the book deals signed, the new stores opened, the fellowships granted, the accoutrements of a burgeoning Black bourgeoisie, a new generation of Black brokers, who, as Glaude notes, excel at parlaying racism "into a lot of money and gain a lot of influence for themselves . . . but do little for Black democratic life."

This is what they do to us. They grant us awards telling us how much we've changed them as they stay the same. They tell us that we're subversive as they subvert us. They sell out our book events as they turn us into sellouts. For however indirectly, we have now come to profit off of racial violence in a nation erected by it, and we sense it corrupting us. We sense that in vesting our Black book business in the lynching business, we have become a subsidiary of America's blood trade—a shareholder watching our stocks rise as the ropes do.

Capitalism's greatest trick, argues essayist Jason England, is its ability to "consume your culture, no matter how subversive, and sell it back to you at a higher cost, as a box containing nothing." Just as Whole Foods grew out of a vegetarian commune movement only to sell out to a despotic Amazon, our Black book movement rooted in the Freedom Struggle now finds itself drowning under corporate co-option. Today a monopolistic literary industry has discovered how to subvert Ida B. Wells's radical legacy, and has commodified her concept of post-lynching literature into a cottage industry.

Always controversial, the Black postmortem publishing exposing American racism's brutality once served as a kind of negative good. For while it did recirculate grotesque images of Black death for profit, it also shocked and scared America into a compassion and solidified Black consciousness. But as the number of these titles proliferates, as the revenue from these books consolidates, it's an open question if this business model of postmortem lynching literature has run its course. It is an open question if those of us in the Black book trade have not overlearned the lesson of publishing Emmett Till's open casket—a practice that, as the historian Brenna Wynn Greer reminds us, was always more "capitalistic than moralistic or altruistic." For today, the postmortem marketing has become so commonplace, so crucial to Black publishers, writers, and booksellers, that when there are no lynchings to publicize and promote our books, it seems that our industries shrink and our sales wilt. How are we to escape our destruction if we, too, have become addicted to it?

Our answer to a corrupting industry cannot be to walk away, to stop writing Black books, or to stop building communities around them. Anyone who has loved Black literature knows that it's too important, too transcendent, to leave behind. Anyone who has been in a Black bookstore knows that these communities are too special and unique to simply let go of.

Just because the supply chain is shot doesn't mean that the product is. The question for us isn't whether we stop writing or selling books—the questions are: How do we get the blood off the pages, how do we get the bodies out of the books, how do we build a free and thriving Black book industry that serves us without swallowing us? To this end, the secrets of Black books' salvation might lie in the books themselves.

Since our days in bondage, Black literature's central contention has been that one need not build a country out of cannibalism, that there is no need for a blood sacrifice at the center of economic life, that one could grow cotton without slaves, reap fruits without whips, build cities without cuffs. For centuries, Black folks have fought to bring this world forth. On farms and foundries, they rejected cannibalism for cooperation, murder for mutualism, the lash for love. Read Black history, and you will discover how they did it, how they forged supply chains with no shackles, how they reimagined prosperity without pain.

For Black communities, nonviolence worked not only as a means of protest but as a means of production. During the Civil Rights era, the same folks that fought to remove brutality from politics sought to strain it out of economics, too. All across the country, Black activists created novel bookstores that supplanted Jim Crow in the same way that Black cooperative farms supplanted sharecropping's spurs in the South. Bookstores like Drum and Spear, Liberation, and Ujamaa Kitabu tapped into the soul of the Freedom Struggle. They pulled from Black economic theories of communalism. They innovated on early models like the antebellum abolitionist bazaars, which sold literature condemning slavery. They experimented with collective, democratic forms of ownership and management. They played with creative forms of culturally relevant marketing. And in the sum of their efforts, they discovered ways to sell Black books without bloodink.

Of course, much like today's bookstores, these Black bookshops of the 1960s and 1970s were forced to reckon with incredible anti-Black violence, but that violence did not define them. Their business models rested not on the productive powers of murder but on the movement's productive potential, not on lynching but on love. For today's booksellers and writers, beleaguered by profiteering and corruption, the paradigm of activist stores of the Black Power era offers one path forward. In their practices, there is a blueprint for how to bind our books with something other than skin and how to build their spines out of something other than bones.

Today, in fits and starts, one can see a new generation of Black bookstores continuing this mission. These bookshops' proprietors aren't among those "whose dreams have been utterly co-opted by the marketplace," as Robin D.G. Kelley writes—those who believe "that 'getting paid' and living ostentatiously was the goal of the Black freedom movement." Take a peek inside The Salt Eaters Bookshop's crafting of a resting ground for Black women and gender-expansive people, study For Keeps Books' free provision of rare titles for public consumption, visit yes, please books' regenerative readings on feminism and socialism, stop in bookshops all around the country; one can see the vision for something different—the blueprints of a twenty-first-century "radical democratic public culture," the outlines of a literary ecosystem where the demand for our books is decoupled from the destruction of our bodies.

What today's community-minded Black bookstores offer, at their best, is an experimental alternative to the vapid corporate culture that so many of us feel corroding us and our literature. These stores serve as lived, embodied havens for Black democratic life: their programming, their ethics, their organizations, their ideas, their debates, their education, their free exchange, their opposition to oppression, their dedication to liberation—all fuse to make these shops places where you can not only buy *Freedom Dreams* but you can also live them. Their walls, wrapped in the Black canon's cipher, surround us in our histories, centering us in a dialogue with our ancestors. These spaces bend time; to quote Sonia Sanchez, they "cut the century in half" and allow us to tap into the free Black spaces of the past, into the mutual-aid societies, into the union-cooperatives, into the earliest Black bookstores, and to understand that what freed them can free us, to understand that in community lies our escape from cannibalism.

Baldwin & Co. in New Orleans, Louisiana.

# FURTHER EXPLORATION

## More Black Bookstores to Visit

**ARIZONA**

Grassrootz Bookstore

**CALIFORNIA**

Octavia's Bookshelf
Protagonist Black
Shades of Afrika Bookstore
Underground Books

**CONNECTICUT**

Bingham's Books & Culture
Kindred Thoughts Bookstore

**DELAWARE**

Books & Bagels
MeJah Books, Inc.

**FLORIDA**

Best Richardson African
    Diaspora Literature &
    Culture Museum
Black English Bookstore
Dare Books
Essence of Knowledge Urban
    Bookstore

**GEORGIA**

Black Dot Cultural Center
Nubian Bookstore
A Small Place Books

**ILLINOIS**

AfriWare Books Co.
Call & Response
Underground Bookstore

**INDIANA**

Akoma Books

Beyond Barcodes Bookstore
Black Worldschoolers Mobile
    Bookstore
Ujamaa Community Bookstore

**LOUISIANA**

Umoja Books and Products

**MARYLAND**

Urban Reads Bookstore
Vinyl and Pages
Wisdom Book Center

**MASSACHUSETTS**

Footprints Bookshop
Frugal Bookstore
Print Ain't Dead

**MICHIGAN**

Black Stone Bookstore &
    Cultural Center
Comma Bookstore & Social
    Hub
Detroit Book City

**MISSOURI**

BLK + BROWN.
EyeSeeMe African American
    Children's Bookstore
The Noir Bookshop
Willa's Books and Vinyl

**NEBRASKA**

Aframerican Book Store

**NEVADA**

The Analog Dope Store
R.D. Talley Books Publishing

**NEW JERSEY**

La Unique African American
    Bookstore & Cultural Center
Source of Knowledge
    Bookstore

**NEW YORK**

Bronx Bound Books
Café con Libros
The Lit. Bar
Sister's Uptown Bookstore
Zawadi Books

**NORTH CAROLINA**

The Next Chapter Books & Art
Rofhiwa Book Café
Urban Reader Bookstore

**OHIO**

Elizabeth's Bookshop &
    Writing Centre
ThirdSpace Reading Room
Ujamaa Book Store

**OKLAHOMA**

Fulton Street Coffee & Books
Nappy Roots Books

**PENNSYLVANIA**

The Black Reserve Bookstore
A Concrete Rose

**TENNESSEE**

Alkebu-Lan Images
Allgood's Used Books and
    Coffee
The Bottom
Cafe Noir

**TEXAS**

BLACKLIT
Black Pearl Books
Class Bookstore
The Dock Bookshop
Pan-African Connection
  Bookstore and Resource
  Center

**VIRGINIA**

Harambee Books & Artworks
House of Consciousness
Positive Vibes
Resist Booksellers

**WASHINGTON**

LOVING ROOM: diaspora
  books + salon

**ONLINE**

AALBC (The African American
  Literature Book Club)
African American Images
  Bookstore
African Bookstore
Aya Coffee + Books
BLK & Company
The Book Bar
Cultured Books

Enda's BOOKtique
Gold Mouf Book Club
The Key Bookstore
Loc'd and Lit
Moore Books
Niche Book Bar
Nkiru Books
Pyramid Books
Rooted MKE
Uhuru Bookstore

Timbuktu: The Black Peoples Bookstore

February is Black Liberation Month

Peoples College Press

# More Black Bookstores Throughout History

**ALABAMA**

Black Classics Books & Gifts
Know Thyself Bookstore
Root & Wings: A Cultural
  Bookplace

**CALIFORNIA**

African Book Mart
The More Bookstore
New Day Bookstore
Phenix Information Center

**COLORADO**

Sundiata Bookstore

**CONNECTICUT**

Assegai Books
New World Bookstore

**DELAWARE**

Haneef's Bookstore

**FLORIDA**

Afro-In Books N' Things

Books for Thought
Montsho Books
Nefertiti Books & Gifts
Ujamaa African Book Store

**GEORGIA**

Cobb Books
Ka'Lors Book Store
Soul Source Bookstore
Timbuktu Market of New Africa

**ILLINOIS**

African-American Book Center
African-American Bookstore
African Caribbean Bookstore
A.J. Williams Bookstore
Azizi Books
Black Bookstore
Books & Stuff
Ellis Book Store
Eye on the Prize African
  American Bookstore &
  Cultural Learning Center
Freedom Found Books
House of Knowledge Bookstore

Timbuktu: The Black People's
  Bookstore

**INDIANA**

The Afro American Bookstore
Alkebu-Lan Images

**KANSAS**

X-pression Bookstore

**KENTUCKY**

Black Market Bookstore
Booklink

**LOUISIANA**

Afro-American Book Stop

**MARYLAND**

Sibanye Inc.

**MASSACHUSETTS**

Afro-American Book Source

## MICHIGAN

Apple Book Center

East and West Bookshoppe

## MISSOURI

Afrocentric Books & Café

## NEVADA

Zaliwa Creations

## NEW JERSEY

La Unique African-American
    Books & Cultural Center

Esteem Books

In Progress

Kujichagulia Bookstore

Mart 247

Nile Valley Books

Nyumba ya Ujamaa

OurStory Books

## NEW YORK

AfroAmerican Book Center

Black Mind Book Boutique

The Blyden Bookstore

Books & Things

Brownstone Books

Freedom Bookstore

Indigo Café and Books

Kitabu Kingdom

Mood Makers Books

Ms. Print

Richardson Books

Written Word Book Store

## NORTH CAROLINA

Ebony Bookstore

Freedom Bookstore

The Know Bookstore

Special Occasions

## OHIO

The Ghetto Bookstore

## OREGON

Reflections Coffee and
    Bookstore

Talking Drum Bookstore

## PENNSYLVANIA

Basic Black Books

Horizon Books

Know Thyself Bookstore and
    Cultural Development
    Center

Liguorius Books

Marcus Garvey's Bookstore

## SOUTH CAROLINA

Doretha's African-American
    Books & Gifts

## TEXAS

Afro Awakenings

Amistad Book Place

Black Bookworm

Folktales

Jokae's African American Books
    and Custom Framing

Nu World of Books

## VIRGINIA

Black Butterfly

## WASHINGTON

Blackbird Books

Parable

## WASHINGTON, D.C.

House of Khamit

Sisterspace and Books

Ujamaa Bookstore & African
    Shop

## WISCONSIN

Cultural Connection Bookstore

Positive Image Books & Gifts

The Reader's Choice

The AfroAmerican Book Center's children's section. Courtesy of Augusta Mann.

# Chapter 1: The Northeast

### D. RUGGLES BOOKS

Blight, David W. *Frederick Douglass: Prophet of Freedom.* New York: Simon & Schuster, 2018.

"David Ruggles (American National Biography)." House Divided: The Civil War Research Engine at Dickinson College. https://hd.housedivided .dickinson.edu/node/19403.

Douglass, Frederick. "What I Found at The Northampton Association (1895)" in *The Frederick Douglass Papers: Series Four: Journalism and Other Writings, Volume 1.* Edited by John R. Kaufman-McKivigan. New Haven: Yale University Press, 2022, 621–31.

Mann, Augusta. *Black Bookstores in Harlem and the Men and Women Who Established Them: 1915–1982.* Chapter 1.

Pasquale, Andrew. "David Ruggles." David Ruggles Center for History and Education. https://davidrugglescenter .org/david-ruggles.

### YOUNG'S BOOK EXCHANGE

"Advertisement 7—no Title." *Outlook (1893–1924),* June 25, 1919, 349.

Allen, Cleveland G. "New York City Has Book Exchange: Rev. W. P. Hayes Celebrates His Fourth Anniversary as Pastor of Church—R. W. Thompson Via Its Gotham." *The Chicago Defender (Big Weekend Edition) (1905–1966),* May 29, 1915, 5.

"George Young Dead; Had Book Exchange: Former Pullman Porter Owned Volumes on Negro—Active for Betterment of Race." *New York Times (1923–),* April 19, 1935, 21.

"Hoover Thanks Young for Douglass Volume." *Amsterdam News (1922–1938),* June 4, 1930.

Mann, Augusta. *Black Bookstores in Harlem and the Men and Women Who Established Them: 1915–1982.*

"Pullman Porter Now a Bookseller." *New York Evening Post,* October 12, 1921.

"Rare Books for Negroes." *New York Times (1857–1922),* November 13, 1921.

### THE SCHOMBURG SHOP AT THE SCHOMBURG CENTER FOR RESEARCH IN BLACK CULTURE

"About the Schomburg Center for Research in Black Culture." The New York Public Library. https://www.nypl .org/about/locations/schomburg.

Mann, Augusta. *Black Bookstores in Harlem and the Men and Women Who Established Them: 1915–1982.*

Masiki, Trent. "The Afroethnic Impulse and Renewal: African American Transculturations in Afro-Latino Bildung Narratives, 1961 to 2013." Doctoral Dissertations, 2017, 925.

Mixon, Virginia. Interview by Katie Mitchell, March 30, 2023, video.

"The Negro Digs Up His Past." Schomburg Center for Research in Black Culture, Manuscripts, Archives, and Rare Books Division, The New York Public Library, New York Public Library Digital Collections.

"Welcome to ABA, Schomburg Shop!" The American Booksellers Association. November 7, 2017. https://www .bookweb.org/news/welcome-aba -schomburg-shop-102223.

### NATIONAL MEMORIAL AFRICAN BOOKSTORE

"125th Street Storeowners on 'Like it is.'" *Amsterdam News (1962–),* December 7, 1974.

"50-Year-Old Bookstore to Close in Harlem." *Afro-American (1893–),* December 14, 1974.

"August 27, 1976 (Page 37 of 655)." *Daily News (1920–),* August 27, 1976.

Baker, Sybil. "Cover Promised for His Books." *Daily News (1920–),* January 8, 1974.

"Black Power: Bookstore Is Headquarters for Harlem Bitterness." *The Daily Home News (1903–1970),* August 9, 1966.

"Bookstore Closing: Owner Guest at NBT." *Amsterdam News (1962–),* January 5, 1974.

Cummings, Judith. "Michaux's Book Store, a Font of Black Culture, to Shut Down: New Facility Promised 'End of Perfect Day' Advice Is Followed Start of Business Recalled Investors Sought." *New York Times (1923–),* November 30, 1974, 33.

Daniels, Ron. "Vantage Point: Feb. 21 Launches 'Year of Malcolm X.'" *Michigan Citizen,* February 17, 1990, 5.

Dier, Richard. "Here's a Guy Who Owns 2 Book Stores." *Afro-American (1893–),* January 27, 1945.

Fraser, C. Gerald. "Lewis Michaux, 92, Dies; Ran Bookstore in Harlem." *New York Times (1923–),* August 27, 1976, 34.

Fraser, C. Gerald. "Lewis Michaux Is Eulogized in Harlem as a Bookseller Who Changed Lives." *New York Times (1923–),* August 31, 1976, 30.

Hamilton, Willie L. "Louis Michaux, A Familiar Face." *Amsterdam News (1962– )*, January 19, 1974, 1.

Hughes, Langston. "Harlem's Bookshops Have a Wealth of Material by and about Negroes." *The Chicago Defender (National Edition) (1921–1967)*, February 14, 1953.

Laura, Harris Hurd. "Rockefeller's Promise Fails; Famous Bookstore Threatened." *Amsterdam News (1962–)*, January 12, 1974, 1.

"Louis H. Michaux, Our Greatest Bookseller." African American Literature Book Club. March 17, 2018. https://aalbc.com/tc/topic/5091-louis-h-michaux-our-greatest-bookseller.

"Michaux Fair Set to Bloom." *Amsterdam News (1962–)*, May 6, 1978, 2.

Michaux, Lewis H. "Cooperation and Unity: A Way Out: Peace, It's Wonderful." *Amsterdam News (1962–)*, July 28, 1962.

Nelson, Vaunda Micheaux, and R. Gregory Christie. *No Crystal Stair*. Minneapolis: Lerner Publishing Group, 2012.

Raymond, Cynthia. "The Schomburg: Hot, Vital, Endangered." *Daily News (1920–)*, August 31, 1975, 92.

"She's Angry!" *Amsterdam News (1962–)*, August 20, 1975.

Tapley, Mel. "Lewis Michaux Buried—4 Decades of Service." *Amsterdam News (1962–)*, September 4, 1976, 2.

## FREDERICK DOUGLASS BOOK CENTER

Birthday dinner invitation, Richard B. Moore papers, Sc MG 397, Schomburg Center for Research in Black Culture, Manuscripts, Archives, and Rare Books Division, The New York Public Library.

Collection notices, Richard B. Moore papers, Sc MG 397, Schomburg Center for Research in Black Culture, Manuscripts, Archives, and Rare Books Division, The New York Public Library.

Frederick Douglass Book Center flier, Richard B. Moore papers, Sc MG 397, Schomburg Center for Research in Black Culture, Manuscripts, Archives, and Rare Books Division, The New York Public Library.

Moore, Richard B. *The Name "Negro": Its Origin and Evil Use*. Baltimore: Black Classic Press, 1992.

Richard B. Moore letters, Richard B. Moore papers, Sc MG 397, Schomburg Center for Research in Black Culture, Manuscripts, Archives, and Rare Books Division, The New York Public Library.

Richard Benjamin Moore, W. Burghardt Turner, and Joyce Moore Turner. *Richard B. Moore, Caribbean Militant in Harlem*. Bloomington: Indiana University Press, 1988.

Turner, W. Burghardt. "The Richard B. Moore Collection and Its Collector." *Caribbean Studies* 15, no. 1 (1975): 135–45.

## THE MARCH COMMUNITY BOOKSHOP

Hughes, Langston. "Harlem's Bookshops Have a Wealth of Material by and about Negroes." *The Chicago Defender (National Edition) (1921–1967)*, February 14, 1953, 10.

Mann, Augusta. *Black Bookstores in Harlem and the Men and Women Who Established Them: 1915–1982*.

"March Community Bookshop." *Negro History Bulletin* 12 no. 6 (March 1, 1949): 137.

## HAKIM'S BOOKSTORE

Blake, Yvonne. Interview by Katie Mitchell, February 8, 2023, video.

Blake, Yvonne. Interview by Katie Mitchell, May 19, 2023, Philadelphia, in person.

## LIBERATION BOOKSTORE

Boyd, Herb. "Is There a Future for Liberation Books?" *Amsterdam News*, July 20, 2000, 4.

Boyd, Herb. "We Are Liberated at Liberation." *Amsterdam News*, July 12, 2001, 3.

Boyd, Herb. "Books Are in Her Blood." *Amsterdam News*, September 26, 2002, 28.

Davis, Joshua Clark. "Una Mulzac, Black Women Booksellers, and Pan-Africanism—AAIHS," September 19, 2016. https://www.aaihs.org/una-mulzac-black-women-booksellers-and-pan-africanism.

"Liberation Bookstore Owner in Harlem Una Mulzac Passes." *Harlem World Magazine*, February 4, 2012. https://www.harlemworldmagazine.com/liberation-bookstore-owner-harlem-una-mulzac-passes.

Mann, Augusta. *Black Bookstores in Harlem and the Men and Women Who Established Them: 1915–1982*.

*Neighborhood Report: Harlem; A Legendary Bookstore Gets a Last-Minute Lease on Life*. New York: New York Times Company, 2000.

Sana, Simba. "African-Centered Bookstores as Weapons of Culture: Applying the Thought of Amilcar Cabral to the Development of Black Cultural Institutions in the U.S." Master's Thesis, Howard University, 1998.

Sinclair, Abiola. "Liberation Bookstore 15th Anniversary." *Amsterdam News (1962–)*, November 20, 1982, 48.

## TREE OF LIFE BOOKSTORE

Browne, J. Zamgba. "Tree of Life Yearning to Return Home to Harlem." *Amsterdam News (1962–)*, October 28, 1989.

BACKGROUND: Hakim's Bookstore Atlanta location. Courtesy of Yvonne Blake.

"Charlie's Angles." City Journal. https://www.city-journal.org/article/charlies-angles.

Johnson, Thomas A. "A Parking Lot Is to Replace the Tree of Life in Harlem." *New York Times (1923–)*, January 24, 1976.

Mann, Augusta. *Black Bookstores in Harlem and the Men and Women Who Established Them: 1915–1982.*

McGhee, Kanya Vashon. "The Tree of Life Bookstore & Education Center of Harlem, NY." https://www.linkedin.com/pulse/20140909191516-78091384-the-tree-of-life-bookstore-education-center-of-harlem-ny.

"Readers Write: For the Tree of Life." *Amsterdam News (1962–)*, April 3, 1976.

Ruby, Dee. "'. . . Swingin' Gently.'" *Amsterdam News (1962–)*, November 19, 1977, 1.

Rule, Sheila. "Bulldozers Destroy Disputed Harlem Bookstore." *New York Times (1923–)*, September 17, 1980, 1.

Tapley, Mel. "About the Arts." *Amsterdam News (1962–)*, October 29, 1977.

Toscano, John. "Harlem Group Protests Plans to Demolish Its Center." *New York Daily News*, October 13, 1977.

"Tree of Life Padlocked." *Amsterdam News (1962–)*, September 20, 1980.

"Tree of Life Vows Not to Be Uprooted." *Amsterdam News (1962–)*, June 23, 1979.

## BLACK BOOKS PLUS

Johnson, Glenderlyn. Interview by Katie Mitchell, April 3, 2023, video.

Johnson, Glenderlyn. Interview by Katie Mitchell, May 22, 2023, Manhattan, in person.

Johnson, Glenderlyn. Interview by Katie Mitchell, September 22, 2023, Manhattan, in person.

## HUE-MAN BOOKSTORE AND CAFÉ

Allen, Marva. Interview by Katie Mitchell, March 21, 2023, video.

Allen, Marva. Interview by Katie Mitchell, September 21, 2023, Manhattan, in person.

Boyd, Herb. "New Hue-Man Opens in Harlem." *Amsterdam News (1962–)*, September 27, 2001, 6.

Ewing, Rita. Interview by Katie Mitchell, April 5, 2023, telephone.

Ewing, Rita. Interview by Katie Mitchell, September 21, 2023, Manhattan, in person.

McCrea, Bridget. "Harlem Haven." Black Enterprise. November 1, 2005. https://www.blackenterprise.com/harlem-haven.

Patrick, Diane. "The Comeback Queens." *Publishers Weekly* 249, no. 47 (November 25, 2002): 22–24.

"Shelf Awareness for Monday, July 2, 2012." https://www.shelf-awareness.com/issue.html?issue=1774#m16664.

Villarosa, Clara, and Linda Villarosa. Interview by Katie Mitchell, June 19, 2023, video.

## FREE BLACK WOMEN'S LIBRARY

Akinmowo, Olaronke. Interview by Katie Mitchell, February 20, 2023, telephone.

## HARRIETT'S BOOKSHOP AND IDA'S BOOKSHOP

Cook, Jeannine. Interview by Katie Mitchell, February 9, 2023, telephone.

"This Black-Owned Bookstore Is Delivering Books on Horseback." Because of Them We Can. November 30, 2021. https://www.becauseofthemwecan.com/blogs/culture/this-black-owned-bookstore-is-delivering-books-on-horseback.

## UNCLE BOBBIE'S COFFEE & BOOKS

Hill, Marc Lamont. Interview by Katie Mitchell, February 23, 2023, video.

Hill, Marc Lamont. Interview by Katie Mitchell, May 18, 2023, Philadelphia, in person.

## ADANNE BOOKSHOP

Okpo, Darlene. Interview by Katie Mitchell, February 1, 2023, video.

Okpo, Darlene. Interview by Katie Mitchell, May 20, 2023, Brooklyn, in person.

## BAILEY STREET BOOKS

Love, Anyabwile. Interview by Katie Mitchell, February 20, 2023, video.

Love, Anyabwile. Interview by Katie Mitchell, May 18, 2023, Philadelphia, in person.

## BEM | BOOKS & MORE

Davenport, Danielle, and Gabrielle Davenport. Interview by Katie Mitchell, June 22, 2023, video.

Muhammad, Nylah Iqbal. "At Brooklyn's BEM Bookstore, Black Food Stories Find Their Home." *Sweet July*. https://stories.sweetjuly.com/editorial/at-brooklyns-bem-bookstore-black-food-stories-find-their-home.

Stewart, Kayla. "This Entire Bookstore Is Dedicated to Black Food Writing," *Bon Appétit*. December 23, 2022.

## DRUM AND SPEAR BOOKSTORE

Beckles, Colin Anthony. "PanAfrican Sites of Resistance: Black Bookstores and the Struggle to Re-Present Black Identity." Order No. 9601388, University of California, Los Angeles, 1995.

Beckles, Colin. "Black Bookstores, Black Power, and the FBI: The Case of Drum and Spear." *Western Journal of Black Studies*, 1996.

Cobb, Charlie. Interview by Joshua Clark Davis, October 16, 2015, location unspecified, in person.

Courtland, Cox. Interview by Katie Mitchell, April 3, 2023, video.

Davis, Joshua C. *From Head Shops to Whole Foods: The Rise and Fall of Activist Entrepreneurs*. New York: Columbia University Press, 2017.

Davis, Joshua Clark. "Black-Owned Bookstores: Anchors of the Black Power Movement." AAIHS. January 28, 2017. https://www.aaihs.org/black-owned-bookstores-anchors-of-the-black-power-movement.

Davis, Joshua Clark. "The FBI's War on Black-Owned Bookstores." *The Atlantic*, February 19, 2018. https://www.theatlantic.com/politics/archive/2018/02/fbi-black-bookstores/553598.

"Drum and Spear Books Founded." SNCC Digital Gateway. https://snccdigital.org/events/drum-and-spear-books-founded.

Hunter, Charlayne. "Blast Victim Regarded as Top Rights Organizer." *New York Times (1923–)*, March 11, 1970.

Gittens, Tony. Interview by Katie Mitchell, March 29, 2023, video.

Gittens, Tony. "Drum and Spear Bookstore" | Black Power Chronicles." https://blackpowerchronicles.org/cool_timelinedrum-and-spear-bookstore.

Lawson, Jennifer. Interview by Katie Mitchell, March 28, 2023, video.

Library of Congress. 2019. *Since 1968: The Drum & Spear Bookstore*. https://www.youtube.com/watch?v=GPdGP_rNrrI.

Manns, Adrienne. "Ghetto Bookstore Finds Untapped Negro Mart." *Washington Post*, August 27, 1968.

Manns, Adrienne. "Writing a New Chapter in Black Children's Books." *The Washington Post, Times Herald (1959–1973)*, December 18, 1973, 2.

Muse, Daphne, and Grant Williams-Yackel. Interview by Katie Mitchell, May 4, 2023, Brentwood, California, in person.

Muse, Daphne, and Grant Williams-Yackel. Interview by Katie Mitchell, March 28, 2023, video.

Richardson, Judy. Interview by Katie Mitchell, March 30, 2023, video.

Richardson, Judy. Interview by Katie Mitchell, April 29, 2024, email.

Turan, Kenneth and Laton McCartney. "You Are What You Read: Sketches of Six Special Bookstores Drum and Spear Book Store." *The Washington Post, Times Herald (1959–1973)*, November 12, 1972.

## THE BLACK BOOK

Coates, Paul. Interview by Katie Mitchell, March 17, 2023, video.

Coates, Paul. Interview by Katie Mitchell, June 17, 2023, video.

Coates, Paul. Interview by Katie Mitchell, May 16, 2023, Washington, D.C., in person.

## PYRAMID BOOKS

Ali, Qadira. Interview by Katie Mitchell, March 18, 2024, telephone.

Ali, Sadiq. Interview by Katie Mitchell, February 24, 2024, telephone.

Barras, Jonetta Rose. "Independent Thought." *Washington City Paper*, September 8, 1995. https://washingtoncitypaper.com/article/297027/independent-thought.

Corey, Mary. "A Boom in Books for Blacks from Best-Seller Lists, to Romance Novels, to More Shelf Space at Book Stores, Black Literature Is Proliferating." *Baltimore Sun*, November 1, 1991. https://www.baltimoresun.com/1991/11/01/a--boom-in-books-for-blacks-from-best-seller-lists-to-romance-novels-to-more-shelf-space-at-book-stores-black-literature-is-proliferating.

"House of Knowledge Opens in Washington." *Washington Informer (Pre-1990)* 20, no. 50 (October 3, 1984): 2.

## EVERYONE'S PLACE

Coates, Ta-Nehisi. *Between the World and Me*. New York: Random House, 2015.

Nati, Brother, and Olakekan Kamau-Nataki. Interview by Katie Mitchell, March 27, 2023, video.

## KARIBU BOOKS

Brown, DeNeen L. "Professor Says Book Club's a Way to Share Ideas on Social Issues." *Fort Worth Star–Telegram*, November 23, 1997.

Glover, Hoke. Interview by Katie Mitchell, November 8, 2023, telephone.

Italie, Hillel. "Black-Interest Book Retail Chain Closes." *Courier Post*, January 24, 2008.

McDaniels, Andrea K. "Karibu Book Chain Is Closing." *Baltimore Sun*, January 24, 2008. https://www.baltimoresun.com/2008/01/24/karibu-book-chain-is-closing.

"News of Karibu's Closing Saddens Customers—Howard University News Service." https://hunewsservice.com/news/news-of-karibus-closing-saddens-customers.

"Owner of Trailblazing Bookstore Chain Pulls the Plug." NPR, February 27, 2008. https://www.npr.org/templates/story/story.php?storyId=57328288.

Sana, Simba. Interview by Katie Mitchell, August 17, 2023, video.

"Shelf Awareness for Wednesday, January 23, 2008." https://www.shelf-awareness.com/issue.html?issue=597#m4041.

"The Karibu Books Chain Comes to an End." 6abc Philadelphia, January 23, 2008. https://6abc.com/archive/5910232.

"Welcome to Karibu Books—Empowering and Educating." The American Booksellers Association, January 4, 2005. https://www.bookweb.org/news/welcome-karibu-books-empowering-and-educating.

Wilkerson-Glover, Karla. Interview by Katie Mitchell, November 28, 2023, telephone.

Young, Ramunda, and Derrick Young. Interview by Katie Mitchell, February 28, 2023, video.

## SANKOFA VIDEO BOOKS & CAFÉ

Gerima, Shirikiana. Interview by Katie Mitchell, March 15, 2023, video.

Mengistu, Yonathan. Interview by Katie Mitchell, June 8, 2023, telephone.

Mengistu, Yonathan. Interview by Katie Mitchell, June 8, 2023, Washington, D.C., in person.

## MAHOGANYBOOKS

Young, Ramunda, and Derrick Young. Interview by Katie Mitchell, February 28, 2023, video.

## LOYALTY BOOKSTORE

Frey, Julie. "Hannah Oliver Depp Wins 2021 WNBA Award." WNBA-Books, May 12, 2021. https://wnba-books.org/hannah-oliver-depp-wins-2021-wnba-award.

Oliver Depp, Hannah. Interview by Katie Mitchell, November 28, 2023, telephone.

# Chapter 3: The South

## MARSHALL'S MUSIC AND BOOKSTORE

Jone Primm, Maati. Interview by Katie Mitchell, February 16, 2023, telephone.

Jone Primm, Maati. Interview by Katie Mitchell, March 30, 2024, Jackson, Mississippi, in person.

## SHRINE OF THE BLACK MADONNA BOOKSTORE AND CULTURAL CENTER

Chui, Mbiyu. Interview by Katie Mitchell, March 1, 2023, video.

Cleage, Pearl. Interview by Katie Mitchell, February 28, 2023, email.

Covington, Germain, and Marie Brown. Interview by Katie Mitchell, February 9, 2023, video.

Covington, Germain, and Marie Brown. Interview by Katie Mitchell, April 10, 2023, Atlanta, in person.

"Shrine of the Black Madonna | American Black Journal." https://www.youtube.com/watch?v=mT5Sr0J_OZs.

## BLACK IMAGES BOOK BAZAAR

"[Dear Mrs. Parks] Booksigning." C-SPAN.org, November 24, 1996. https://www.c-span.org/video/?77015-1/dear-mrs-parks-booksigning.

Rodgers, Emma. Interview by Katie Mitchell, August 28, 2023, video.

Sana, Simba. "African-Centered Bookstores as Weapons of Culture: Applying the Thought of Amilcar Cabral to the Development of Black Cultural Institutions in the U.S." Master's Thesis, Howard University, 1998.

Tosihwe, Ashira. Interview by Katie Mitchell, August 30, 2023, telephone.

## COMMUNITY BOOK CENTER

Flaherty, Jordan. "Overlooked Spaces." Colorlines, March 2007, 10.

Larson, Susan. "Strength in Stories; Like Everything Else, the Local Literary Infrastructure—Libraries, Festivals, Publishers, Bookstores and Writing Programs—Had to Rebuild After Katrina.

It's More Buff than You Might Expect." Times-Picayune, October 28, 2006.

Maloney, Stephen. "Bayou Road Shops Receive $400,000 to Reopen." New Orleans CityBusiness, December 18, 2006, 1.

Simmons, Ann M. "The Nation; After Katrina, a Lesson in Business, Hope; Stanford MBA Students Go to New Orleans to Try to Help a Bookstore and Several Other Small Enterprises Rebound." Los Angeles Times, March 29, 2007.

"Top Female Achievers." New Orleans Magazine, July 2010, 58–69.

Turner, Jennifer. Interview by Katie Mitchell, April 15, 2023, New Orleans, in person.

Warren-Williams, Vera. Interview by Katie Mitchell, April 15, 2023, New Orleans, in person.

## FIRST WORLD BOOKSTORES

Alexander, Jim. Interview by Katie Mitchell, April 5, 2023, video.

Alexander, Jim. Interview by Katie Mitchell, April 15, 2023, East Point, Georgia, in person.

## PYRAMID ART, BOOKS & CUSTOM FRAMING

Hearne, Garbo. Interview by Katie Mitchell, April 4, 2023, video.

## MEDU BOOKSTORE

Damali, Nia. Interview by Katie Mitchell, March 21, 2023, video.

Damali, Nia. Interview by Katie Mitchell, April 12, 2023, Atlanta, in person.

## 44TH & 3RD BOOKSELLERS

Lee, Warren, and Cheryl Lee. Interview by Katie Mitchell, February 13, 2023, video.

Lee, Warren, Cheryl Lee, Allyce Lee, and Lorin Brown. Interview by Katie Mitchell, April 10, 2023, Atlanta, in person.

## FOR KEEPS BOOKS

Duffy, Rosa. Interview by Katie Mitchell, February 15, 2023, Atlanta, in person.

Duffy, Rosa. Interview by Katie Mitchell, April 12, 2023, Atlanta, in person.

## LIBERATION STATION BOOKSTORE

"Black-Owned Children's Bookstore in Raleigh Moving after Threats, Owner Says." WRAL.com, April 2, 2024. https://www.wral.com/story/black-owned-children-s-bookstore-in-raleigh-moving-after-threats-owner-says/21358758.

Scott-Miller, Victoria. Interview by Katie Mitchell, September 11, 2023, video.

## BALDWIN & CO.

Johnson, DJ (@baldwinandcompany). "Today marks a special celebration at Baldwin & Co." Instagram, February 20, 2024. http://instagram.com/baldwinandcompany.

Johnson, DJ. Interview by Katie Mitchell, November 22, 2022, video.

Johnson, DJ. Interview by Katie Mitchell, April 15, 2023, New Orleans, in person.

## KINDRED STORIES

Hamm, Terri. Interview by Katie Mitchell, March 23, 2023, video.

## YES, PLEASE BOOKS

jones, lauren. Interview by Katie Mitchell, March 28, 2023, video.

jones, lauren. Interview by Katie Mitchell, March 28, 2023, Decatur, Georgia, in person.

# Chapter 4: The Midwest

## VAUGHN'S BOOKSTORE

"Interview with Ed Vaughn." Digital.wustl.edu. http://digital.wustl.edu/e/eii/eiiweb/vau5427.0309.166edvaughn.html.

"Interview with Edward Vaughn." Repository.wustl.edu. http://repository.wustl.edu/concern/videos/47429d93b.

Livengood, Chad. "Still Rebuilding: Detroit's Nascent Comeback Hinges on Rebuilding a Vast Network of Small Businesses That Were Lost in the Aftermath of 1967." *Crain's Detroit Business* 33 (26) (June 26, 2017): 1.

*Negro Digest.* "Second Annual Black Arts Convention," June 1967.

Vaughn, Ed. Interview by Katie Mitchell, March 26, 2023, Atlanta, in person.

"Vaughn's Bookstore." Jacob Torkelson. https://www.jwtorkelson.com/vaughns-bookstore.

"Weekly List 2023 08 11—National Register of Historic Places." U.S. National Park Service.

## AFROCENTRIC BOOKSTORE

Beaven, Stephen. "A Cultural Haven on College Ave." *Indianapolis Business Journal* 19, no. 17 (July 13, 1998).

Chinn, Lesley R. "Afrocentric Bookstore Closes." *Chicago Citizen*, July 23, 2008.

Greggs, LaTicia D. "Afrocentric Bookstore Celebrates New Site." *Chicago Defender (Daily Edition) (1973–),* April 22, 1997.

Greggs, LaTicia D. "Afrocentric Bookstore to Hold 'Raise the Roof Birthday Book Bash.'" *Chicago Defender (Daily Edition) (1973–),* July 13, 1999.

Hutson, Wendell. "Afrocentric Bookstore Set to Close Next Month." *Chicago Defender (Daily Edition) (1973–),* July 9, 2008.

Richards, Rhonda. "Taking Care of Business." *Essence,* 9 (1994): 66.

Ridgell, Olivia. "300 Harris, Cleage Fans at Afrocentric's 'Literaturely Speaking.'" *Chicago Defender (Daily Edition) (1973–),* July 17, 2001.

Sanders, Desiree. Interview by Katie Mitchell, February 28, 2023, telephone.

Sanders, Desiree. Interview by Katie Mitchell, June 4, 2023, Chicago, in person.

Starling, Kelly. "Success Secrets of Young Entrepreneurs." *Ebony*, September 1999, 165–168+.

Walls, Sunya. "Black Bookstore Owner Fills Important Niche." *Chicago Weekend*, February 11, 1996.

## DA BOOK JOINT

"After Nearly Closing, Black Bookstores Semicolon and Da Book Joint Have Been Able to Pivot and 'Stick It Out.'" *Chicago Tribune*, January 26, 2024. https://www.chicagotribune.com/2024/01/26/after-nearly-closing-black-bookstores-semicolon-and-da-book-joint-have-been-able-to-pivot-and-stick-it-out.

Evans, Maxwell. "Vic Mensa Surprises Da Book Joint with Check to Cover a Year's Rent." Block Club Chicago, March 21, 2024. https://blockclubchicago.org/2024/03/21/vic-mensa-surprises-da-book-joint-with-check-to-cover-a-years-rent.

Singletary, Verlean. Interview by Katie Mitchell, February 13, 2023, video.

Singletary, Verlean, and Courtney Woods. Interview by Katie Mitchell, June 4, 2023, Chicago, in person.

"TODAY Surprises Mother-Daughter behind Community Bookshop." https://www.youtube.com/watch?v=_mTGknCn41M.

Woods, Courtney (@dabookjoint). ". . . we decided to keep fighting . . ." Instagram, January 3, 2024. http://instagram.com/dabookjoint.

## SEMICOLON BOOKSTORE & GALLERY

"After Nearly Closing, Black Bookstores Semicolon and Da Book Joint Have Been Able to Pivot and 'Stick It Out.'" *Chicago Tribune*, January 26, 2024. https://www.chicagotribune.com/2024/01/26/after-nearly-closing-black-bookstores-semicolon-and-da-book-joint-have-been-able-to-pivot-and-stick-it-out.

Mullen, Danielle. Interview by Katie Mitchell, November 1, 2022, video.

Mullen, Danielle. Interview by Katie Mitchell, June 5, 2023, Chicago, in person.

Mullen, Danielle (@semicolonchi). "The cat is outta the bag: Semicolon has moved to a fully nonprofit model!" Instagram photo, June 2, 2023. https://www.instagram.com/p/Cs_hHRkrcAp.

Mullen, Danielle (@semicolonchi). "People keep asking how I feel . . ." Instagram, August 15, 2024.

## SOCIALIGHT SOCIETY

Lawrence, Nyshell. Interview by Katie Mitchell, February 6, 2023, video.

## BLACK GARNET BOOKS

Sims, Dione. Interview by Katie Mitchell, February 3, 2023, video.

# Chapter 5: The West

## AQUARIAN BOOKSHOP

"All the Lights the Light: Oral History Transcript: Alfred Ligon." Oac.cdlib.org. https://oac.cdlib.org/view?docId=hb4g5009q6&brand=oac4&doc.view=entire_text.

Boyer, Edward J., and Andrea Ford Times. "Black-Owned Businesses Pay a Heavy Price." *Los Angeles Times (1923–1995)*, May 8, 1992.

Doc Young, A. S. "The Burning of Aquarian." *Los Angeles Sentinel (1934–)*, May 21, 1992.

"Dr. Alfred Ligon 'Returns Home.'" *Weekend Chicago Defender (1980–2008)*, August 28, 1982.

Duty, Juana E. "Aquarian Book Shop Survives but 'It's a Starvation Business.'"

*Los Angeles Times (1923–1995)*, May 4, 1982.

Idelson, Karen. "Out of the Ashes/Donations Pour In to Rebuild Black Bookstore Gutted During L.A. Riots." *Houston Chronicle (Pre-1997 Full text)*, May 28, 1992.

Johnson, Sharon, and Martha Southgate. "Alfred Ligon." *Essence*, September 1989, 32.

Martin, Douglas. "Bookstore Owner Promoted Black Culture." *National Post*, September 3, 2002.

Mydans, Seth. "Riot Leveled a Font of Black Culture." *New York Times (1923–)*, August 5, 1992.

Oliver, Myrna. "Bernice Ligon of Early Black-Owned Bookstore Dies; Culture: Her Husband Founded the Aquarian

Book Shop in 1941. It Became an L.A. Haven for Intellectuals." *Los Angeles Times*, November 10, 2000.

"Photo Standalone 2—no Title." *Los Angeles Sentinel (1934–)*, June 4, 1992.

Samuels, Alisa. "Black Bookstore Renaissance: Publishing: After Slow Sales in the 1970s and '80s, Shops Are Benefiting from an Upswing in African-American Interest." *Los Angeles Times (1923–1995)*, February 10, 1990.

"The Aquarian Age." Los Angeles Archivists Collective, May 30, 2017. https://www.laacollective.org/work/the-aquarian-age-alfred-and-bernice-ligon.

Tipton, Toni. "10 Benchmarks and Landmarks: Black History on View in L.A." *Los Angeles Times (1923–1995)*, January 15, 1987.

## HUGH GORDON BOOKSHOP

"Adele R. Young Opens Book Shop." *Los Angeles Sentinel (1934–)*, June 10, 1948.

"Black History." *Los Angeles Sentinel (1934–)*, September 25, 1969.

de Lavallade, Carmen. Interview by Katie Mitchell. June 27, 2023, telephone.

Hughes, Langston. "The Negro Mother."

Hugh Gordon Bookshop (Los Angeles, California). Letter from Hugh Gordon Bookshop to W.E.B. Du Bois, March 11, 1950. W.E.B. Du Bois Papers (MS 312). Special Collections and University Archives, University of Massachusetts Amherst Libraries.

"Hugh Gordon, circa 1930—UCLA Library Digital Collections."

Whitley, Helen. "Hugh Gordon Book Store: Ghetto's Cultural Center." *Afro-American (1893–)*, September 10, 1966.

## MARCUS BOOKS

Baldwin, James. *The Fire Next Time.* New York: Dial, 1967.

"Ghosts in the Schoolyard: A Conversation with Eve L. Ewing & Ta-Nehisi Coates." https://www.youtube.com/watch?v=RCuZFD4CX2M.

Hubbard, Lee. "Black Bookstores Fight to Stay Alive." *Atlanta Daily World (1932–)*, September 10, 2000.

Johnson, Jasmine. Interview by Katie Mitchell, April 19, 2023, video.

"Marcus Books." C-SPAN.org, November 2, 2015. https://www.c-span.org/video/?402682-1/marcus-books.

"Marcus Books / Jimbo's Bop City Building Receives Historic Landmark Approval." San Francisco Planning Department. https://content.govdelivery.com/accounts/CASFPD/bulletins/a2129f.

"Marcus Books of San Francisco Evicted." San Francisco Bay Guardian Archive 1966–2014. https://sfbgarchive.48hills.org/sfbgarchive/2014/05/08/marcus-books-san-francisco-evicted.

"Our History | Marcus Books." https://www.marcusbooks.com/store-history.

Ulansky, Gene. "Marcus Garvey's Man in San Francisco." *Encore American & Worldwide News*, May 19, 1975, 36.

Wheeler, André. "'Economic Duress Is Nothing New': Can America's Oldest Black Bookstore Survive the Pandemic?" *The Guardian*, May 15, 2020, sec. Books. https://www.theguardian.com/books/2020/may/15/marcus-books-oakland-oldest-black-bookstore.

Woo, David. *Marcus Books, the Nation's Oldest Black Bookstore*. https://www.foundsf.org/index.php?title=Marcus_Books,_the_Nation%E2%80%99s_Oldest_Black_Bookstore.

## THIRD WORLD ETHNIC BOOKS

"Black History Trove, a Life's Work, Seeks Museum." *New York Times*, December 13, 2006.

Coopersmith, Sandra. "Celebrating Mayme A. Clayton's Legacy." *Culver City Observer*, March 7, 2019. https://www.culvercityobserver.com/story/2019/03/07/news/celebrating-mayme-a-claytons-legacy/7991.html.

Harnisch, Larry. "A Miracle of Black History; Mayme Clayton's Mission Lives On at Old Culver City Courthouse." *Los Angeles Times*, July 25, 2012.

Hunt, Paul. "Collectors and Characters." Bookstore Memories, March 14, 2024. http://bookstorememories.com/blog/?cat=36.

Kerr, Leah M. "Collectors' Contributions to Archiving Early Black Film." *Black Camera* 5, no. 1 (Fall, 2013): 274–84, 293–94.

Matchstick, Ben. "Dr. Mayme Clayton, Renegade Librarian and Icon of Black History Preservation." Goddard College, February 18, 2021. https://www.goddard.edu/blog/alumni-news/dr-mayme-claytons-legacy-of-black-history-preservation.

"Mayme Clayton." The History Makers, October 7, 2004. https://www.thehistorymakers.org/biography/mayme-clayton-40.

"Mayme Clayton: Americans in Focus." Accessed April 7, 2024. https://www.youtube.com/watch?v=oLHomNl_GaQ&t=1s.

"Preserving African-American History: The Legacy of Mayme A. Clayton." PBS SoCal, June 30, 2016. https://www.pbssocal.org/shows/lost-la/preserving-african-american-history-the-legacy-of-mayme-a-clayton.

Williford, Stanley. "Mayme Clayton: Collecting Bits of Black History." *Los Angeles Sentinel (1934–)*, May 30, 1974.

Woo, Elaine. Special from the *Los Angeles Times*. "Mayme Clayton, 83, Collector, Chronicler of Black Americana; Museum to House Eclectic Inventory." *The Record*, October 22, 2006.

Woo, Elaine. "Mayme Clayton; Founded Center for Preservation of Black History." *The Washington Post (1974–)*, October 24, 2006.

Woo, Elaine. "The State; A Champion of Black History; Librarian Mayme Clayton, Who Scoured Stores, Attics and Even Dumps to Amass a Prized Collection That She Kept in Her Garage, Has Died." *Los Angeles Times*, October 21, 2006.

## OASIS IN THE DIASPORA

Muse, Daphne, and Grant Williams-Yackel. Interview by Katie Mitchell, March 28, 2023, video.

Muse, Daphne, and Grant Williams-Yackel. Interview by Katie Mitchell, May 4, 2023, Brentwood, California, in-person.

## HUE-MAN EXPERIENCE

"Briefing." *Denver Post*, October 14, 1994.

"Dream, Girl Bonus Footage: The Full Clara Villarosa Interview (November 2014)." https://www.youtube.com/watch?v=gRgRL66BEJw.

Holsendolph, Ernest. "Small Bookshops Turn the Page to Survival." *Emerge*, June 1995, 20.

Luins Small, Mary. "Denver's Black Bookstore and More." *American Visions*, February 1, 1989, 42.

Villarosa, Clara, and Linda Villarosa. Interview by Katie Mitchell, June 19, 2023, video.

Wheeler, Sheba R. "Hue-Man Experience Founder Heads to N.Y." *Denver Post*, July 10, 2000.

Woods, Paula L. "Black-Owned Shops Fight to Survive Super Bookstores." *Emerge*, February 1999, 104–5.

## ESO WON BOOKS

Albeck-Ripka, Livia. "A Beloved Black-Run Bookstore in Los Angeles Is Closing: California Today." *New York Times*, July 1, 2022.

Anderson, Makebra. "L.A.'s Leading Black Bookstore Bans Popular Author Over Review." *Los Angeles Sentinel*, May 30, 2002.

Beckles, Colin Anthony. "PanAfrican Sites of Resistance: Black Bookstores and the Struggle to Re-Present Black Identity." Order No. 9601388, University of California, Los Angeles, 1995.

Brown, Ann. "Final Chapter." *Black Enterprise (Online)*, February 5, 2008.

Fugate, James. Interview by Katie Mitchell, March 6, 2023, video.

Fugate, James. Interview by Katie Mitchell, May 1, 2023, Los Angeles, in person.

Kaplan, Erin Aubry. "The Enduring Legacy of L.A.'s Eso Won Books." *Los Angeles Times*, June 17, 2022.

Mitchell, John L. "L.A. Black-Focus Bookshop May Close; Eso Won Welcomed Presidents, Candidates and Entertainers, but the Independent Bookseller Finds It Hard to Compete with Chains, Internet." *Los Angeles Times*, October 5, 2007.

Njeri, Itabari. "Violent Message Finds Success: Books: Shahrazad Ali's 'Guide' Urging Submission of Black Women to Black Men Is Selling Briskly." *Los Angeles Times (1923–1995)*, July 30, 1990.

Sabathia, Christine G. "Only the Community Can Save Black Bookstore." *Los Angeles Sentinel*, October 2007.

Samuels, Alisa. "Black Bookstore Renaissance." *Los Angeles Times*, February 10, 1990.

## MALIK BOOKS

De.aR. *Malik Books*. https://www.youtube.com/watch?v=yLIRJXGdiwI.

Ligon. "Frustration & Fire: The 1992 Los Angeles Uprising." Rediscovering Black History, April 29, 2022. https://rediscovering-black-history.blogs.archives.gov/2022/04/29/frustration-fire-the-1992-los-angeles-uprising.

Muhammad, Malik. Interview by Katie Mitchell, February 2, 2023, video.

Muhammad, Malik, and April Muhammad. Interview by Katie Mitchell, May 2, 2023, Los Angeles, in person.

## REPARATIONS CLUB

McGilbert, Jazzi. Interview by Katie Mitchell, February 6, 2023, video.

McGilbert, Jazzi. Interview by Katie Mitchell, May 2, 2023, Los Angeles, in person.

## SISTAH SCIFI

Asare, Isis. Interview by Katie Mitchell, February 1, 2023, video.

Asare, Isis. Interview by Katie Mitchell, May 3, 2023, Oakland, California, in person.

## THIRD EYE BOOKS AND GIFTS

"Black Exclusion Laws in Oregon." https://www.oregonencyclopedia.org/articles/exclusion_laws.

Hannah, Charles, and Michelle Lewis. Interview by Katie Mitchell, February 20, 2023, video.

## THE SALT EATERS BOOKSHOP

Bambara, Toni Cade. *The Salt Eaters*. New York: Random House Trade, 1980.

"Donate to Help Establish The Salt Eaters Bookshop, Organized by The Salt Eaters Bookshop." https://www.gofundme.com/f/help-establish-the-salt-eaters-bookshop.

Grant, Asha. Interview by Katie Mitchell, February 13, 2023, video.

Grant, Asha. Interview by Katie Mitchell, May 2, 2023, Los Angeles, in person.

Kashanie, Kamilah. "Remembering Latasha Harlins, Whose Death Helped Set Off Unrest in Los Angeles." NPR.org, April 29, 2022. https://www.npr.org/2022/04/29/1095444468/storycorps-remembering-15-year-old-latasha-harlins.

## RADICAL HOOD LIBRARY

Matos, Natalie. Interview by Katie Mitchell, February 7, 2023, video.

"Prison Program—Noname Book Club." https://nonamebooks.com/Prison-Program.

BOTTOM BACKGROUND:
Courtesy of Malik Muhammad.

3/26/23

4/12/23

Daphne Muse   Katie M

Brentwood, CA

Katie Mitchell
Ed Vaughn   Vaughn's
Bookstore

Katie M + Rosa D
For keeps Books
Atlanta, GA

Oasis in the Diaspora
Prose to the People 5/4/12

5/16/23

5/18/23

5/16/23

Katie M   Paul Coates
The Black Book

Marc Hill   Katie M
Uncle Bobbie's
Philly

Makala   Katie
Christina/Joy   Yonathan
Sankofa   D.C.

D.C.
5/20/23

5/21/23

5/2.1/23

Darlene Okpo Katie M
Adanne
Brooklyn

Danielle   Katie   Gabrielle
BEM
Brooklyn

Katie M + Jazzi M
Papi Tacos & Churros
Los Angeles (Rep Club)

When I set out to write *Prose,* I wanted the book to be a microcosm of the Black bookstore itself—full of different genres, media, and voices. In this pursuit, I encountered countless coconspirators without whom *Prose to the People* would have remained an idea scribbled in my journal.

First, heartfelt gratitude to the remarkable bookstores that generously opened their doors and shared their stories, making this book a reality. Your passion for books and your commitment to fostering vibrant literary communities is truly inspiring. To the bookstore owners, employees, and customers who took the time to share their insights and anecdotes, you've enriched this project immeasurably.

I'd also like to express my sincere gratitude to the readers who continue to support independent Black bookstores. May this book inspire many more adventures in the world of Black books and Black bookstores.

*Prose* is the newest addition to works about Black bookstores, but it's certainly not the first. I'd like to thank some of those whose scholarship on Black bookstores came before *Prose:* Augusta Mann, Colin Beckles, Simba Sana, Joshua Clark Davis, Rosemary M. Stevenson, Vincent Copeland, and Char Adams.

Thank you to each contributor who wrote an essay or poem for *Prose.* Your thoughtful reflections have added depth and richness to this exploration of Black bookstores in the United States. In writing about a specific community, I've found a community of writers who've supported this project in ways I couldn't have predicted. From Lynell George ("Closed Door, Open Window") introducing me to Michael A. Gonzales ("The Adventures of Book Boy") or Joshua Clark Davis ("The Lies—and Surprising Truths—of Surveillance Files on Black Bookstores") introducing me to the Drum and Spear collective and Paul Coates, the butterfly effects of your kind gestures unfolded beautifully in *Prose.* Speaking of Paul, his simple question, "How do you define a Black bookstore?" changed the course of this book. Thank you for asking the right question at the right time.

I'd also like to thank the late Toni Morrison, whose oft-quoted advice to write the book you want to read gave me the permission—nay, the directive—to write *Prose* in the first place.

Thank you to everyone who opened their homes to me as I journeyed across the United States to document the bookstores in *Prose:* Ndidi Enyinnia (Brooklyn), Angela Owens (Washington, D.C.), Paul Coates (Washington, D.C.), Daphne Muse (Brentwood, California), James Fugate (Los Angeles), Desiree Sanders (Chicago), Anyabwile Love (Philadelphia), and Edward and Randall Vaughn (Atlanta).

As I bounced from city to city, state to state, I found myself in libraries, scouring the archives for Black bookstore histories. Thank you for opening your doors and databases: Auburn Avenue Research Library, Newberry Library, Stuart A. Rose Manuscripts, Archives, and Rare Books Library, UCLA Library Special Collections,

5/21/24

Katie   Glen Johnson
Black Books   Manhattan
Plus

Schomburg Center for Research in Black Culture. Barrye Brown at the Schomburg introduced me to Glenderlyn Johnson of Black Books Plus, and that connection led to one of my favorite profiles in *Prose*. The Bibliographical Society of America funded my research on New York bookstores through the Dorothy Porter Wesley Fellowship. Thank you for your generous financial support.

I always wanted *Prose* to transport the reader to the bookstores profiled. Thank you to the many generous photographers who shared the images that turned pictures into portals.

Before I ever put pen to paper, my mother, Katherine, instilled in me a love for Black books, and, more importantly, Black people. Thank you for seeing me through this yearslong process. Thank you for writing *Prose*'s dedication and pull quotes by hand. Thank you for loving me.

Aaron Ross Coleman, thank you for nurturing this idea from its very inception. Thank you for being a thought partner, a sounding board, a reader, an editor, and IT support. You're my favorite writer. Your editorial process made me sharper and more decisive, but your love made me whole.

Most importantly: thank You, Jesus, thank You, Jesus, thank You, Jesus—for saving me, for keeping me, for giving me these hot lines. All good things flow through You. Only the mistakes have been mine.

## ABOUT THE AUTHOR

**KATIE MITCHELL** is a storyteller and bookseller based in Atlanta, Georgia. Her online and pop-up Black bookstore, Good Books, has been featured in *The New York Times*, NBC, NPR, and PBS, and many other outlets. Katie is a Dorothy Porter Wesley fellow.

# Rosa Parks At Shrine Bookstore Fri.

## Bookstore Hosts Local Writers

First World Bookstore will host Dr. Richard Long at an afternoon Booksigning/lecture on February 9 froom 3-5 p.m.

## African Spectrum Bookstore Expands Business In South DeKalb

Photo Courtesy of Nemasengeri Mutota

Nemasengeri Mutota, (second from right) owner of the African Spectrum bookstore in Clarkston, works to empower Black entrepreneurship in DeKalb County. Here, Mutota and his wife, Fanta, host authors (from left) Walter Moseley and Agyman Kaman at the 1999 Book Club Conference.

## Hakims; A Hub For African American Historical Facts

### AUTHOR IN ATLANTA

Inside is a collection of books, records, tapes and art that is a timeless table of black history. On its walls hang pictures of African Kings, black activists and famous black political leaders.

It's atmosphere is that of a museum. The only difference is one's curiosity assumes the role of tour guide.

This celler of vintaged literature is called Hakims Book Store.

Author/poet John Chena will read from and sign recently published book poetry "The Invisible M Returns" on Sunday, Nov from 3-5 p.m. at First Wo Bookstore, 86 Upper Alaba Street in Underground Atlan Chenault is a Cincinn playwright, essayist and aut of numerous articles. He columnist and section editor ArtRage Magazine in Lond England, and author of "B Blackness," a collection poetry published in 1969. booksigning and reading sponsored by First Wo Bookstore.

## At Shrine Bookstore

### Hunter-Gault Visits To Sign New Book

Charlayne Hunter-Gault, national correspondent for PBS's MacNeil/Lehrer News-Hour and one of two Black Students to integrate the University of Georgia, will sign copies of her autobiography, In My Place, Saturday, November 7, 3:30 p.m. to 5:00 p.m., at the Shrines of the Black Madonna Bookstore, 946 Abernathy Blvd. SW. For more information, call 752-6125.

## Medu Bookstore Celebrates 4 Years At Greenbriar

### MEET THE AUTHOR

### Shrine Of Black Madonna Bookstore Hosting Book Party For T.M. Alexander

### New Bookstore Features Many Black Authors

## Giovanni Blesses Medu With Signin

### Shrine Celebrates Life, Teachings Of Marcus Garvey

### I.B.W. Opens Bookstore

### Help Wante

## Bookstore, Cultural Center To Honor Black History Month

### Need For AUC Bookstore Cited

### Sweet Auburn Avenue; A Smile With Tooth Decay

### WHO LOVES YOU?

See The Stars At Dark, Splash In A Duck Pond, And See Yourself In The Mirror And Know Who Loves You!

Who Loves You! By Evelyn Wilson A Basic Study Book For PRE SCHOOL-ERS & FIRST GRADERS And A Founda-tion Guide For Parents & Educators